T0188646

The Autobiography

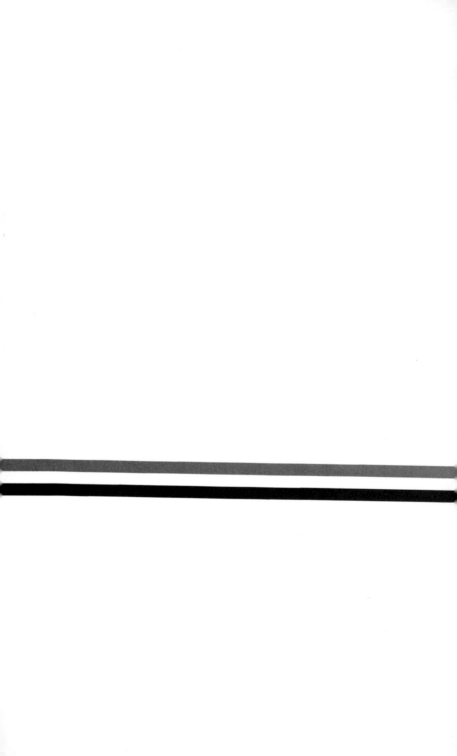

Benjamin Franklin
The Autobiography

WITH AN INTRODUCTION BY
Daniel Aaron

LIBRARY OF AMERICA PAPERBACK CLASSICS

Introduction copyright © 1990 by Daniel Aaron

Chronology, Note on the Text, and Notes copyright © 1987 by Literary
Classics of the United States, New York, NY. All rights reserved.

The Introduction by Daniel Aaron was originally published in the
memership bulletin of the American Academy of Arts and Sciences.

Distributed to the trade in the United States by Penguin Group (USA) Inc.
and in Canada by Penguin Books Canada Ltd.

Library of Congress Control Number: 2010939603
978-1-59853-095-7

Library of America Paperback Classics are printed on acid-free paper.

FIRST LIBRARY OF AMERICA PAPERBACK CLASSIC EDITION
January 2011
Third printing

Manufactured in the United States of America

J. A. Leo Lemay
PREPARED THE NOTES WHICH APPEAR
AT THE END OF THIS VOLUME

Contents

INTRODUCTION

by Daniel Aaron

I didn't read Benjamin Franklin until my early twenties and only then because I was required to. Of course he'd been a familiar since childhood, a kind of national artifact all mixed up with kites and electricity and maxims, one of the Founders commemorated in the names of towns and counties, but of his subtlety and complexity I hadn't a show.

The man I haven't yet "discovered" and probably never shall is not Franklin the exemplar and patron saint of Yankee-dom; not the mathematician of morals and consummate rationalizer; not D. H. Lawrence's snuff-colored John Wana-maker Franklin; not Horatio Alger Franklin; not Franklin the PR man; and certainly not "Honest Ben" Franklin, the common man's common man. These and unmentioned personae are certainly there. But I shall focus on a less familiar Frank-lin, the proud and powerful Dr. Franklin—alert, tenacious of purpose, ambitious, self-controlled—our first republican man of letters (so David Hume called him), the ambivalent ally of flawed mankind, a man, if not for *all* seasons, for *our* season and good medicine for anyone living in these distempered times.

Benjamin Franklin neither exalted nor despised his fellow men. He took them good-humoredly as they were—fallible creatures, self-deluded, cruel, thoughtless, yet capable of en-lightenment. From Newtonian analogies he inferred a provi-dential design in the universe and publicly acknowledged a friendly and reasonable deity (not unlike Franklin himself), who delighted in the happiness of His creatures. The world Franklin came to terms with, however, was a rough place, where the strong ate the weak and Privilege was in the saddle. It could be made more bearable not through spiritual revivals, not by burnt offerings, but by harnessing aspiration to possi-bility, by small, gradual, and unmomentous remedial acts, by self-discipline and self-trust. God was best served by doing good to men, Franklin said—and then added dryly: "but Praying is thought an easier Service, and therefore more generally chosen." The survivor of a shipwreck, he suggested, would be better advised to erect a lighthouse than to build a church.

Hence throughout his life, even during the years when he was deeply involved in his most important political and diplomatic assignments, Franklin's mind turned to such mundane projects as draining swamps or improving watering troughs for horses or curing smoky chimneys or cleaning streets. I particularly like his answer in his *Autobiography* to those, he says, who "think these trifling matters not worth minding or relating." They may appear to be of small consequence, he goes on to say, but

> Human felicity is produc'd not so much by great pieces of good fortune that seldom happen, as by little advantages that occur every day. Thus, if you teach a poor young man to shave himself, and keep his razor in order, you may contribute more to the happiness of his life than in giving him a thousand guineas. The money may be soon spent, the regret only remaining of having foolishly consumed it; but in the other case, he escapes a frequent vexation of waiting for barbers, and of their sometimes dirty fingers, offensive breaths, and dull razors; he shaves when most convenient to him, and enjoys daily the pleasure of its being done with a good instrument.

And Franklin was a master persuader, skilled in the art of making his readers accept his ideas as their own. Writing for him was a form of action. If he hadn't possessed remarkable literary gifts, his contemporary and subsequent reputation, in all likelihood, would have been considerably less. How he taught himself to write his lucid and serviceable prose is described in the *Autobiography*, and the happy results are evident in his solid expository pieces, in his satires and hoaxes, in his bagatelles (those witty and artful trifles he dashed off for his French lady friends) and above all in his incomparable letters, treasured by all of his correspondents. The accomplished writer subjected himself to an arduous apprenticeship as an editor of almanacs and newspapers. His exposure to London's Grub Street—the same world of playhouses, coffeehouses, reviews, and pamphlets where Daniel Defoe learned his craft—

sharpened his sense of what would please an audience. It also taught him what language could conceal as well as reveal.

Autobiography: the title of this famous and influential work is a little misleading since the book ends around 1757, long before Franklin had taken on many of his important public roles. Furthermore, it omits episodes in his life that predate 1757—his celebrated kite experiment, for example—and the monologue of the narrator is interpolated with little fictions, not to mention misrememberings. In short, the *Autobiography* is neither a chronological nor a strictly accurate report of Franklin's career but a conduct book, grounded in facts and designed to show America's youth how they, too, might rise from obscurity to eminence.

Franklin has transformed himself into an emblematic figure, a "character," if you will, just as Whitman in "Song of Myself" invented a character, "Walt of Mannahatta." Minor characters in the *Autobiography* are based on real people, but they are also types who are intended to stand for specific human traits.

Franklin called his *Autobiography* a "rambling series of digressions." It might more accurately be defined as an account of a histrionic life—not in the sense of exaggerated or emotional but dramatic—in which he acted out various and illustrative roles on the stage of history. One of them was the smart-aleck adolescent testing his powers, another the hustling entrepreneur learning how to get ahead, a third the promoter of public projects. The elderly speaker recollecting his earlier selves sounds a little complacent about his accomplishments, but his prevailing tone is amiable and unserious. He seems amused in retrospect by his ambitious and youthful effronteries. The reader-audience watches the Yankee Proteus as he passes through his successive incarnations—printer, tradesman, civic leader—in each of which a part of the mature autobiographer is foreshadowed.

I don't think it's too farfetched to see the *Autobiography* as a kind of secular and less allegorical *Pilgrim's Progress* (a work Franklin knew well), the Heavenly City of Bunyan's tale changed into an industrious, orderly community with just a touch of Vanity Fair. Both Franklin and Bunyan were intent upon the moral purport of their entertaining narratives, although, in Franklin's case, a bit of self-gratulation accompanies the instruction.

Take, for example, two accounts of young Franklin's arrival in Philadelphia. One is the familiar story he relates in the *Autobiography*. The other appeared thirteen years earlier as an anecdote in an English magazine. It is told in the third person, but scholars have decided that it came from Franklin himself.

In this early version, Franklin doesn't come to Philadelphia by boat; he walks all the way. When he gets there, he buys a simple meal, falls asleep in a Quaker meetinghouse, and is awakened by the sexton. A benevolent Quaker gentleman invites him to dinner and thereafter starts young Franklin on his way to wealth and fame. In the *Autobiography*, the narrator, Benjamin Franklin, also falls asleep in the meetinghouse, but this time he's not *befriended* by the venerable Quaker. Instead, he *asks* his advice about where he should stay and is advised where *not* to stay. He then eats his dinner and goes to sleep.

In the early account, Franklin's *luck* is emphasized, in the second, his *initiative*. What actually occurred is of less matter than the autobiographer's message: a person's fate is largely determined by his own acts. God helps those who help themselves. Or, to put it another way, life is a game. The *Autobiography* is a treatise in which the hazards of living are set down along with the strategies to circumvent them. To win the game, the player has to synchronize his habits with the processes of nature and to learn its rules.

This notion of sticking to the rules is succinctly summarized in Franklin's bagatelle "The Morals of Chess," in which a chess game becomes a metaphor for human life. To play it well requires foresight and caution because, he observes, "If you touch a Piece, you must move it somewhere; if you set it down, you must let it stand." Chess is also a metaphor for war: if the player puts himself into a dangerous position, his enemy won't allow him to pull back his troops. Yet chess also teaches the player not to despair but to search for alternative moves; in fact, a temporary setback may teach him to act with greater "care & attention." Needless to say, the player must not expect special favors, or make false moves, or disturb his adversary by whistling or singing, or insult him, or gloat after beating him. Indeed, the player is some cases might be advised to lose deliberately to a weak opponent if by so doing he can win his affection.

Franklin's writings are filled with prudential hints on how to sidestep obstacles and survive in a world full of fools and frauds. "Poor Richard," Franklin's most widely known persona, is no flatterer of human nature—including his own. "Are you angry that others disappoint you?" he asks. "Remember you cannot depend upon yourself." "He that has neither fools, whores nor beggars among his kindred is the son of a Thunder gust." "A wolf eats sheep now and then, / Ten Thousand are devour'd by men." "A Mob's a Monster; Heads enough, but no Brains." "He that understands the World, least likes it." "Nothing humbler than *Ambition*, when it is about to climb." "Much virtue in Herbs, little in men." "To be intimate with a foolish Friend, is like going to bed with a Razor."

Given this unreliable mix of humanity, no wonder the wise man proceeds cautiously, keeps his own counsel, guards his tongue. As Poor Richard puts it: "He makes a Foe who makes a jest." "*Friendship* cannot live with *Ceremony*, nor without *Civility*." "Humility makes great men twice honourable." "If you have no Honey in your Pot, have some in your Mouth." "Be rarely warm in censure or in Praise. / Few men deserve our Passion either ways." "Beware of him that is slow to anger: He is angry for something, and will not be pleased for nothing." "The Wit of Conversation consists more in finding it in others, than shewing a good deal yourself. He who goes out of your Company pleased with his own facetiousness and Ingenuity will the sooner come into it again."

Many have concluded from these and comparable maxims that their author was a cunning soft-soaper who practiced virtue for reasons of utility and dispensed with truth if it wasn't useful. This seems to me a gross misreading of the author's character. Franklin never claimed to know the "truth" of anything. He observed his own times and studied past times; he analyzed his own conduct to find out what useful lessons could be extracted from his successes and blunders. (The "blunders," be it noted, he subsumed in the printer's term *errata*; his ancestors had called them sins.) Lessons derived from personal experience and extensive reading lay behind his hypotheses and tentative formulas for sensible behavior. He was neither credulous nor cynical. Human happiness (which he boiled down to health, wealth, and wisdom) might be approximated by cultivating useful habits; errata might be corrected. He discerned a moral pattern in the universe but entertained small hope in the moral prospects of mankind.

The Autobiography

Part One

Twyford, at the Bishop
of St Asaph's
1771.

Dear Son,

I have ever had a Pleasure in obtaining any little Anecdotes of my Ancestors. You may remember the Enquiries I made among the Remains of my Relations when you were with me in England; and the Journey I took for that purpose. Now imagining it may be equally agreable to you to know the Circumstances of *my* Life, many of which you are yet unacquainted with; and expecting a Weeks uninterrupted Leisure in my present Country Retirement, I sit down to write them for you. To which I have besides some other Inducements. Having emerg'd from the Poverty & Obscurity in which I was born & bred, to a State of Affluence & some Degree of Reputation in the World, and having gone so far thro' Life with a considerable Share of Felicity, the conducing Means I made use of, which, with the Blessing of God, so well succeeded, my Posterity may like to know, as they may find some of them suitable to their own Situations, & therefore fit to be imitated.—That Felicity, when I reflected on it, has induc'd me sometimes to say, that were it offer'd to my Choice, I should have no Objection to a Repetition of the same Life from its Beginning, only asking the Advantage Authors have in a second Edition to correct some Faults of the first. So would I if I might, besides corr^g the Faults, change some sinister Accidents & Events of it for others more favourable, but tho' this were deny'd, I should still accept the Offer. However, since such a Repetition is not to be expected, the Thing most like living one's Life over again, seems to be a *Recollection* of that Life; and to make that Recollection as durable as possible, the putting it down in Writing.—Hereby, too, I shall indulge the Inclination so natural in old Men, to be talking of themselves and their own past Actions, and I shall indulge it, without being troublesome to others who thro' respect to Age might think themselves oblig'd to give me a Hearing, since this may be read or not as any one pleases.

And lastly, (I may as well confess it, since my Denial of it will be believ'd by no body) perhaps I shall a good deal gratify my own *Vanity*. Indeed I scarce ever heard or saw the introductory Words, *Without Vanity I may say*, &c. but some vain thing immediately follow'd. Most People dislike Vanity in others whatever Share they have of it themselves, but I give it fair Quarter wherever I meet with it, being persuaded that it is often productive of Good to the Possessor & to others that are within his Sphere of Action: And therefore in many Cases it would not be quite absurd if a Man were to thank God for his Vanity among the other Comforts of Life.—

And now I speak of thanking God, I desire with all Humility to acknowledge, that I owe the mention'd Happiness of my past Life to his kind Providence, which led me to the Means I us'd & gave them Success.—My Belief of This, induces me to *hope*, tho' I must not *presume*, that the same Goodness will still be exercis'd towards me in continuing that Happiness, or in enabling me to bear a fatal Reverso, which I may experience as others have done, the Complexion of my future Fortune being known to him only: and in whose Power it is to bless to us even our Afflictions.

The Notes one of my Uncles (who had the same kind of Curiosity in collecting Family Anecdotes) once put into my Hands, furnish'd me with several Particulars, relating to our Ancestors. From those Notes I learnt that the Family had liv'd in the same Village, Ecton in Northamptonshire, for 300 Years, & how much longer he knew not, (perhaps from the Time when the Name *Franklin* that before was the Name of an Order of People, was assum'd by them for a Surname, when others took Surnames all over the Kingdom.—*) on a

---

*As a proof that FRANKLIN was anciently the common name of an order or rank in England, see Judge Fortescue, *De laudibus Legum Angliae*, written about the year 1412, in which is the following passage, to show that good juries might easily be formed in any part of England.

"Regio etiam illa, ita respersa refertaque est *possessoribus terrarum* et agrorum, quod in ea, villula tam parva reperiri non poterit, in qua non est *miles*, *armiger*, vel pater-familias, qualis ibidem *Franklin* vulgariter nuncupatur, magnis ditatus possessionibus, nec non libere tenentes et alii *valecti* plurimi, suis patrimoniis sufficientes ad faciendum juratam, in forma praenotata."

"Moreover, the same country is so filled and replenished with landed

Freehold of about 30 Acres, aided by the Smith's Business which had continued in the Family till his Time, the eldest Son being always bred to that Business. A Custom which he & my Father both followed as to their eldest Sons.—When I search'd the Register at Ecton, I found an Account of their Births, Marriages and Burials, from the Year 1555 only, there being no Register kept in that Parish at any time preceding.—By that Register I perceiv'd that I was the youngest Son of the youngest Son for 5 Generations back. My Grandfather Thomas, who was born in 1598, lived at Ecton till he grew too old to follow Business longer, when he went to live with his Son John, a Dyer at Banbury in Oxfordshire, with whom my Father serv'd an Apprenticeship. There my Grandfather died and lies buried. We saw his Gravestone in 1758. His eldest Son Thomas liv'd in the House at Ecton, and left it with the Land to his only Child, a Daughter, who with her Husband, one Fisher of Wellingborough sold it to Mr Isted, now Lord of the Manor there. My Grandfather had 4 Sons that grew up, viz. Thomas, John, Benjamin and Josiah. I will give you what Account I can of them at this distance from my Papers, and if those are not lost in my Absence, you will among them find many more Particulars. Thomas was bred a Smith under his Father, but being ingenious, and encourag'd in Learning (as all his Brothers like wise werre,) by an Esquire Palmer then the principal Gentleman in that Parish, he qualify'd himself for the Business of Scrivener, became a con-

---

menne, that therein so small a Thorpe cannot be found werein dweleth not a knight, an esquire, or such a householder, as is there commonly called a *Franklin*, enriched with great possessions; and also other freeholders and many yeomen able for their livelihoods to make a jury in form aforementioned."—(*Old Translation*.)

Chaucer too calls his Country Gentleman, a *Franklin*, and after describing his good housekeeping thus characterises him:

> "This worthy Franklin bore a purse of silk,
> Fix'd to his girdle, white as morning milk.
> Knight of the Shire, first Justice at th' Assize,
> To help the poor, the doubtful to advise.
> In all employments, generous, just, he proved;
> Renown'd for courtesy, by all beloved."

siderable Man in the County Affairs, was a chief Mover of all publick Spirited Undertakings, for the County or Town of Northampton & his own Village, of which many Instances were told us at Ecton and he was much taken Notice of and patroniz'd by the then Lord Halifax. He died in 1702 Jan. 6. old Stile, just 4 Years to a Day before I was born. The Account we receiv'd of his Life & Character from some old People at Ecton, I remember struck you as something extraordinary from its Similarity to what you knew of mine. Had he died on the same Day, you said one might have suppos'd a Transmigration.—John was bred a Dyer, I believe of Woollens. Benjamin, was bred a Silk Dyer, serving an Apprenticeship at London. He was an ingenious Man, I remember him well, for when I was a Boy he came over to my Father in Boston, and lived in the House with us some Years. He lived to a great Age. His Grandson Samuel Franklin now lives in Boston. He left behind him two Quarto Volumes, M.S. of his own Poetry, consisting of little occasional Pieces address'd to his Friends and Relations, of which the following sent to me, is a Specimen.

Sent to My Name upon a Report
of his Inclination to Martial affaires
7 July 1710

Beleeve me Ben. It is a Dangerous Trade
The Sword has Many Marr'd as well as Made
By it doe many fall Not Many Rise
Makes Many poor few Rich and fewer Wise
Fills Towns with Ruin, fields with blood beside
Tis Sloths Maintainer, And the Shield of pride
Fair Cities Rich to Day, in plenty flow
War fills with want, Tomorrow, & with woe
Ruin'd Estates, The Nurse of Vice, broke limbs & scarss
   Are the Effects of Desolating Warrs

Sent to B. F. in N. E. 15 July 1710

B   e to thy parents an Obedient Son
E   ach Day let Duty constantly be Done
N   ever give Way to sloth or lust or pride

I f free you'd be from Thousand Ills beside
A bove all Ills be sure Avoide the shelfe
M ans Danger lyes in Satan sin and selfe
I n vertue Learning Wisdome progress Make
N ere shrink at Suffering for thy saviours sake
F raud and all Falshood in thy Dealings Flee
R eligious Always in thy station be
A dore the Maker of thy Inward part
N ow's the Accepted time, Give him thy Heart
K eep a Good Consceince 'tis a constant Frind
L ike Judge and Witness This Thy Acts Attend
I n Heart with bended knee Alone Adore
N one but the Three in One Forevermore.

He had form'd a Shorthand of his own, which he taught me, but never practicing it I have now forgot it. I was nam'd after this Uncle, there being a particular Affection between him and my Father. He was very pious, a great Attender of Sermons of the best Preachers, which he took down in his Shorthand and had with him many Volumes of them. —He was also much of a Politician, too much perhaps for his Station. There fell lately into my Hands in London a Collection he had made of all the principal Pamphlets relating to Publick Affairs from 1641 to 1717. Many of the Volumes are wanting, as appears by the Numbering, but there still remains 8 Vols. Folio, and 24 in 4to & 8vo.—A Dealer in old Books met with them, and knowing me by my sometimes buying of him, he brought them to me. It seems my Uncle must have left them here when he went to America, which was above 50 Years since. There are many of his Notes in the Margins.—

This obscure Family of ours was early in the Reformation, and continu'd Protestants thro' the Reign of Queen Mary, when they were sometimes in Danger of Trouble on Account of their Zeal against Popery. They had got an English Bible, & to conceal & secure it, it was fastned open with Tapes under & within the Frame of a Joint Stool. When my Great Great Grandfather read in it to his Family, he turn'd up the

Joint Stool upon his Knees, turning over the Leaves then under the Tapes. One of the Children stood at the Door to give
Notice if he saw the Apparitor coming, who was an Officer
of the Spiritual Court. In that Case the Stool was turn'd
down again upon its feet, when the Bible remain'd conceal'd
under it as before. This Anecdote I had from my Uncle Benjamin.—The Family continu'd all of the Church of England
till about the End of Charles the 2^{ds} Reign, when some of the
Ministers that had been outed for Nonconformity, holding
Conventicles in Northamptonshire, Benjamin & Josiah ad-
her'd to them, and so continu'd all their Lives. The rest of
the Family remain'd with the Episcopal Church.

Josiah, my Father, married young, and carried his Wife
with three Children unto New England, about 1682. The
Conventicles having been forbidden by Law, & frequently
disturbed, induced some considerable Men of his Acquaintance to remove to that Country, and he was prevail'd with to
accompany them thither, where they expected to enjoy their
Mode of Religion with Freedom.—By the same Wife he had
4 Children more born there, and by a second Wife ten more,
in all 17, of which I remember 13 sitting at one time at his
Table, who all grew up to be Men & Women, and married;—
I was the youngest Son and the youngest Child but two, &
was born in Boston, N. England.

My Mother the 2^{d} Wife was Abiah Folger, a Daughter of
Peter Folger, one of the first Settlers of New England, of
whom honourable mention is made by Cotton Mather, in his
Church History of that Country, (entitled Magnalia Christi
Americana) as a *godly learned Englishman*, if I remember the
Words rightly.—I have heard that he wrote sundry small occasional Pieces, but only one of them was printed which I saw
now many Years since. It was written in 1675, in the home-
spun Verse of that Time & People, and address'd to those
then concern'd in the Government there. It was in favour of
Liberty of Conscience, & in behalf of the Baptists, Quakers,
& other Sectaries, that had been under Persecution; ascribing
the Indian Wars & other Distresses, that had befallen the
Country to that Persecution, as so many Judgments of God,
to punish so heinous an Offence; and exhorting a Repeal
of those uncharitable Laws. The whole appear'd to me as

written with a good deal of Decent Plainness & manly Freedom. The six last concluding Lines I remember, tho' I have
forgotten the two first of the Stanza, but the Purport of them
was that his Censures proceeded from *Goodwill*, & therefore
he would be known as the Author,

>   because to be a Libeller, (says he)
>   I hate it with my Heart.
>   From *Sherburne Town where now I dwell,
>   My Name I do put here,
>   Without Offence, your real Friend,
>   It is Peter Folgier.

*In the Island of Nantucket.

My elder Brothers were all put Apprentices to different
Trades. I was put to the Grammar School at Eight Years of
Age, my Father intending to devote me as the Tithe of his
Sons to the Service of the Church. My early Readiness in
learning to read (which must have been very early, as I do
not remember when I could not read) and the Opinion of all
his Friends that I should certainly make a good Scholar, encourag'd him in this Purpose of his. My Uncle Benjamin too
approv'd of it, and propos'd to give me all his Shorthand Volumes of Sermons I suppose as a Stock to set up with, if I
would learn his Character. I continu'd however at the Grammar School not quite one Year, tho' in that time I had risen
gradually from the Middle of the Class of that Year to be the
Head of it, and farther was remov'd into the next Class above
it, in order to go with that into the third at the End of the
Year. But my Father in the mean time, from a View of the
Expence of a College Education which, having so large a
Family, he could not well afford, and the mean Living many
so educated were afterwards able to obtain, Reasons that he
gave to his Friends in my Hearing, altered his first Intention,
took me from the Grammar School, and sent me to a School
for Writing & Arithmetic kept by a then famous Man, Mr
Geo. Brownell, very successful in his Profession generally, and
that by mild encouraging Methods. Under him I acquired fair
Writing pretty soon, but I fail'd in the Arithmetic, & made
no Progress in it.—At Ten Years old, I was taken home to

assist my Father in his Business, which was that of a Tallow Chandler and Sope-Boiler. A Business he was not bred to, but had assumed on his Arrival in New England & on finding his Dying Trade would not maintain his Family, being in little Request. Accordingly I was employed in cutting Wick for the Candles, filling the Dipping Mold, & the Molds for cast Candles, attending the Shop, going of Errands, &c.—I dislik'd the Trade and had a strong Inclination for the Sea; but my Father declar'd against it; however, living near the Water, I was much in and about it, learnt early to swim well, & to manage Boats, and when in a Boat or Canoe with other Boys I was commonly allow'd to govern, especially in any case of Difficulty; and upon other Occasions I was generally a Leader among the Boys, and sometimes led them into Scrapes, of wch I will mention one Instance, as it shows an early projecting public Spirit, tho' not then justly conducted. There was a Salt Marsh that bounded part of the Mill Pond, on the Edge of which at Highwater, we us'd to stand to fish for Minews. By much Trampling, we had made it a mere Quagmire. My Proposal was to build a Wharf there fit for us to stand upon, and I show'd my Comrades a large Heap of Stones which were intended for a new House near the Marsh, and which would very well suit our Purpose. Accordingly in the Evening when the Workmen were gone, I assembled a Number of my Playfellows, and working with them diligently like so many Emmets, sometimes two or three to a Stone, we brought them all away and built our little Wharff.— The next Morning the Workmen were surpriz'd at Missing the Stones; which were found in our Wharff; Enquiry was made after the Removers; we were discovered & complain'd of; several of us were corrected by our Fathers; and tho' I pleaded the Usefulness of the Work, mine convinc'd me that nothing was useful which was not honest.—

I think you may like to know something of his Person & Character. He had an excellent Constitution of Body, was of middle Stature, but well set and very strong. He was ingenious, could draw prettily, was skill'd a little in Music and had a clear pleasing Voice, so that when he play'd Psalm Tunes on his Violin & sung withal as he some times did in an Evening after the Business of the Day was over, it was extreamly agreable to hear. He had a mechanical Genius too, and on occasion was very handy in the Use of other Tradesmen's Tools. But his great Excellence lay in a sound Understanding, and solid Judgment in prudential Matters, both in private & publick Affairs. In the latter indeed he was never employed, the numerous Family he had to educate & the Straitness of his Circumstances, keeping him close to his Trade, but I remember well his being frequently visited by leading People, who consulted him for his Opinion on Affairs of the Town or of the Church he belong'd to & show'd a good deal of Respect for his Judgment and Advice. He was also much consulted by private Persons about their Affairs when any Difficulty occur'd, & frequently chosen an Arbitrator between contending Parties.—At his Table he lik'd to have as often as he could, some sensible Friend or Neighbour, to converse with, and always took care to start some ingenious or useful Topic for Discourse, which might tend to improve the Minds of his Children. By this means he turn'd our Attention to what was good, just, & prudent in the Conduct of Life; and little or no Notice was ever taken of what related to the Victuals on the Table, whether it was well or ill drest, in or out of season, of good or bad flavour, preferable or inferior to this or that other thing of the kind; so that I was bro't up in such a perfect Inattention to those Matters as to be quite Indifferent what kind of Food was set before me; and so unobservant of it, that to this Day, if I am ask'd I can scarce tell, a few Hours after Dinner, what I din'd upon.— This has been a Convenience to me in travelling, where my Companions have been sometimes very unhappy for want of a suitable Gratification of their more delicate because better instructed Tastes and Appetites.—

My Mother had likewise an excellent Constitution. She suckled all her 10 Children. I never knew either my Father or Mother to have any Sickness but that of which they dy'd, he at 89 & she at 85 Years of age. They lie buried together at Boston, where I some Years since plac'd a Marble stone over their Grave with this Inscription

Josiah Franklin
And Abiah his Wife

Lie here interred.
They lived lovingly together in Wedlock
Fifty-five Years.—
Without an Estate or any gainful Employment,
By constant Labour and Industry,
With God's Blessing,
They maintained a large Family
Comfortably;
And brought up thirteen Children,
And seven Grandchildren
Reputably.
From this Instance, Reader,
Be encouraged to Diligence in thy Calling,
And distrust not Providence.
He was a pious & prudent Man,
She a discreet and virtuous Woman.
Their youngest Son,
In filial Regard to their Memory,
Places this Stone.
J. F. born 1655—Died 1744. Ætat 89
A. F. born 1667—died 1752——85

By my rambling Digressions I perceive my self to be grown
old. I us'd to write more methodically.—But one does not
dress for private Company as for a publick Ball. 'Tis perhaps
only Negligence.—

To return. I continu'd thus employ'd in my Father's Business for two Years, that is till I was 12 Years old; and my
Brother John, who was bred to that Business having left my
Father, married and set up for himself at Rhodeisland, there
was all Appearance that I was destin'd to supply his Place and
be a Tallow Chandler. But my Dislike to the Trade continuing, my Father was under Apprehensions that if he did not
find one for me more agreable, I should break away and get
to Sea, as his Son Josiah had done to his great Vexation. He
therefore sometimes took me to walk with him, and see Join-
ers, Bricklayers, Turners, Braziers, &c. at their Work, that he
might observe my Inclination, & endeavour to fix it on some
Trade or other on Land.—It has ever since been a Pleasure

to me to see good Workmen handle their Tools; and it has been useful to me, having learnt so much by it, as to be able to do little Jobs my self in my House, when a Workman could not readily be got; & to construct little Machines for my Experiments while the Intention of making the Experiment was fresh & warm in my Mind. My Father at last fix'd upon the Cutler's Trade, and my Uncle Benjamin's Son Samuel who was bred to that Business in London being about that time establish'd in Boston, I was sent to be with him some time on liking. But his Expectations of a Fee with me displeasing my Father, I was taken home again.—

From a Child I was fond of Reading, and all the little Money that came into my Hands was ever laid out in Books. Pleas'd with the Pilgrim's Progress, my first Collection was of John Bunyan's Works, in separate little Volumes. I afterwards sold them to enable me to buy R. Burton's Historical Collections; they were small Chapmen's Books and cheap, 40 or 50 in all.—My Father's little Library consisted chiefly of Books in polemic Divinity, most of which I read, and have since often regretted, that at a time when I had such a Thirst for Knowledge, more proper Books had not fallen in my Way, since it was now resolv'd I should not be a Clergyman. Plutarch's Lives there was, in which I read abundantly, and I still think that time spent to great Advantage. There was also a Book of Defoe's called an Essay on Projects and another of Dr Mather's call'd Essays to do Good, which perhaps gave me a Turn of Thinking that had an Influence on some of the principal future Events of my Life.

This Bookish Inclination at length determin'd my Father to make me a Printer, tho' he had already one Son, (James) of that Profession. In 1717 my Brother James return'd from England with a Press & Letters to set up his Business in Boston. I lik'd it much better than that of my Father, but still had a Hankering for the Sea.—To prevent the apprehended Effect of such an Inclination, my Father was impatient to have me bound to my Brother. I stood out some time, but at last was persuaded and signed the Indentures, when I was yet but 12 Years old.—I was to serve as an Apprentice till I was 21 Years of Age, only I was to be allow'd Journeyman's Wages during the last Year. In a little time I made great Proficiency in the

Business, and became a useful Hand to my Brother. I now had Access to better Books. An Acquaintance with the Apprentices of Booksellers, enabled me sometimes to borrow a small one, which I was careful to return soon & clean. Often I sat up in my Room reading the greatest Part of the Night, when the Book was borrow'd in the Evening & to be return'd early in the Morning lest it should be miss'd or wanted.—And after some time an ingenious Tradesman* who had a pretty Collection of Books, & who frequented our Printing House, took Notice of me, invited me to his Library, & very kindly lent me such Books as I chose to read. I now took a Fancy to Poetry, and made some little Pieces. My Brother, thinking it might turn to account encourag'd me, & put me on composing two occasional Ballads. One was called the *Light House Tragedy*, & contain'd an Acc^t of the drowning of Capt. Worthilake with his Two Daughters; the other was a Sailor Song on the Taking of *Teach* or Blackbeard the Pirate. They were wretched Stuff, in the Grubstreet Ballad Stile, and when they were printed he sent me about the Town to sell them. The first sold wonderfully, the Event being recent, having made a great Noise. This flatter'd my Vanity. But my Father discourag'd me, by ridiculing my Performances, and telling me Verse-makers were generally Beggars; so I escap'd being a Poet, most probably a very bad one. But as Prose Writing has been a great Use to me in the Course of my Life, and was a principal Means of my Advancement, I shall tell you how in such a Situation I acquir'd what little Ability I have in that Way.

There was another Bookish Lad in the Town, John Collins by Name, with whom I was intimately acquainted. We sometimes disputed, and very fond we were of Argument, & very desirous of confuting one another. Which disputacious Turn, by the way, is apt to become a very bad Habit, making People often extreamly disagreable in Company, by the Contradiction that is necessary to bring it into Practice, & thence, besides souring & spoiling the Conversation, is productive of Disgusts & perhaps Enmities where you may have occasion for Friendship. I had caught it by reading my Father's Books

*Mr Matthew Adams

of Dispute about Religion. Persons of good Sense, I have since observ'd, seldom fall into it, except Lawyers, University Men, and Men of all Sorts that have been bred at Edinborough. A Question was once some how or other started between Collins & me, of the Propriety of educating the Female Sex in Learning, & their Abilities for Study. He was of Opinion that it was improper; & that they were naturally unequal to it. I took the contrary Side, perhaps a little for Dispute sake. He was naturally more eloquent, had a ready Plenty of Words, and sometimes as I thought bore me down more by his Fluency than by the Strength of his Reasons. As we parted without settling the Point, & were not to see one another again for some time, I sat down to put my Arguments in Writing, which I copied fair & sent to him. He answer'd & I reply'd. Three or four Letters of a Side had pass'd, when my Father happen'd to find my Papers, and read them. Without entring into the Discussion, he took occasion to talk to me about the Manner of my Writing, observ'd that tho' I had the Advantage of my Antagonist in correct Spelling & pointing (which I ow'd to the Printing House) I fell far short in elegance of Expression, in Method and in Perspicuity, of which he convinc'd me by several Instances. I saw the Justice of his Remarks, & thence grew more attentive to the *Manner* in Writing, and determin'd to endeavour at Improvement.—

About this time I met with an odd Volume of the Spectator. I had never before seen any of them. I bought it, read it over and over, and was much delighted with it. I thought the Writing excellent, & wish'd if possible to imitate it. With that View, I took some of the Papers, & making short Hints of the Sentiment in each Sentence, laid them by a few Days, and then without looking at the Book, try'd to compleat the Papers again, by expressing each hinted Sentiment at length & as fully as it had been express'd before, in any suitable Words that should come to hand.

Then I compar'd my Spectator with the Original, discover'd some of my Faults & corrected them. But I found I wanted a Stock of Words or a Readiness in recollecting & using them, which I thought I should have acquir'd before that time, if I had gone on making Verses, since the continual

Occasion for Words of the same Import but of different Length, to suit the Measure, or of different Sound for the Rhyme, would have laid me under a constant Necessity of searching for Variety, and also have tended to fix that Variety in my Mind, & make me Master of it. Therefore I took some of the Tales & turn'd them into Verse: And after a time, when I had pretty well forgotten the Prose, turn'd them back again. I also sometimes jumbled my Collections of Hints into Confusion, and after some Weeks, endeavour'd to reduce them into the best Order, before I began to form the full Sentences & compleat the Paper. This was to teach me Method in the Arrangement of Thoughts. By comparing my Work afterwards with the original, I discover'd many faults and amended them; but I sometimes had the Pleasure of Fancying that in certain Particulars of small Import, I had been lucky enough to improve the Method or the Language and this encourag'd me to think I might possibly in time come to be a tolerable English Writer, of which I was extreamly ambitious.

My Time for these Exercises & for Reading, was at Night after Work, or before Work began in the Morning; or on Sundays, when I contrived to be in the Printing House alone, evading as much as I could the common Attendance on publick Worship, which my Father used to exact of me when I was under his Care:—And which indeed I still thought a Duty; tho' I could not, as it seemed to me, afford the Time to practise it.

When about 16 Years of Age, I happen'd to meet with a Book written by one Tryon, recommending a Vegetable Diet. I determined to go into it. My Brother being yet unmarried, did not keep House, but boarded himself & his Apprentices in another Family. My refusing to eat Flesh occasioned an Inconveniency, and I was frequently chid for my singularity. I made my self acquainted with Tryon's Manner of preparing some of his Dishes, such as Boiling Potatoes, or Rice, making Hasty Pudding, & a few others, and then propos'd to my Brother, that if he would give me Weekly half the Money he paid for my Board, I would board my self. He instantly agreed to it, and I presently found that I could save half what he paid me. This was an additional Fund for buying Books:

But I had another Advantage in it. My Brother and the rest
going from the Printing House to their Meals, I remain'd
there alone, and dispatching presently my light Repast,
(which often was no more than a Bisket or a Slice of Bread,
a Handful of Raisins or a Tart from the Pastry Cook's, and a
Glass of Water) had the rest of the Time till their Return, for
Study, in which I made the greater Progress from that greater
Clearness of Head & quicker Apprehension which usually at-
tend Temperance in Eating & Drinking. And now it was that
being on some Occasion made asham'd of my Ignorance in
Figures, which I had twice fail'd in learning when at School,
I took Cocker's Book of Arithmetick, & went thro' the whole
by my self with great Ease. — I also read Seller's & Sturmy's
Books of Navigation, & became acquainted with the little
Geometry they contain, but never proceeded far in that
Science. — And I read about this Time Locke on Human
Understanding and the Art of Thinking by Messrs du Port
Royal.

While I was intent on improving my Language, I met with
an English Grammar (I think it was Greenwood's) at the End
of which there were two little Sketches of the Arts of Rheto-
ric and Logic, the latter finishing with a Specimen of a Dispute in the Socratic Method. And soon after I procur'd
Xenophon's Memorable Things of Socrates, wherein there are
many Instances of the same Method. I was charm'd with it,
adopted it, dropt my abrupt Contradiction, and positive Argumentation, and put on the humble Enquirer & Doubter.
And being then, from reading Shaftsbury & Collins, become
a real Doubter in many Points of our Religious Doctrine, I
found this Method safest for my self & very embarassing to
those against whom I used it, therefore I took a Delight in it,
practis'd it continually & grew very artful & expert in drawing People even of superior Knowledge into Concessions the
Consequences of which they did not foresee, entangling them
in Difficulties out of which they could not extricate themselves, and so obtaining Victories that neither my self nor my
Cause always deserved. — I continu'd this Method some few
Years, but gradually left it, retaining only the Habit of expressing my self in Terms of modest Diffidence, never using
when I advance any thing that may possibly be disputed, the

Words, *Certainly*, *undoubtedly*, or any others that give the Air of Positiveness to an Opinion; but rather say, *I conceive*, or *I apprehend* a Thing to be so or so, *It appears to me*, or *I should think it so or so for such & such Reasons*, or *I imagine* it to be so, or *it is so* if *I am not mistaken.*—This Habit I believe has been of great Advantage to me, when I have had occasion to inculcate my Opinions & persuade Men into Measures that I have been from time to time engag'd in promoting.—And as the chief Ends of Conversation are to *inform*, or to be *informed*, to *please* or to *persuade*, I wish well meaning sensible Men would not lessen their Power of doing Good by a Positive assuming Manner that seldom fails to disgust, tends to create Opposition, and to defeat every one of those Purposes for which Speech was given us, to wit, giving or receiving Information, or Pleasure: For If you would *inform*, a positive dogmatical Manner in advancing your Sentiments, may provoke Contradiction & prevent a candid Attention. If you wish Information & Improvement from the Knowledge of others and yet at the same time express your self as firmly fix'd in your present Opinions, modest sensible Men, who do not love Disputation, will probably leave you undisturb'd in the Possession of your Error; and by such a Manner you can seldom hope to recommend your self in *pleasing* your Hearers, or to persuade those whose Concurrence you desire.—Pope says, judiciously,

> *Men should be taught as if you taught them not,*
> *And things unknown propos'd as things forgot,*—

farther recommending it to us,

> *To speak tho' sure, with seeming Diffidence.*

And he might have couple'd with this Line that which he has coupled with another, I think less properly,

> *For want of Modesty is want of Sense.*

If you ask why *less properly*, I must repeat the Lines;

> "Immodest Words admit of *no* Defence;
> "*For* Want of Modesty is Want of Sense."

Now is not *Want of Sense*, (where a Man is so unfortunate as to want it) some Apology for his *Want of Modesty*? and would not the Lines stand more justly thus?

> Immodest Words admit *but this* Defence,
> That Want of Modesty is Want of Sense.

This however I should submit to better Judgments.—

My Brother had in 1720 or 21, begun to print a Newspaper. It was the second that appear'd in America, & was called *The New England Courant*. The only one before it, was *the Boston News Letter*. I remember his being dissuaded by some of his Friends from the Undertaking, as not likely to succeed, one Newspaper being in their Judgment enough for America.— At this time 1771 there are not less than five & twenty.—He went on however with the Undertaking, and after having work'd in composing the Types & printing off the Sheets I was employ'd to carry the Papers thro' the Streets to the Customers.—He had some ingenious Men among his Friends who amus'd themselves by writing little Pieces for this Paper, which gain'd it Credit, & made it more in Demand; and these Gentlemen often visited us.—Hearing their Conversations, and their Accounts of the Approbation their Papers were receiv'd with, I was excited to try my Hand among them. But being still a Boy, & suspecting that my Brother would object to printing any Thing of mine in his Paper if he knew it to be mine, I contriv'd to disguise my Hand, & writing an anonymous Paper I put it in at Night under the Door of the Printing House. It was found in the Morning & communicated to his Writing Friends when they call'd in as Usual. They read it, commented on it in my Hearing, and I had the exquisite Pleasure, of finding it met with their Approbation, and that in their different Guesses at the Author none were named but Men of some Character among us for Learning & Ingenuity.—I suppose now that I was rather lucky in my Judges: And that perhaps they were not really so very good ones as I then esteem'd them. Encourag'd however by this, I wrote and convey'd in the same Way to the Press several more Papers, which were equally approv'd, and I kept my Secret till my small Fund of Sense for such Performances was pretty well exhausted, & then I discovered it; when I began to be considered a little more by my Brother's Acquaintance, and in a manner that did not quite please him, as he thought, probably with reason, that it tended to make me too vain. And perhaps this might be one Occasion of the Differences that we began to have about this Time. Tho' a Brother, he considered himself as my Master, & me as his Apprentice; and accordingly expected the same Services from me as he would from another; while I thought he demean'd me too much in some he requir'd of me, who from a Brother expected more Indulgence. Our Disputes were often brought before our Father, and I fancy I was either generally in the right, or else a better Pleader, because the Judgment was generally in my favour: But my Brother was passionate & had often beaten me, which I took extreamly amiss; * and thinking my Apprenticeship very tedious, I was continually wishing for some Opportunity of shortening it, which at length offered in a manner unexpected.

One of the Pieces in our News-Paper, on some political Point which I have now forgotten, gave Offence to the Assembly. He was taken up, censur'd and imprison'd for a Month by the Speaker's Warrant, I suppose because he would not discover his Author. I too was taken up & examin'd before the Council; but tho' I did not give them any Satisfaction, they contented themselves with admonishing me, and dismiss'd me; considering me perhaps as an Apprentice who was bound to keep his Master's Secrets. During my Brother's Confinement, which I resented a good deal, notwithstanding our private Differences, I had the Management of the Paper, and I made bold to give our Rulers some Rubs in it, which my Brother took very kindly, while others began to consider me in an unfavourable Light, as a young Genius that had a Turn for Libelling & Satyr. My Brother's Discharge was accompany'd with an Order of the House, (a very odd one) *that James Franklin should no longer print the Paper called the New England Courant.* There was a Consultation held in our Printing House among his Friends what he should do in this

---

*I fancy his harsh & tyrannical Treatment of me, might be a means of impressing me with that Aversion to arbitrary Power that has stuck to me thro' my whole Life.

Case. Some propos'd to evade the Order by changing the Name of the Paper; but my Brother seeing Inconveniences in that, it was finally concluded on as a better Way, to let it be printed for the future under the Name of *Benjamin Franklin*. And to avoid the Censure of the Assembly that might fall on him, as still printing it by his Apprentice, the Contrivance was, that my old Indenture should be return'd to me with a full Discharge on the Back of it, to be shown on Occasion; but to secure to him the Benefit of my Service I was to sign new Indentures for the Remainder of the Term, wch were to be kept private. A very flimsy Scheme it was, but however it was immediately executed, and the Paper went on accordingly under my Name for several Months. At length a fresh Difference arising between my Brother and me, I took upon me to assert my Freedom, presuming that he would not venture to produce the new Indentures. It was not fair in me to take this Advantage, and this I therefore reckon one of the first Errata of my Life: But the Unfairness of it weigh'd little with me, when under the Impressions of Resentment, for the Blows his Passion too often urg'd him to bestow upon me. Tho' He was otherwise not an ill-natur'd Man: Perhaps I was too saucy & provoking.—

When he found I would leave him, he took care to prevent my getting Employment in any other Printing-House of the Town, by going round & speaking to every Master, who accordingly refus'd to give me Work. I then thought of going to New York as the nearest Place where there was a Printer: and I was the rather inclin'd to leave Boston, when I reflected that I had already made my self a little obnoxious, to the governing Party; & from the arbitrary Proceedings of the Assembly in my Brother's Case it was likely I might if I stay'd soon bring my self into Scrapes; and farther that my indiscrete Disputations about Religion began to make me pointed at with Horror by good People, as an Infidel or Atheist; I determin'd on the Point: but my Father now siding with my Brother, I was sensible that if I attempted to go openly, Means would be used to prevent me. My Friend Collins therefore undertook to manage a little for me. He agreed with the Captain of a New York Sloop for my Passage, under the Notion of my being a young Acquaintance of his that had got a naughty

Girl with Child, whose Friends would compel me to marry her, and therefore I could not appear or come away publickly. So I sold some of my Books to raise a little Money, Was taken on board privately, and as we had a fair Wind, in three Days I found my self in New York near 300 Miles from home, a Boy of but 17, without the least Recommendation to or Knowledge of any Person in the Place, and with very little Money in my Pocket.—

My Inclinations for the Sea, were by this time worne out, or I might now have gratify'd them.—But having a Trade, & supposing my self a pretty good Workman, I offer'd my Service to the Printer of the Place, old Mr W.ᵐ Bradford.—He could give me no Employment, having little to do, and Help enough already: But, says he, my Son at Philadelphia has lately lost his principal Hand, Aquila Rose, by Death. If you go thither I believe he may employ you.—Philadelphia was 100 Miles farther. I set out, however, in a Boat for Amboy; leaving my Chest and Things to follow me round by Sea. In crossing the Bay we met with a Squall that tore our rotten Sails to pieces, prevented our getting into the Kill, and drove us upon Long Island. In our Way a drunken Dutchman, who was a Passenger too, fell over board; when he was sinking I reach'd thro' the Water to his shock Pate & drew him up so that we got him in again.—His Ducking sober'd him a little, & he went to sleep, taking first out of his Pocket a Book which he desir'd I would dry for him. It prov'd to be my old favourite Author Bunyan's Pilgrim's Progress in Dutch, finely printed on good Paper with copper Cuts, a Dress better than I had ever seen it wear in its own Language. I have since found that it has been translated into most of the Languages of Europe, and suppose it has been more generally read than any other Book except perhaps the Bible.—Honest John was the first that I know of who mix'd Narration & Dialogue, a Method of Writing very engaging to the Reader, who in the most interesting Parts finds himself as it were brought into the Company, & present at the Discourse. De foe in his Cruso, his Moll Flanders, Religious Courtship, Family Instructor, & other Pieces, has imitated it with Success. And Richardson has done the same in his Pamela, &c.—

When we drew near the Island we found it was at a Place

where there could be no Landing, there being a great Surff
on the stony Beach. So we dropt Anchor & swung round
towards the Shore. Some People came down to the Water
Edge & hallow'd to us, as we did to them. But the Wind was
so high & the Surff so loud, that we could not hear so as to
understand each other. There were Canoes on the Shore, &
we made Signs & hallow'd that they should fetch us, but they
either did not understand us, or thought it impracticable. So
they went away, and Night coming on, we had no Remedy
but to wait till the Wind should abate, and in the mean time
the Boatman & I concluded to sleep if we could, and so
crouded into the Scuttle with the Dutchman who was still
wet, and the Spray beating over the Head of our Boat, leak'd
thro' to us, so that we were soon almost as wet as he. In this
Manner we lay all Night with very little Rest. But the Wind
abating the next Day, we made a Shift to reach Amboy before
Night, having been 30 Hours on the Water without Victuals,
or any Drink but a Bottle of filthy Rum:—The Water we
sail'd on being salt.—

In the Evening I found my self very feverish, & went ill
to Bed. But having read somewhere that cold Water drank
plentifully was good for a Fever, I follow'd the Prescription,
sweat plentifully most of the Night, my Fever left me, and in
the Morning crossing the Ferry, proceeded on my Journey,
on foot, having 50 Miles to Burlington, where I was told I
should find Boats that would carry me the rest of the Way to
Philadelphia.

It rain'd very hard all the Day, I was thoroughly soak'd,
and by Noon a good deal tir'd, so I stopt at a poor Inn,
where I staid all Night, beginning now to wish I had never
left home. I cut so miserable a Figure too, that I found by
the Questions ask'd me I was suspected to be some runaway
Servant, and in danger of being taken up on that Suspicion.—However I proceeded the next Day, and got in the
Evening to an Inn within 8 or 10 Miles of Burlington, kept
by one Dr Brown.—

He entred into Conversation with me while I took some
Refreshment, and finding I had read a little, became very sociable and friendly. Our Acquaintance continu'd as long as he
liv'd. He had been, I imagine, an itinerant Doctor, for there

was no Town in England, or Country in Europe, of which he could not give a very particular Account. He had some Letters, & was ingenious, but much of an Unbeliever, & wickedly undertook some Years after to travesty the Bible in doggrel Verse as Cotton had done Virgil.—By this means he set many of the Facts in a very ridiculous Light, & might have hurt weak minds if his Work had been publish'd:—but it never was.—At his House I lay that Night, and the next Morning reach'd Burlington.—But had the Mortification to find that the regular Boats were gone, a little before my coming, and no other expected to go till Tuesday, this being Saturday. Wherefore I return'd to an old Woman in the Town of whom I had bought Gingerbread to eat on the Water, & ask'd her Advice; she invited me to lodge at her House till a Passage by Water should offer; & being tired with my foot Travelling, I accepted the Invitation. She understanding I was a Printer, would have had me stay at that Town & follow my Business, being ignorant of the Stock necessary to begin with. She was very hospitable, gave me a Dinner of Ox Cheek with great Goodwill, accepting only of a Pot of Ale in return. And I tho't my self fix'd till Tuesday should come. However walking in the Evening by the Side of the River a Boat came by, which I found was going towards Philadelphia, with several People in her. They took me in, and as there was no Wind, we row'd all the Way; and about Midnight not having yet seen the City, some of the Company were confident we must have pass'd it, and would row no farther, the others knew not where we were, so we put towards the Shore, got into a Creek, landed near an old Fence with the Rails of which we made a Fire, the Night being cold, in October, and there we remain'd till Daylight. Then one of the Company knew the Place to be Cooper's Creek a little above Philadelphia, which we saw as soon as we got out of the Creek, and arriv'd there about 8 or 9 a Clock, on the Sunday morning, and landed at the Market street Wharff.—

I have been the more particular in this Description of my Journey, & shall be so of my first Entry into that City, that you may in your Mind compare such unlikely Beginning with the Figure I have since made there. I was in my working Dress, my best Cloaths being to come round by Sea. I was dirty from my Journey; my Pockets were stuff'd out with Shirts & Stockings; I knew no Soul, nor where to look for Lodging. I was fatigu'd with Travelling, Rowing & Want of Rest. I was very hungry, and my whole Stock of Cash consisted of a Dutch Dollar and about a Shilling in Copper. The latter I gave the People of the Boat for my Passage, who at first refus'd it on Acc^t of my Rowing; but I insisted on their taking it, a Man being sometimes more generous when he has but a little Money than when he has plenty, perhaps thro' Fear of being thought to have but little. Then I walk'd up the Street, gazing about, till near the Market House I met a Boy with Bread. I had made many a Meal on Bread, & inquiring where he got it, I went immediately to the Baker's he directed me to in second Street; and ask'd for Bisket, intending such as we had in Boston, but they it seems were not made in Philadelphia, then I ask'd for a threepenny Loaf, and was told they had none such: so not considering or knowing the Difference of Money & the greater Cheapness nor the Names of his Bread, I bad him give me three pennyworth of any sort. He gave me accordingly three great Puffy Rolls. I was surpriz'd at the Quantity, but took it, and having no Room in my Pockets, walk'd off, with a Roll under each Arm, & eating the other. Thus I went up Market Street as far as fourth Street, passing by the Door of Mr Read, my future Wife's Father, when she standing at the Door saw me, & thought I made as I certainly did a most awkward ridiculous Appearance. Then I turn'd and went down Chestnut Street and part of Walnut Street, eating my Roll all the Way, and coming round found my self again at Market street Wharff, near the Boat I came in, to which I went for a Draught of the River Water, and being fill'd with one of my Rolls, gave the other two to a Woman & her Child that came down the River in the Boat with us and were waiting to go farther. Thus refresh'd I walk'd again up the Street, which by this time had many clean dress'd People in it who were all walking the same Way; I join'd them, and thereby was led into the great Meeting House of the Quakers near the Market. I sat down among them, and after looking round a while & hearing nothing said, being very drowsy thro' Labour & want of Rest the preceding Night, I fell fast asleep, and continu'd so till the

Meeting broke up, when one was kind enough to rouse me.
This was therefore the first House I was in or slept in, in
Philadelphia.—

Walking again down towards the River, & looking in the
Faces of People, I met a young Quaker Man whose Countenance I lik'd, and accosting him requested he would tell me
where a Stranger could get Lodging. We were then near the
Sign of the Three Mariners. Here, says he, is one Place that
entertains Strangers, but it is not a reputable House; if thee
wilt walk with me, I'll show thee a better. He brought me to
the Crooked Billet in Water-Street. Here I got a Dinner. And
while I was eating it, several sly Questions were ask'd me, as
it seem'd to be suspected from my youth & Appearance, that
I might be some Runaway. After Dinner my Sleepiness return'd: and being shown to a Bed, I lay down without un-
dressing, and slept till Six in the Evening; was call'd to
Supper; went to Bed again very early and slept soundly till
the next Morning. Then I made my self as tidy as I could,
and went to Andrew Bradford the Printer's.—I found in the
Shop the old Man his Father, whom I had seen at New York,
and who travelling on horse back had got to Philadelphia before me.—He introduc'd me to his Son, who receiv'd me civ-
illy, gave me a Breakfast, but told me he did not at present
want a Hand, being lately supply'd with one. But there was
another Printer in town lately set up, one Keimer, who perhaps might employ me; if not, I should be welcome to lodge
at his House, & he would give me a little Work to do now &
then till fuller Business should offer.

The old Gentleman said, he would go with me to the new
Printer: And when we found him, Neighbour, says Bradford,
I have brought to see you a young Man of your Business,
perhaps you may want such a One. He ask'd me a few Questions, put a Composing Stick in my Hand to see how I
work'd, and then said he would employ me soon, tho' he had
just then nothing for me to do. And taking old Bradford
whom he had never seen before, to be one of the Towns
People that had a Good Will for him, enter'd into a Conversation on his present Undertaking & Prospects; while Bradford not discovering that he was the other Printer's Father;

on Keimer's Saying he expected soon to get the greatest Part
of the Business into his own Hands, drew him on by artful
Questions and starting little Doubts, to explain all his Views,
what Interest he rely'd on, & in what manner he intended to
proceed.—I who stood by & heard all, saw immediately that
one of them was a crafty old Sophister, and the other a mere
Novice. Bradford left me with Keimer, who was greatly surpriz'd when I told him who the old Man was.

Keimer's Printing House I found, consisted of an old shat-
ter'd Press, and one small worn-out Fount of English, which
he was then using himself, composing in it an Elegy on
Aquila Rose before-mentioned, an ingenious young Man of
excellent Character much respected in the Town, Clerk of the
Assembly, & a pretty Poet. Keimer made Verses, too, but very
indifferently.—He could not be said to write them, for his
Manner was to compose them in the Types directly out of his
Head; so there being no Copy, but one Pair of Cases, and
the Elegy likely to require all the Letter, no one could help
him.—I endeavour'd to put his Press (which he had not yet
us'd, & of which he understood nothing) into Order fit to be
work'd with; & promising to come & print off his Elegy as
soon as he should have got it ready, I return'd to Bradford's
who gave me a little Job to do for the present, & there I
lodged & dieted. A few Days after Keimer sent for me to print
off the Elegy. And now he had got another Pair of Cases, and
a Pamphlet to reprint, on which he set me to work.—

These two Printers I found poorly qualified for their Business. Bradford had not been bred to it, & was very illiterate;
and Keimer tho' something of a Scholar, was a mere Compositor, knowing nothing of Presswork. He had been one of
the French Prophets and could act their enthusiastic Agita-
tions. At this time he did not profess any particular Religion,
but something of all on occasion; was very ignorant of the
World, & had, as I afterwards found, a good deal of the
Knave in his Composition. He did not like my Lodging at
Bradford's while I work'd with him. He had a House indeed,
but without Furniture, so he could not lodge me: But he got
me a Lodging at Mr Read's before-mentioned, who was the
Owner of his House. And my Chest & Clothes being come

by this time, I made rather a more respectable Appearance in the Eyes of Miss Read, than I had done when she first happen'd to see me eating my Roll in the Street.—

I began now to have some Acquaintance among the young People of the Town, that were Lovers of Reading with whom I spent my Evenings very pleasantly and gaining Money by my Industry & Frugality, I lived very agreably, forgetting Boston as much as I could, and not desiring that any there should know where I resided except my Friend Collins who was in my Secret, & kept it when I wrote to him.—At length an Incident happened that sent me back again much sooner than I had intended.—

I had a Brother-in-law, Robert Holmes, Master of a Sloop, that traded between Boston and Delaware. He being at New Castle 40 Miles below Philadelphia, heard there of me, and wrote me a Letter, mentioning the Concern of my Friends in Boston at my abrupt Departure, assuring me of their Goodwill to me, and that every thing would be accommodated to my Mind if I would return, to which he exhorted me very earnestly.—I wrote an Answer to his Letter, thank'd him for his Advice, but stated my Reasons for quitting Boston fully, & in such a Light as to convince him I was not so wrong as he had apprehended.—Sir William Keith Governor of the Province, was then at New Castle, and Capt. Holmes happening to be in Company with him when my Letter came to hand, spoke to him of me, and show'd him the Letter. The Governor read it, and seem'd surpriz'd when he was told my Age. He said I appear'd a young Man of promising Parts, and therefore should be encouraged: The Printers at Philadelphia were wretched ones, and if I would set up there, he made no doubt I should succeed; for his Part, he would procure me the publick Business, & do me every other Service in his Power. This my Brother-in-Law afterwards told me in Boston. But I knew as yet nothing of it; when one Day Keimer and I being at Work together near the Window, we saw the Governor and another Gentleman (which prov'd to be Col. French, of New Castle) finely dress'd, come directly across the Street to our House, & heard them at the Door. Keimer ran down immediately, thinking it a Visit to him. But the Governor enquir'd for me, came up, & with a Condescension &

Politeness I had been quite unus'd to, made me many Compliments, desired to be acquainted with me, blam'd me kindly for not having made my self known to him when I first came to the Place, and would have me away with him to the Tavern where he was going with Col. French to taste as he said some excellent Madeira. I was not a little surpriz'd, and Keimer star'd like a Pig poison'd. I went however with the Governor & Col. French, to a Tavern the Corner of Third Street, and over the Madeira he propos'd my Setting up my Business, laid beforre me the Probabilities of Success, & both he & Col French, assur'd me I should have their Interest & Influence in procuring the Publick Business of both Governments. On my doubting whether my Father would assist me in it, Sir William said he would give me a Letter to him, in which he would state the Advantages,—and he did not doubt of prevailing with him. So it was concluded I should return to Boston in the first Vessel with the Governor's Letter recommending me to my Father. In the mean time the Intention was to be kept secret, and I went on working with Keimer as usual, the Governor sending for me now & then to dine with him, a very great Honour I thought it, and conversing with me in the most affable, familiar, & friendly manner imaginable. About the End of April 1724. a little Vessel offer'd for Boston. I took Leave of Keimer as going to see my Friends. The Governor gave me an ample Letter, saying many flattering things of me to my Father, and strongly recommending the Project of my setting up at Philadelphia, as a Thing that must make my Fortune.—We struck on a Shoal in going down the Bay & sprung a Leak, we had a blustring time at Sea, and were oblig'd to pump almost continually, at which I took my Turn.—We arriv'd safe however at Boston in about a Fortnight.—I had been absent Seven Months and my Friends had heard nothing of me, for my Br. Holmes was not yet return'd; and had not written about me. My unexpected Appearance surpriz'd the Family; all were however very glad to see me and made me Welcome, except my Brother. I went to see him at his Printing-House: I was better dress'd than ever while in his Service, having a genteel new Suit from Head to foot, a Watch, and my Pockets lin'd with near Five Pounds Sterling in Silver. He receiv'd me not very frankly, look'd me all over, and turn'd to his Work again. The Journey-Men were inquisitive where I had been, what sort of a Country it was, and how I lik'd it? I prais'd it much, & the happy Life I led in it; expressing strongly my Intention of returning to it; and one of them asking what kind of Money we had there, I produc'd a handful of Silver, and spread it before them, which was a kind of Raree-Show they had not been us'd to, Paper being the Money of Boston. Then I took an Opportunity of letting them see my Watch: and lastly, (my Brother still grum & sullen) I gave them a Piece of Eight to drink & took my Leave.—This Visit of mine offended him extreamly. For when my Mother some time after spoke to him of a Reconciliation, & of her Wishes to see us on good Terms together, & that we might live for the future as Brothers, he said, I had insulted him in such a Manner before his People that he could never forget or forgive it.—In this however he was mistaken.—

My Father receiv'd the Governor's Letter with some apparent Surprize; but said little of it to me for some Days; when Capt. Homes returning, he show'd it to him, ask'd if he knew Keith, and what kind of a Man he was: Adding his Opinion that he must be of small Discretion, to think of setting a Boy up in Business who wanted yet 3 Years of being at Man's Estate. Homes said what he could in fav^r of the Project; but my Father was clear in the Impropriety of it; and at last gave a flat Denial to it. Then he wrote a civil Letter to Sir William thanking him for the Patronage he had so kindly offered me, but declining to assist me as yet in Setting up, I being in his Opinion too young to be trusted with the Management of a Business so important; & for which the Preparation must be so expensive.—

My Friend & Companion Collins, who was a Clerk at the Post-Office, pleas'd with the Account I gave him of my new Country, determin'd to go thither also:—And while I waited for my Fathers Determination, he set out before me by Land to Rhodeisland, leaving his Books which were a pretty Collection of Mathematicks & Natural Philosophy, to come with mine & me to New York where he propos'd to wait for me. My Father, tho' he did not approve Sir William's Proposition was yet pleas'd that I had been able to obtain so advantageous

a Character from a Person of such Note where I had resided,
and that I had been so industrious & careful as to equip my
self so handsomely in so short a time: therefore seeing no
Prospect of an Accommodation between my Brother & me,
he gave his Consent to my Returning again to Philadelphia,
advis'd me to behave respectfully to the People there, endeavour to obtain the general Esteem, & avoid lampooning
& libelling to which he thought I had too much Inclination;— telling me, that by steady Industry and a prudent Par-
simony, I might save enough by the time I was One and
Twenty to set me up, & that if I came near the Matter he
would help me out with the Rest.—This was all I could obtain, except some small Gifts as Tokens of his & my Mother's
Love, when I embark'd again for New-York, now with their
Approbation & their Blessing.—

The Sloop putting in at Newport, Rhodeisland, I visited
my Brother John, who had been married & settled there some
Years. He received me very affectionately, for he always lov'd
me.—A Friend of his, one Vernon, having some Money due
to him in Pensilvania, about 35 Pounds Currency, desired I
would receive it for him, and keep it till I had his Directions
what to remit it in. Accordingly he gave me an Order.—This
afterwards occasion'd me a good deal of Uneasiness.—At
Newport we took in a Number of Passengers for New York:
Among which were two young Women, Companions, and a
grave, sensible Matron-like Quaker-Woman with her Atten-
dants.—I had shown an obliging Readiness to do her some
little Services which impress'd her I suppose with a degree of
Good-will towards me.—Therefore when she saw a daily
growing Familiarity between me & the two Young Women,
which they appear'd to encourage, she took me aside & said,
Young Man, I am concern'd for thee, as thou has no Friend
with thee, and seems not to know much of the World, or of
the Snares Youth is expos'd to; depend upon it those are very
bad Women, I can see it in all their Actions, and if thee art
not upon thy Guard, they will draw thee into some Danger:
they are Strangers to thee,—and I advise thee in a friendly
Concern for thy Welfare, to have no Acquaintance with
them.—As I seem'd at first not to think so ill of them as she
did, she mention'd some Things she had observ'd & heard

that had escap'd my Notice; but now convinc'd me she was right. I thank'd her for her kind Advice, and promis'd to follow it.—When we arriv'd at New York, they told me where they liv'd, & invited me to come and see them: but I avoided it. And it was well I did: For the next Day, the Captain miss'd a Silver Spoon & some other Things that had been taken out of his Cabbin, and knowing that these were a Couple of Strumpets, he got a Warrant to search their Lodgings, found the stolen Goods, and had the Thieves punish'd.—So tho' we had escap'd a sunken Rock which we scrap'd upon in the Passage, I thought this Escape of rather more Importance to me. At New York I found my Friend Collins, who had arriv'd there some Time before me. We had been intimate from Children, and had read the same Books together. But he had the Advantage of more time for Reading, & Studying and a wonderful Genius for Mathematical Learning in which he far outstript me. While I liv'd in Boston most of my Hours of Leisure for Conversation were spent with him, & he continu'd a sober as well as an industrious Lad; was much respected for his Learning by several of the Clergy & other Gentlemen, & seem'd to promise making a good Figure in Life: but during my Absence he had acquir'd a Habit of Sotting with Brandy; and I found by his own Account & what I heard from others, that he had been drunk every day since his Arrival at New York, & behav'd very oddly. He had gam'd too and lost his Money, so that I was oblig'd to discharge his Lodgings, & defray his Expences to and at Philadelphia: —Which prov'd extreamly inconvenient to me.—The then Governor of N York, Burnet, Son of Bishop Burnet hearing from the Captain that a young Man, one of his Passengers, had a great many Books, desired he would bring me to see him. I waited upon him accordingly, and should have taken Collins with me but that he was not sober. The Gov.ʳ treated me with greet Civility, show'd me his Library, which was a very large one, & we had a good deal of Conversation about Books & Authors. This was the second Governor who had done me the Honour to take Notice of me, which to a poor Boy like me was very pleasing.—We proceeded to Philadelphia. I received on the Way Vernon's Money, without which we could hardly have finish'd our Journey.—Collins wish'd to be employ'd in some Counting House; but whether they discover'd his Dramming by his Breath, or by his Behaviour, tho' he had some Recommendations, he met with no Success in any Application, and continu'd Lodging & Boarding at the same House with me & at my Expence. Knowing I had that Money of Vernon's he was continually borrowing of me, still promising Repayment as soon as he should be in Business. At length he had got so much of it, that I was distress'd to think what I should do, in case of being call'd on to remit it.—His Drinking continu'd, about which we sometimes quarrel'd, for when a little intoxicated he was very fractious. Once in a Boat on the Delaware with some other young Men, he refused to row in his Turn: I will be row'd home, says he. We will not row you, says I. You must says he, or stay all Night on the Water, just as you please. The others said, Let us row; What signifies it? But my Mind being soured with his other Conduct, I continu'd to refuse. So he swore he would make me row, or throw me overboard; and coming along stepping on the Thwarts towards me, when he came up & struck at me, I clapt my Hand under his Crutch, and rising pitch'd him head-foremost into the River. I knew he was a good Swimmer, and so was under little Concern about him; but before he could get round to lay hold of the Boat, we had with a few Strokes pull'd her out of his Reach.—And ever when he drew near the Boat, we ask'd if he would row, striking a few Strokes to slide her away from him.—He was ready to die with Vexation, & obstinately would not promise to row; however seeing him at last beginning to tire, we lifted him in; and brought him home dripping wet in the Evening. We hardly exchang'd a civil Word afterwards; and a West India Captain who had a Commission to procure a Tutor for the Sons of a Gentleman at Barbadoes, happening to meet with him, agreed to carry him thither. He left me then, promising to remit me the first Money he should receive in order to discharge the Debt. But I never heard of him after.—The Breaking into this Money of Vernon's was one of the first great Errata of my Life. And this Affair show'd that my Father was not much out in his Judgment when he suppos'd me too Young to manage Business of Importance. But Sir William, on reading his Letter, said he was too prudent. There was great Difference in Persons, and Discretion did not always accompany Years, nor was Youth always without it. And since he will not set you up, says he, I will do it my self. Give me an Inventory of the Things necessary to be had from England, and I will send for them. You shall repay me when you are able; I am resolv'd to have a good Printer here, and I am sure you must succeed. This was spoken with such an Appearance of Cordiality, that I had not the least doubt of his meaning what he said.—I had hitherto kept the Proposition of my Setting up a Secret in Philadelphia, & I still kept it. Had it been known that I depended on the Governor, probably some Friend that knew him better would have advis'd me not to rely on him, as I afterwards heard it as his known Character to be liberal of Promises which he never meant to keep.—Yet unsolicited as he was by me, how could I think his generous Offers insincere? I believ'd him one of the best Men in the World.—

I presented him an Inventory of a little Print.ᵍ House, amounting by my Computation to about 100£ Sterling. He lik'd it, but ask'd me if my being on the Spot in England to chuse the Types & see that every thing was good of the kind, might not be of some Advantage. Then, says he, when there, you may make Acquaintances & establish Correspondencies in the Bookselling, & Stationary Way. I agreed that this might be advantageous. Then says he, get yourself ready to go with Annis; which was the annual Ship, and the only one at that Time usually passing between London and Philadelphia. But it would be some Months before Annis sail'd, so I continu'd working with Keimer, fretting about the Money Collins had got from me, and in daily Apprehensions of being call'd upon by Vernon, which however did not happen for some Years after.—

I believe I have omitted mentioning that in my first Voyage from Boston, being becalm'd off Block Island, our People set about catching Cod & hawl'd up a great many. Hitherto I had stuck to my Resolution of not eating animal Food; and on this Occasion, I consider'd with my Master Tryon, the taking every Fish as a kind of unprovok'd Murder, since none of them had or ever could do us any Injury that might justify the Slaughter.— All this seem'd very reasonable.—But I had formerly been a great Lover of Fish, & when this came hot out of the Frying Pan, it smelt admirably well. I balanc'd some time between Principle & Inclination: till I recollected, that when the Fish were opened, I saw smaller Fish taken out of their Stomachs:—Then, thought I, if you eat one another, I don't see why we mayn't eat you. So I din'd upon Cod very heartily and continu'd to eat with other People, returning only now & then occasionally to a vegetable Diet. So convenient a thing it is to be a *reasonable Creature*, since it enables one to find or make a Reason for every thing one has a mind to do.—

Keimer & I liv'd on a pretty good familiar Footing & agreed tolerably well: for he suspected nothing of my Setting up. He retain'd a great deal of his old Enthusiasms, and lov'd an Argumentation. We therefore had many Disputations. I us'd to work him so with my Socratic Method, and had trapann'd him so often by Questions apparently so distant from any Point we had in hand, and yet by degrees led to the Point, and brought him into Difficulties & Contradictions, that at last he grew ridiculously cautious, and would hardly answer me the most common Question, without asking first, *What do you intend to infer from that?* However it gave him so high an Opinion of my Abilities in the Confuting Way, that he seriously propos'd my being his Colleague in a Project he had of setting up a new Sect. He was to preach the Doctrines, and I was to confound all Opponents. When he came to explain with me upon the Doctrines, I found several Conundrums which I objected to, unless I might have my Way a little too, and introduce some of mine. Keimer wore his Beard at full Length, because somewhere in the Mosaic Law it is said, *thou shalt not mar the Corners of thy Beard*. He likewise kept the seventh day Sabbath; and these two Points were Essentials with him.—I dislik'd both, but agreed to admit them upon Condition of his adopting the Doctrine of using no animal Food. I doubt, says he, my Constitution will not bear that. I assur'd him it would, & that he would be the better for it. He was usually a great Glutton, and I promis'd my self some Diversion in half-starving him. He agreed to try the Practice if I would keep him Company. I did so and we held it for three Months. We had our Victuals dress'd and brought to us regularly by a Woman in the Neighbourhood, who had from me a List of 40 Dishes to be prepar'd for us at different times, in all which there was neither Fish Flesh nor Fowl, and the Whim suited me the better at this time from the Cheapness of it, not costing us above 18^d Sterling each, per Week.—I have since kept several Lents most strictly, Leaving the common Diet for that, and that for the common, abruptly, without the least Inconvenience: So that I think there is little in the Advice of making those Changes by easy Gradations.—I went on pleasantly, but Poor Keimer suffer'd grievously, tir'd of the Project, long'd for the Flesh Pots of Egypt, and order'd a roast Pig; He invited me & two Women Friends to dine with him, but it being brought too soon upon table, he could not resist the Temptation, and ate it all up before we came.—

I had made some Courtship during this time to Miss Read, I had a great Respect & Affection for her, and had some Reason to believe she had the same for me: but as I was about to take a long Voyage, and we were both very young, only a little above 18. it was thought most prudent by her Mother to prevent our going too far at present, as a Marriage if it was to take place would be more convenient after my Return, when I should be as I expected set up in my Business. Perhaps too she thought my Expectations not so well founded as I imagined them to be.—

My chief Acquaintances at this time were, Charles Osborne, Joseph Watson, & James Ralph; All Lovers of Reading. The two first were Clerks to an eminent Scrivener or Conveyancer in the Town, Charles Brogden; the other was Clerk to a Merchant. Watson was a pious sensible young Man, of great Integrity.—The others rather more lax in their Principles of Religion, particularly Ralph, who as well as Collins had been unsettled by me, for which they both made me suffer.—Osborne was sensible, candid, frank, sincere, and affectionate to his Friends; but in litterary Matters too fond of Criticising. Ralph, was ingenious, genteel in his Manners, & extreamly eloquent; I think I never knew a prettier Talker.— Both of them great Admirers of Poetry, and began to try their Hands in little Pieces. Many pleasant Walks we four had together, on Sundays into the Woods near Skuylkill, where we read to one another & conferr'd on what we read. Ralph was inclin'd to pursue the Study of Poetry, not doubting but he might become eminent in it and make his Fortune by it, alledging that the best Poets must when they first began to write, make as many Faults as he did.—Osborne dissuaded him, assur'd him he had no Genius for Poetry, & advis'd him to think of nothing beyond the Business he was bred to; that in the mercantile way tho' he had no Stock, he might by his Diligence & Punctuality recommend himself to Employment as a Factor, and in time acquire wherewith to trade on his own Account. I approv'd the amusing one's Self with Poetry now & then, so far as to improve one's Language, but no farther. On this it was propos'd that we should each of us at our next Meeting produce a Piece of our own Composing, in order to improve by our mutual Observations, Criticisms & Corrections. As Language & Expression was what we had in View, we excluded all Considerations of Invention, by agreeing that the Task should be a Version of the 18th Psalm, which describes the Descent of a Deity. When the Time of our Meeting drew nigh, Ralph call'd on me first, & let me know his Piece was ready. I told him I had been busy, & having little Inclination had done nothing.—He then show'd me his Piece for my Opinion; and I much approv'd it, as it appear'd to me to have great Merit. Now, says he, Osborne never will allow the least Merit in any thing of mine, but makes 1000 Criticisms out of mere Envy. He is not so jealous of you. I wish therefore you would take this Piece, & produce it as yours. I will pretend not to have had time, & so produce nothing: We shall then see what he will say to it.—It was agreed, and I immediately transcrib'd it that it might appear in my own hand. We met. Watson's Performance was read: there were some Beauties in it: but many Defects. Osborne's was read: It was much better. Ralph did it Justice, remark'd some Faults, but applauded the Beauties. He himself had nothing to produce. I was backward, seem'd desirous of being excus'd, had not had sufficient Time to correct; &c. but no Excuse could be admitted, produce I must. It was read and repeated; Watson and Osborne gave up the Contest; and join'd in applauding it immoderately. Ralph only made some Criticisms & propos'd some Amendments, but I defended my

Text. Osborne was against Ralph, & told him he was no better a Critic than Poet; so he dropt the Argument. As they two went home together, Osborne express'd himself still more strongly in favour of what he thought my Production, having restrain'd himself before as he said, lest I should think it Flattery. But who would have imagin'd, says he, that Franklin had been capable of such a Performance; such Painting, such Force! such Fire! he has even improv'd the Original! In his common Conversation, he seems to have no Choice of Words; he hesitates and blunders; and yet, good God, how he writes!—When we next met, Ralph discover'd the Trick we had plaid him, and Osborne was a little laught at. This Transaction fix'd Ralph in his Resolution of becoming a Poet. I did all I could to dissuade him from it, but He continu'd scribbling Verses, till *Pope* cur'd him.—He became however a pretty good Prose Writer. More of him hereafter. But as I may not have occasion again to mention the other two, I shall just remark here, that Watson died in my Arms a few Years after, much lamented, being the best of our Set. Osborne went to the West Indies, where he became an eminent Lawyer & made Money, but died young. He and I had made a serious Agreement, that the one who happen'd first to die, should if possible make a friendly Visit to the other, and acquaint him how he found things in that separate State. But he never fulfill'd his Promise.

The Governor, seeming to like my Company, had me frequently to his House; & his Setting me up was always mention'd as a fix'd thing. I was to take with me Letters recommendatory to a Number of his Friends, besides the Letter of Credit, to furnish me with the necessary Money for purchasing the Press & Types, Paper, &c. For these Letters I was appointed to call at different times, when they were to be ready, but a future time was still named.—Thus we went on till the Ship whose Departure too had been several times postponed was on the Point of sailing. Then when I call'd to take my Leave & receive the Letters, his Secretary, Dr Bard, came out to me and said the Governor was extreamly busy, in writing, but would be down at Newcastle before the Ship, & there the Letters would be delivered to me.

Ralph, tho' married & having one Child, had determined

to accompany me in this Voyage. It was thought he intended to establish a Correspondence, & obtain Goods to sell on Commission. But I found afterwards, that thro' some Discontent with his Wifes Relations, he purposed to leave her on their Hands, & never return again.—Having taken leave of my Friends, & interchang'd some Promises with Miss Read, I left Philadelphia in the Ship, which anchor'd at Newcastle. The Governor was there. But when I went to his Lodging, the Secretary came to me from him with the civillest Message in the World, that he could not then see me being engag'd in Business of the utmost Importance, but should send the Letters to me on board, wish'd me heartily a good Voyage and a speedy Return, &c. I return'd on board, a little puzzled, but still not doubting.—

Mr Andrew Hamilton, a famous Lawyer of Philadelphia, had taken Passage in the same Ship for himself and Son: and with Mr Denham a Quaker Merchant, & Messrs Onion & Russel Masters of an Iron Work in Maryland, had engag'd the Great Cabin; so that Ralph and I were forc'd to take up with a Birth in the Steerage:—And none on board knowing us, were considered as ordinary Persons.—But Mr Hamilton & his Son (it was James, since Governor) return'd from New Castle to Philadelphia, the Father being recall'd by a great Fee to plead for a seized Ship.—And just before we sail'd Col. French coming on board, & showing me great Respect, I was more taken Notice of, and with my Friend Ralph invited by the other Gentlemen to come into the Cabin, there being now Room. Accordingly we remov'd thither.

Understanding that Col. French had brought on board the Governor's Dispatches, I ask'd the Captain for those Letters that were to be under my Care. He said all were put into the Bag together; and he could not then come at them; but before we landed in England, I should have an Opportunity of picking them out. So I was satisfy'd for the present, and we proceeded on our Voyage. We had a sociable Company in the Cabin, and lived uncommonly well, having the Addition of all Mr Hamilton's Stores, who had laid in plentifully. In this Passage Mr Denham contracted a Friendship for me that continued during his Life. The Voyage was otherwise not a pleasant one, as we had a great deal of bad Weather.—

When we came into the Channel, the Captain kept his Word with me, & gave me an Opportunity of examining the Bag for the Governor's Letters. I found none upon which my Name was put, as under my Care; I pick'd out 6 or 7 that by the Handwriting I thought might be the promis'd Letters, especially as one of them was directed to Basket the King's Printer, and another to some Stationer. We arriv'd in London the 24th of December, 1724.—I waited upon the Stationer who came first in my Way, delivering the Letter as from Gov. Keith. I don't know such a Person, says he: but opening the Letter, O, this is from Riddlesden; I have lately found him to be a compleat Rascal, and I will have nothing to do with him, nor receive any Letters from him. So putting the Letter into my Hand, he turn'd on his Heel & left me to serve some Customer.—I was surprized to find these were not the Governor's Letters. And after recollecting and comparing Circumstances, I began to doubt his Sincerity.—I found my Friend Denham, and opened the whole Affair to him. He let me into Keith's Character, told me there was not the least Probability that he had written any Letters for me, that no one who knew him had the smallest Dependance on him, and he laught at the Notion of the Governor's giving me a Letter of Credit, having as he said no Credit to give.—On my expressing some Concern about what I should do: He advis'd me to endeavour getting some Employment in the Way of my Business. Among the Printers here, says he, you will improve yourself; and when you return to America, you will set up to greater Advantage.—

We both of us happen'd to know, as well as the Stationer, that Riddlesden the Attorney, was a very Knave. He had half ruin'd Miss Read's Father by drawing him in to be bound for him. By his Letter it appear'd, there was a secret Scheme on foot to the Prejudice of Hamilton, (Suppos'd to be then coming over with us,) and that Keith was concern'd in it with Riddlesden. Denham, who was a Friend of Hamilton's, thought he ought to be acquainted with it. So when he arriv'd in England, which was soon after, partly from Resentment & Ill-Will to Keith & Riddlesden, & partly from Good Will to him: I waited on him, and gave him the Letter. He thank'd me cordially, the Information being of Importance to him. And from that time he became my Friend, greatly to my Advantage afterwards on many Occasions.

But what shall we think of a Governor's playing such pitiful Tricks, & imposing so grossly on a poor ignorant Boy! It was a Habit he had acquired. He wish'd to please every body; and having little to give, he gave Expectations.—He was otherwise an ingenious sensible Man, a pretty good Writer, & a good Governor for the People, tho' not for his Constituents the Proprietaries, whose Instructions he sometimes disregarded.—Several of our best Laws were of his Planning, and pass'd during his Administration.—

Ralph and I were inseparable Companions. We took Lodgings together in Little Britain at 3/6 per Week, as much as we could then afford.—He found some Relations, but they were poor & unable to assist him. He now let me know his Intentions of remaining in London, and that he never meant to return to Philad.ª—He had brought no Money with him, the whole he could muster having been expended in paying his Passage.—I had 15 Pistoles: So he borrowed occasionally of me, to subsist while he was looking out for Business.—He first endeavoured to get into the Playhouse, believing himself qualify'd for an Actor; but Wilkes, to whom he apply'd, advis'd him candidly not to think of that Employment, as it was impossible he should succeed in it.—Then he propos'd to Roberts, a Publisher in Paternoster Row, to write for him a Weekly Paper like the Spectator, on certain Conditions, which Roberts did not approve. Then he endeavour'd to get Employm.ᵗ as a Hackney Writer to copy for the Stationers & Lawyers about the Temple: but could find no Vacancy.—

I immediately got into Work at Palmer's then a famous Printing House in Bartholomew Close; and here I continu'd near a Year. I was pretty diligent; but spent with Ralph a good deal of my Earnings in going to Plays & other Places of Amusement. We had together consum'd all my Pistoles, and now just rubb'd on from hand to mouth. He seem'd quite to forget his Wife & Child, and I by degrees my Engagements wᵗʰ Miss Read, to whom I never wrote more than one Letter, & that was to let her know I was not likely soon to return. This was another of the great Errata of my Life, which I should wish to correct if I were to live it over again.—In fact, by our Expences, I was constantly kept unable to pay my Passage.

At Palmer's I was employ'd in Composing for the second Edition of Woollaston's Religion of Nature. Some of his Reasonings not appearing to me well-founded, I wrote a little metaphysical Piece, in which I made Remarks on them. It was entitled, *A Dissertation on Liberty & Necessity, Pleasure and Pain.*—I inscrib'd it to my Friend Ralph.—I printed a small Number. It occasion'd my being more consider'd by Mr Palmer, as a young Man of some Ingenuity, tho' he seriously expostulated with me upon the Principles of my Pamphlet which to him appear'd abominable. My printing this Pamphlet was another Erratum.

While I lodg'd in Little Britain I made an Acquaintance with one Wilcox a Bookseller, whose Shop was at the next Door. He had an immense Collection of second-hand Books. Circulating Libraries were not then in Use; but we agreed that on certain reasonable Terms which I have now forgotten, I might take, read & return any of his Books. This I esteem'd a great Advantage, & I made as much Use of it as I could.—

My Pamphlet by some means falling into the Hands of one Lyons, a Surgeon, Author of a Book intituled *The Infallibility of Human Judgment*, it occasioned an Acquaintance between us; he took great Notice of me, call'd on me often, to converse on these Subjects, carried me to the Horns a pale Ale-House in   Lane, Cheapside, and introduc'd me to Dr Mandevile, Author of the Fable of the Bees who had a Club there, of which he was the Soul, being a most facetious entertaining Companion. Lyons too introduc'd me to Dr Pemberton, at Batson's Coffee House, who promis'd to give me an Opportunity some time or other of seeing Sir Isaac Newton, of which I was extreamly desirous; but this never happened.

I had brought over a few Curiosities among which the principal was a Purse made of the Asbestos, which purifies by Fire. Sir Hans Sloane heard of it, came to see me, and invited me to his House in Bloomsbury Square; where he show'd me all his Curiosities, and persuaded me to let him add that to the Number, for which he paid me handsomely.—

In our House there lodg'd a young Woman; a Millener,

who I think had a Shop in the Cloisters. She had been gen-
teelly bred; was sensible & lively, and of most pleasing Conversation.—Ralph read Plays to her in the Evenings, they
grew intimate, she took another Lodging, and he follow'd
her. They liv'd together some time, but he being still out of
Business, & her Income not sufficient to maintain them with
her Child, he took a Resolution of going from London, to
try for a Country School, which he thought himself well qualify'd to undertake, as he wrote an excellent Hand, & was a
Master of Arithmetic & Accounts.—This however he deem'd
a Business below him, & confident of future better Fortune
when he should be unwilling to have it known that he once
was so meanly employ'd, he chang'd his Name, & did me the
Honour to assume mine.—For I soon after had a Letter from
him, acquainting me, that he was settled in a small Village in
Berkshire, I think it was, where he taught reading & writing
to 10 or a dozen Boys at 6 pence each per Week, recommending Mrs T. to my Care, and desiring me to write to him
directing for Mr Franklin Schoolmaster at such a Place. He
continu'd to write frequently, sending me large Specimens of
an Epic Poem, which he was then composing, and desiring
my Remarks & Corrections.—These I gave him from time to
time, but endeavour'd rather to discourage his Proceeding.
One of Young's Satires was then just publish'd. I copy'd &
sent him a great Part of it, which set in a strong Light the
Folly of pursuing the Muses with any Hope of Advancement
by them. All was in vain. Sheets of the Poem continu'd to
come by every Post. In the mean time Mrs T. having on his
Account lost her Friends & Business, was often in Distresses,
& us'd to send for me, and borrow what I could spare to help
her out of them. I grew fond of her Company, and being at
this time under no Religious Restraints, & presuming on my
Importance to her, I attempted Familiarities, (another Erratum) which she repuls'd with a proper Resentment, and
acquainted him with my Behaviour. This made a Breach
between us, & when he return'd again to London, he let me
know he thought I had cancel'd all the Obligations he had
been under to me.—So I found I was never to expect his
Repaying me what I lent to him or advanc'd for him. This
was however not then of much Consequence, as he was

totally unable.—And in the Loss of his Friendship I found my self reliev'd from a Burthen. I now began to think of getting a little Money beforehand; and expecting better Work, I left Palmer's to work at Watts's near Lincoln's Inn Fields, a still greater Printing House. Here I continu'd all the rest of my Stay in London.

At my first Admission into this Printing House, I took to working at Press, imagining I felt a Want of the Bodily Exercise I had been us'd to in America, where Presswork is mix'd with Composing. I drank only Water; the other Workmen, near 50 in Number, were great Guzzlers of Beer. On occasion I carried up & down Stairs a large Form of Types in each hand, when others carried but one in both Hands. They wonder'd to see from this & several Instances that the Water-American as they call'd me was *stronger* than themselves who drunk *strong* Beer. We had an Alehouse Boy who attended always in the House to supply the Workmen. My Companion at the Press, drank every day a Pint before Breakfast, a Pint at Breakfast with his Bread and Cheese; a Pint between Breakfast and Dinner; a Pint at Dinner; a Pint in the Afternoon about Six o'clock, and another when he had done his Day's-Work. I thought it a detestable Custom.—But it was necessary, he suppos'd, to drink *strong* Beer that he might be *strong* to labour. I endeavour'd to convince him that the Bodily Strength afforded by Beer could only be in proportion to the Grain or Flour of the Barley dissolved in the Water of which it was made; that there was more Flour in a Pennyworth of Bread, and therefore if he would eat that with a Pint of Water, it would give him more Strength than a Quart of Beer.—He drank on however, & had 4 or 5 Shillings to pay out of his Wages every Saturday Night for that muddling Liquor; an Expence I was free from.—And thus these poor Devils keep themselves always under.

Watts after some Weeks desiring to have me in the Composing-Room, I left the Pressmen. A new *Bienvenu* or Sum for Drink, being 5/, was demanded of me by the Compostors. I thought it an Imposition, as I had paid below. The Master thought so too, and forbad my Paying it. I stood out two or three Weeks, was accordingly considered as an Excommunicate, and had so many little Pieces of private Mischief done

me, by mixing my Sorts, transposing my Pages, breaking my
Matter, &c. &c. if I were ever so little out of the Room, &
all ascrib'd to the Chapel Ghost, which they said ever haunted
those not regularly admitted, that notwithstanding the Master's Protection, I found myself oblig'd to comply and pay
the Money; convinc'd of the Folly of being on ill Terms with
those one is to live with continually. I was now on a fair
Footing with them, and soon acquir'd considerable Influence.
I propos'd some reasonable Alterations in their * Chapel
Laws, and carried them against all Opposition. From my Example a great Part of them, left their muddling Breakfast of
Beer & Bread & Cheese, finding they could with me be supply'd from a neighbouring House with a large Porringer of
hot Water-gruel, sprinkled with Pepper, crumb'd with Bread,
& a Bit of Butter in it, for the Price of a Pint of Beer, viz,
three halfpence. This was a more comfortable as well as
cheaper Breakfast, & kept their Heads clearer.—Those who
continu'd sotting with Beer all day, were often, by not paying, out of Credit at the Alehouse, and us'd to make Interest
with me to get Beer, *their Light*, as they phras'd it, *being out*.
I watch'd the Pay table on Saturday Night, & collected what
I stood engag'd for them, having to pay some times near
Thirty Shillings a Week on their Accounts.—This, and my
being esteem'd a pretty good Riggite, that is a jocular verbal
Satyrist, supported my Consequence in the Society.—My
constant Attendance, (I never making a St. Monday), recommended me to the Master; and my uncommon Quickness at
Composing, occasion'd my being put upon all Work of Dispatch which was generally better paid. So I went on now very
agreably.—

My Lodging in Little Britain being too remote, I found
another in Duke-street opposite to the Romish Chapel. It was
two pair of Stairs backwards at an Italian Warehouse. A
Widow Lady kept the House; she had a Daughter & a Maid
Servant, and a Journey-man who attended the Warehouse, but
lodg'd abroad.—After sending to enquire my Character at
the House where I last lodg'd, she agreed to take me in at the
same Rate 3/6 per Week, cheaper as she said from the Pro-

*A Printing House is always called a Chappel by the Workmen.—

tection she expected in having a Man lodge in the House. She was a Widow, an elderly Woman, had been bred a Protestant, being a Clergyman's Daughter, but was converted to the Catholic Religion by her Husband, whose Memory she much revered, had lived much among People of Distinction, and knew a 1000 Anecdotes of them as far back as the Times of Charles the second. She was lame in her Knees with the Gout, and therefore seldom stirr'd out of her Room, so sometimes wanted Company; and hers was so highly amusing to me; that I was sure to spend an Evening with her whenever she desired it. Our Supper was only half an Anchovy each, on a very little Strip of Bread & Butter, and half a Pint of Ale between us.—But the Entertainment was in her Conversation. My always keeping good Hours, and giving little Trouble in the Family, made her unwilling to part with me; so that when I talk'd of a Lodging I had heard of, nearer my Business, for 2/ a Week, which, intent as I now was on saving Money, made some Difference; she bid me not think of it, for she would abate me two Shillings a Week for the future, so I remain'd with her at 1/6 as long as I staid in London.—

In a Garret of her House there lived a Maiden Lady of 70 in the most retired Manner, of whom my Landlady gave me this Account, that she was a Roman-Catholic, had been sent abroad when young & lodg'd in a Nunnery with an Intent of becoming a Nun: but the Country not agreeing with her, she return'd to England, where there being no Nunnery, she had vow'd to lead the Life of a Nun as near as might be done in those Circumstances: Accordingly She had given all her Estate to charitable Uses, reserving only Twelve Pounds a Year to live on, and out of this Sum she still gave a great deal in Charity, living her self on Watergruel only, & using no Fire but to boil it.—She had lived many Years in that Garret, being permitted to remain there gratis by successive catholic Tenants of the House below, as they deem'd it a Blessing to have her there. A Priest visited her, to confess her every Day. I have ask'd her, says my Landlady, how she, as she liv'd, could possibly find so much Employment for a Confessor? O, says she, it is impossible to avoid *vain Thoughts*. I was permitted once to visit her: She was chearful & polite, & convers'd pleasantly. The Room was clean, but had no other

Furniture than a Matras, a Table with a Crucifix & Book, a
Stool, which she gave me to sit on, and a Picture over the
Chimney of St. *Veronica*, displaying her Handkerchief with
the miraculous Figure of Christ's bleeding Face on it, which
she explain'd to me with great Seriousness. She look'd pale,
but was never sick, and I give it as another Instance on how
small an Income Life & Health may be supported.—

At Watts's Printinghouse I contracted an Acquaintance
with an ingenious young Man, one Wygate, who having
wealthy Relations, had been better educated than most Printers, was a tolerable Latinist, spoke French, & lov'd Reading.
I taught him, & a Friend of his, to swim, at twice going into
the River, & they soon became good Swimmers. They introduc'd me to some Gentlemen from the Country who went to
Chelsea by Water to see the College and Don Saltero's Curiosities. In our Return, at the Request of the Company, whose
Curiosity Wygate had excited, I stript & leapt into the River,
& swam from near Chelsea to Blackfryars, performing on the
Way many Feats of Activity both upon & under Water, that
surpriz'd & pleas'd those to whom they were Novelties.—I
had from a Child been ever delighted with this Exercise, had
studied & practis'd all Thevenot's Motions & Positions,
added some of my own, aiming at the graceful & easy, as well
as the Useful.—All these I took this Occasion of exhibiting
to the Company, & was much flatter'd by their Admiration.—And Wygate, who was desirous of becoming a Master, grew more & more attach'd to me, on that account, as
well as from the Similarity of our Studies. He at length propos'd to me travelling all over Europe together, supporting
ourselves every where by working at our Business. I was once
inclin'd to it. But mentioning it to my good Friend Mr Denham, with whom I often spent an Hour, when I had Leisure.
He dissuaded me from it; advising me to think only of return^g
to Pensilvania, which he was now about to do.—

I must record one Trait of this good Man's Character. He
had formerly been in Business at Bristol, but fail'd in Debt to
a Number of People, compounded and went to America.
There, by a close Application to Business as a Merchant, he
acquir'd a plentiful Fortune in a few Years. Returning to England in the Ship with me, He invited his old Creditors to an

Entertainment, at which he thank'd them for the easy Composition they had favour'd him with, & when they expected
nothing but the Treat, every Man at the first Remove, found
under his Plate an Order on a Banker for the full Amount of
the unpaid Remainder with Interest.

He now told me he was about to return to Philadelphia,
and should carry over a great Quantity of Goods in order to
open a Store there: He propos'd to take me over as his Clerk,
to keep his Books (in which he would instruct me) copy his
Letters, and attend the Store. He added, that as soon as I
should be acquainted with mercantile Business he would promote me by sending me with a Cargo of Flour & Bread &c
to the West Indies, and procure me Commissions from others; which would be profitable, & if I manag'd well, would
establish me handsomely. The Thing pleas'd me, for I was
grown tired of London, remember'd with Pleasure the happy
Months I had spent in Pennsylvania, and wish'd again to see
it. Therefore I immediately agreed, on the Terms of Fifty
Pounds a Year Pensylvania Money; less indeed than my then
present Gettings as a Compostor, but affording a better
Prospect.—

I now took Leave of Printing, as I thought for ever, and
was daily employ'd in my new Business; going about with
Mr Denham among the Tradesmen, to purchase various
Articles, & see them pack'd up, doing Errands, calling upon
Workmen to dispatch, &c. and when all was on board, I had
a few Days Leisure. On one of these Days I was to my Surprize sent for by a great Man I knew only by Name, a Sir
William Wyndham and I waited upon him. He had heard by
some means or other of my Swimming from Chelsey to
Blackfryars, and of my teaching Wygate and another young
Man to swim in a few Hours. He had two Sons about to set
out on their Travels; he wish'd to have them first taught
Swimming; and propos'd to gratify me handsomely if I
would teach them.—They were not yet come to Town and
my Stay was uncertain, so I could not undertake it. But from
this Incident I thought it likely, that if I were to remain in
England and open a Swimming School, I might get a good
deal of Money.—And it struck me so strongly, that had the
Overture been sooner made me, probably I should not so

soon have returned to America.—After Many Years, you & I had something of more Importance to do with one of these Sons of Sir William Wyndham, become Earl of Egremont, which I shall mention in its Place.—

Thus I spent about 18 Months in London. Most Part of the Time, I work'd hard at my Business, & spent but little upon my self except in seeing Plays, & in Books.—My Friend Ralph had kept me poor. He owed me about 27 Pounds; which I was now never likely to receive; a great Sum out of my small Earnings. I lov'd him notwithstanding, for he had many amiable Qualities.—tho' I had by no means improv'd my Fortune.—But I had pick'd up some very ingenious Acquaintance whose Conversation was of great Advantage to me, and I had read considerably.

We sail'd from Gravesend on the 23^d of July 1726.—For The Incidents of the Voyage, I refer you to my Journal, where you will find them all minutely related. Perhaps the most important Part of that Journal is the *Plan* to be found in it which I formed at Sea, for regulating my future Conduct in Life. It is the more remarkable, as being form'd when I was so young, and yet being pretty faithfully adhered to quite thro' to old Age.—We landed in Philadelphia the 11th of October, where I found sundry Alterations. Keith was no longer Governor, being superceded by Major Gordon: I met him walking the Streets as a common Citizen. He seem'd a little asham'd at seeing me, but pass'd without saying any thing. I should have been as much asham'd at seeing Miss Read, had not her Fr.^{ds} despairing with Reason of my Return, after the Receipt of my Letter, persuaded her to marry another, one Rogers, a Potter, which was done in my Absence. With him however she was never happy, and soon parted from him, refusing to cohabit with him, or bear his Name It being now said that he had another Wife. He was a worthless Fellow tho' an excellent Workman which was the Temptation to her Friends. He got into Debt, and ran away in 1727 or 28, went to the West Indies, and died there. Keimer had got a better House, a Shop well supply'd with Stationary, plenty of new Types, a number of Hands tho' none good, and seem'd to have a great deal of Business.

Mr Denham took a Store in Water Street, where we open'd

our Goods. I attended the Business diligently, studied Accounts, and grew in a little Time expert at selling.—We lodg'd and boarded together, he counsell'd me as a Father, having a sincere Regard for me: I respected & lov'd him: and we might have gone on together very happily: But in the Beginning of Feb.ᵞ 172⁶⁄₇ when I had just pass'd my 21ˢᵗ Year, we both were taken ill. My Distemper was a Pleurisy, which very nearly carried me off:—I suffered a good deal, gave up the Point in my own mind, & was rather disappointed when I found my self recovering; regretting in some degree that I must now sometime or other have all that disagreable Work to do over again.—I forget what his Distemper was. It held him a long time, and at length carried him off. He left me a small Legacy in a nuncupative Will, as a Token of his Kindness for me, and he left me once more to the wide World. For the Store was taken into the Care of his Executors, and my Employment under him ended:—My Brother-in-law Homes, being now at Philadelphia, advis'd my Return to my Business. And Keimer tempted me with an Offer of large Wages by the Year to come & take the Management of his Printing-House that he might better attend his Stationer's Shop.—I had heard a bad Character of him in London, from his Wife & her Friends, & was not fond of having any more to do with him. I try'd for farther Employment as a Merchant's Clerk; but not readily meeting with any, I clos'd again with Keimer.—

I found in *his* House these Hands; Hugh Meredith a Welsh-Pensilvanian, 30 Years of Age, bred to Country Work: honest, sensible, had a great deal of solid Observation, was something of a Reader, but given to drink:—Stephen Potts, a young Country Man of full Age, bred to the Same:—of uncommon natural Parts, & great Wit & Humour, but a little idle.—These he had agreed with at extream low Wages, per Week, to be rais'd a Shilling every 3 Months, as they would deserve by improving in their Business, & the Expectation of these high Wages to come on hereafter was what he had drawn them in with.—Meredith was to work at Press, Potts at Bookbinding, which he by Agreement, was to teach them, tho' he knew neither one nor t'other. John ——— a wild Irishman brought up to no Business, whose Service for 4

Years Keimer had purchas'd from the Captain of a Ship. He too was to be made a Pressman. George Webb, an Oxford Scholar, whose Time for 4 Years he had likewise bought, intending him for a Compositor: of whom more presently. And David Harry, a Country Boy, whom he had taken Apprentice. I soon perceiv'd that the Intention of engaging me at Wages so much higher than he had been us'd to give, was to have these raw cheap Hands form'd thro' me, and as soon as I had instructed them, then, they being all articled to him, he should be able to do without me.—I went on however, very chearfully; put his Printing House in Order, which had been in great Confusion, and brought his Hands by degrees to mind their Business and to do it better.

It was an odd Thing to find an Oxford Scholar in the Situation of a bought Servant. He was not more than 18 Years of Age, & gave me this Account of himself; that he was born in Gloucester, educated at a Grammar School there, had been distinguish'd among the Scholars for some apparent Superiority in performing his Part when they exhibited Plays; belong'd to the Witty Club there, and had written some Pieces in Prose & Verse which were printed in the Gloucester Newspapers.—Thence he was sent to Oxford; there he continu'd about a Year, but not well-satisfy'd, wishing of all things to see London & become a Player. At length receiving his Quarterly Allowance of 15 Guineas, instead of discharging his Debts, he walk'd out of Town, hid his Gown in a Furz Bush, and footed it to London, where having no Friend to advise him, he fell into bad Company, soon spent his Guineas, found no means of being introduc'd among the Players, grew necessitous, pawn'd his Cloaths & wanted Bread. Walking the Street very hungry, & not knowing what to do with himself, a Crimp's Bill was put into his Hand, offering immediate Entertainment & Encouragement to such as would bind themselves to serve in America. He went directly, sign'd the Indentures, was put into the Ship & came over; never writing a Line to acquaint his Friends what was become of him. He was lively, witty, good-natur'd and a pleasant Companion; but idle, thoughtless & imprudent to the last Degree.

John the Irishman soon ran away. With the rest I began to live very agreably; for they all respected me, the more as they found Keimer incapable of instructing them, and that from me they learnt something daily. We never work'd on a Saturday, that being Keimer's Sabbath. So I had two Days for Reading. My Acquaintance with ingenious People in the Town, increased. Keimer himself treated me with great Civility & apparent Regard; and nothing now made me uneasy but my Debt to Vernon, which I was yet unable to pay being hitherto but a poor Oeconomist.—He however kindly made no Demand of it.

Our Printing-House often wanted Sorts, and there was no Letter Founder in America. I had seen Types cast at James's in London, but without much Attention to the Manner: However I now contriv'd a Mould, made use of the Letters we had, as Puncheons, struck the Matrices in Lead, and thus supply'd in a pretty tolerable way all Deficiencies. I also engrav'd several Things on occasion. I made the Ink, I was Warehouse-man & every thing, in short quite a Factotum.—

But however serviceable I might be, I found that my Services became every Day of less Importance, as the other Hands improv'd in the Business. And when Keimer paid my second Quarter's Wages, he let me know that he felt them too heavy, and thought I should make an Abatement. He grew by degrees less civil, put on more of the Master, frequently found Fault, was captious and seem'd ready for an Out-breaking. I went on nevertheless with a good deal of Patience, thinking that his incumber'd Circumstances were partly the Cause. At length a Trifle snapt our Connexion. For a great Noise happening near the Courthouse, I put my Head out of the Window to see what was the Matter. Keimer being in the Street look'd up & saw me, call'd out to me in a loud Voice and angry Tone to mind my Business, adding some reproachful Words, that nettled me the more for their Publicity, all the Neighbours who were looking out on the same Occasion being Witnesses how I was treated. He came up immediately into the Printing-House, continu'd the Quarrel, high Words pass'd on both Sides, he gave me the Quarter's Warning we had stipulated, expressing a Wish that he had not been oblig'd to so long a Warning: I told him his Wish was unnecessary for I would leave him that Instant; and so taking my Hat walk'd out of Doors; desiring Meredith whom I saw

below to take care of some Things I left, & bring them to my
Lodging.—

Meredith came accordingly in the Evening, when we talk'd
my Affair over. He had conceiv'd a great Regard for me, &
was very unwilling that I should leave the House while he
remain'd in it. He dissuaded me from returning to my native
Country which I began to think of. He reminded me that
Keimer was in debt for all he possess'd, that his Creditors
began to be uneasy, that he kept his Shop miserably, sold
often without Profit for ready Money, and often trusted without keeping Account. That he must therefore fail; which
would make a Vacancy I might profit of.—I objected my
Want of Money. He then let me know, that his Father had a
high Opinion of me, and from some Discourse that had
pass'd between them, he was sure would advance Money to
set us up, if I would enter into Partnership with him.—My
Time, says he, will be out with Keimer in the Spring. By that
time we may have our Press & Types in from London:—I
am sensible I am no Workman. If you like it, Your Skill in the
Business shall be set against the Stock I furnish; and we will
share the Profits equally.—The Proposal was agreable, and I
consented. His Father was in Town, and approv'd of it, the
more as he saw I had great Influence with his Son, had prevail'd on him to abstain long from Dramdrinking, and he
hop'd might break him of that wretched Habit entirely,
when we came to be so closely connected. I gave an Inventory to the Father, who carry'd it to a Merchant; the Things
were sent for; the Secret was to be kept till they should arrive, and in the mean time I was to get Work if I could at
the other Printing House.—But I found no Vacancy there,
and so remain'd idle a few Days, when Keimer, on a Prospect of being employ'd to print some Paper-money, in New
Jersey, which would require Cuts & various Types that I
only could supply, and apprehending Bradford might engage
me & get the Jobb from him, sent me a very civil Message,
that old Friends should not part for a few Words the Effect
of sudden Passion, and wishing me to return. Meredith persuaded me to comply, as it would give more Opportunity
for his Improvement under my daily Instructions.—So I return'd, and we went on more smoothly than for some time

before.—The New Jersey Jobb was obtain'd. I contriv'd a Copper-Plate Press for it, the first that had been seen in the Country.—I cut several Ornaments and Checks for the Bills. We went together to Burlington, where I executed the Whole to Satisfaction, & he received so large a Sum for the Work, as to be enabled thereby to keep his Head much longer above Water.—

At Burlington I made an Acquaintance with many principal People of the Province. Several of them had been appointed by the Assembly a Committee to attend the Press, and take Care that no more Bills were printed than the Law directed. They were therefore by Turns constantly with us, and generally he who attended brought with him a Friend or two for Company. My Mind having been much more improv'd by Reading than Keimer's, I suppose it was for that Reason my Conversation seem'd to be more valu'd. They had me to their Houses, introduc'd me to their Friends and show'd me much Civility, while he, tho' the Master, was a little neglected. In truth he was an odd Fish, ignorant of common Life, fond of rudely opposing receiv'd Opinions, slovenly to extream dirtiness, enthusiastic in some Points of Religion, and a little Knavish withal. We continu'd there near 3 Months, and by that time I could reckon among my acquired Friends, Judge Allen, Samuel Bustill, the Secretary of the Province, Isaac Pearson, Joseph Cooper & several of the Smiths, Members of Assembly, and Isaac Decow the Surveyor General. The latter was a shrewd sagacious old Man, who told me that he began for himself when young by wheeling Clay for the Brickmakers, learnt to write after he was of Age, carry'd the Chain for Surveyors, who taught him Surveying, and he had now by his Industry acquir'd a good Estate; and says he, I foresee, that you will soon work this Man out of his Business & make a Fortune in it at Philadelphia. He had not then the least Intimation of my Intention to set up there or any where.— These Friends were afterwards of great Use to me, as I occasionally was to some of them.—They all continued their Regard for me as long as they lived.—

Before I enter upon my public Appearance in Business, it may be well to let you know the then State of my Mind, with regard to my Principles and Morals, that you may see how

far those influenc'd the future Events of my Life. My Parent's
had early given me religious Impressions, and brought me
through my Childhood piously in the Dissenting Way. But I
was scarce 15 when, after doubting by turns of several Points
as I found them disputed in the different Books I read, I began to doubt of Revelation it self. Some Books against Deism
fell into my Hands; they were said to be the Substance of
Sermons preached at Boyle's Lectures. It happened that they
wrought an Effect on me quite contrary to what was intended
by them: For the Arguments of the Deists which were quoted
to be refuted, appeared to me much Stronger than the Refu-
tations. In short I soon became a thorough Deist. My Arguments perverted some others, particularly Collins & Ralph:
but each of them having afterwards wrong'd me greatly without the least Compunction, and recollecting Keith's Conduct
towards me, (who was another Freethinker) and my own towards Vernon & Miss Read which at Times gave me great
Trouble, I began to suspect that this Doctrine tho' it might
be true, was not very useful.—My London Pamphlet, which
had for its Motto those Lines of Dryden

> ——Whatever is, is right
> Tho' purblind Man / Sees but a Part of
> The Chain, the nearest Link,
> His Eyes not carrying to the equal Beam,
> That poizes all, above.

And from the Attributes of God, his infinite Wisdom,
Goodness & Power concluded that nothing could possibly
be wrong in the World, & that Vice & Virtue were empty
Distinctions, no such Things existing: appear'd now not so
clever a Performance as I once thought it; and I doubted
whether some Error had not insinuated itself unperceiv'd,
into my Argument, so as to infect all that follow'd, as is common in metaphysical Reasonings.—I grew convinc'd that
Truth, Sincerity & *Integrity* in Dealings between Man & Man,
were of the utmost Importance to the Felicity of Life, and I
form'd written Resolutions, (wch still remain in my Journal
Book) to practise them ever while I lived. Revelation had indeed no weight with me as such; but I entertain'd an Opinion, that tho' certain Actions might not be bad *because* they

were forbidden by it, or good *because* it commanded them; yet probably those Actions might be forbidden *because* they were bad for us, or commanded *because* they were beneficial to us, in their own Natures, all the Circumstances of things considered. And this Persuasion, with the kind hand of Providence, or some guardian Angel, or accidental favourable Circumstances & Situations, or all together, preserved me (thro' this dangerous Time of Youth & the hazardous Situations I was sometimes in among Strangers, remote from the Eye & Advice of my Father,) without any *wilful* gross Immorality or Injustice that might have been expected from my Want of Religion.—I say *wilful*, because the Instances I have mentioned, had something of *Necessity* in them, from my Youth, Inexperience, & the Knavery of others.—I had therefore a tolerable Character to begin the World with, I valued it properly, & determin'd to preserve it.—

We had not been long return'd to Philadelphia, before the New Types arriv'd from London.—We settled with Keimer, & left him by his Consent before he heard of it.—We found a House to hire near the Market, and took it. To lessen the Rent, (which was then but 24£ a Year tho' I have since known it let for 70) We took in Thos Godfrey a Glazier, & his Family, who were to pay a considerable Part of it to us, and we to board with them. We had scarce opened our Letters & put our Press in Order, before George House, an Acquaintance of mine, brought a Countryman to us; whom he had met in the Street enquiring for a Printer. All our Cash was now expended in the Variety of Particulars we had been obliged to procure, & this Countryman's Five Shillings, being our First Fruits & coming so seasonably, gave me more Pleasure than any Crown I have since earn'd; and from the Gratitude I felt towards House, has made me often more ready than perhaps I should otherwise have been to assist young Beginners.—

There are Croakers in every Country always boding its Ruin. Such a one then lived in Philadelphia, a Person of Note, an elderly Man, with a wise Look and very grave Manner of Speaking. His Name was Samuel Mickle. This Gentleman, a Stranger to me, stopt one Day at my Door, and ask'd me if I was the young Man who had lately opened a new

Printing-house: Being answer'd in the Affirmative; He said he was sorry for me; because it was an expensive Undertaking, & the Expence would be lost, for Philadelphia was a sinking Place, the People already half Bankrupts or near being so; all Appearances of the contrary such as new Buildings & the Rise of Rents, being to his certain Knowledge fallacious, for they were in fact among the Things that would soon ruin us. And he gave me such a Detail of Misfortunes now existing or that were soon to exist, that he left me half-melancholy. Had I known him before I engag'd in this Business, probably I never should have done it.—This Man continu'd to live in this decaying Place, & to declaim in the same Strain, refusing for many Years to buy a House there, because all was going to Destruction, and at last I had the Pleasure of seeing him give five times as much for one as he might have bought it for when he first began his Croaking.—

I should have mention'd before, that in the Autumn of the preceding Year, I had form'd most of my ingenious Acquaintance into a Club, for mutual Improvement, which we call'd the Junto. We met on Friday Evenings. The Rules I drew up, requir'd that every Member in his Turn should produce one or more Queries on any Point of Morals, Politics or Natural Philosophy, to be discuss'd by the Company, and once in three Months produce and read an Essay of his own Writing on any Subject he pleased. Our Debates were to be under the Direction of a President, and to be conducted in the sincere Spirit of Enquiry after Truth, without fondness for Dispute, or Desire of Victory; and to prevent Warmth, all Expressions of Positiveness in Opinion, or of direct Contradiction, were after some time made contraband & prohibited under small pecuniary Penalties. The first Members were, Joseph Brientnal, a Copyer of Deeds for the Scriveners; a good-natur'd friendly middle-ag'd Man, a great Lover of Poetry, reading all he could meet with, & writing some that was tolerable; very ingenious in many little Nicknackeries, & of sensible Conversation. Thomas Godfrey, a self-taught Mathematician, great in his Way, & afterwards Inventor of what is now call'd Hadley's Quadrant. But he knew little out of his way, and was not a pleasing Companion, as like most Great Mathematicians I have met with, he expected unusual Precision in every thing said, or was forever denying or distinguishing upon Trifles, to the Disturbance of all Conversation.—He soon left us.—Nicholas Scull, a Surveyor, afterwards Surveyor-General, Who lov'd Books, & sometimes made a few Verses. William Parsons, bred a Shoemaker, but loving Reading, had acquir'd a considerable Share of Mathematics, which he first studied with a View to Astrology that he afterwards laught at. He also became Surveyor General.—William Maugridge, a Joiner, & a most exquisite Mechanic, & a solid sensible Man. Hugh Meredith, Stephen Potts, & George Webb, I have Characteris'd before. Robert Grace, a young Gentleman of some Fortune, generous, lively & witty, a Lover of Punning and of his Friends. And William Coleman, then a Merchant's Clerk, about my Age, who had the coolest clearest Head, the best Heart, and the exactest Morals, of almost any Man I ever met with. He became afterwards a Merchant of great Note, and one of our Provincial Judges: Our Friendship continued without Interruption to his Death, upwards of 40 Years. And the Club continu'd almost as long and was the best School of Philosophy, Morals & Politics that then existed in the Province; for our Queries which were read the Week preceding their Discussion, put us on reading with Attention upon the several Subjects, that we might speak more to the purpose: and here too we acquired better Habits of Conversation, every thing being studied in our Rules which might prevent our disgusting each other. From hence the long Continuance of the Club, which I shall have frequent Occasion to speak farther of hereafter; But my giving this Account of it here, is to show something of the Interest I had, every one of these exerting themselves in recommending Business to us.—Brientnal particularly procur'd us from the Quakers, the Printing 40 Sheets of their History, the rest being to be done by Keimer: and upon this we work'd exceeding hard, for the Price was low. It was a Folio, Pro Patria Size, in Pica with Long Primer Notes. I compos'd of it a Sheet a Day, and Meredith work'd it off at Press. It was often 11 at Night and sometimes later, before I had finish'd my Distribution for the next days Work: For the little Jobbs sent in by our other Friends now & then put us back. But so determin'd I was to continue doing a Sheet a Day of the Folio, that one Night when having impos'd my Forms, I thought my Days Work over, one of them by accident was broken and two Pages reduc'd to Pie, I immediately distributed & compos'd it over again before I went to bed. And this Industry visible to our Neighbours began to give us Character and Credit; particularly I was told, that mention being made of the new Printing Office at the Merchants Every-night-Club, the general Opinion was that it must fail, there being already two Printers in the Place, Keimer & Bradford; but Doctor Baird (whom you and I saw many Years after at his native Place, St. Andrews in Scotland) gave a contrary Opinion; for the Industry of that Franklin, says he, is superior to any thing I ever saw of the kind: I see him still at work when I go home from Club; and he is at Work again before his Neighbours are out of bed. This struck the rest, and we soon after had Offers from one of them to supply us with Stationary. But as yet we did not chuse to engage in Shop Business.

I mention this Industry the more particularly and the more freely, tho' it seems to be talking in my own Praise, that those of my Posterity who shall read it, may know the Use of that Virtue, when they see its Effects in my Favour throughout this Relation.—

George Webb, who had found a Friend that lent him wherewith to purchase his Time of Keimer, now came to offer himself as a Journeyman to us. We could not then imploy him, but I foolishly let him know, as a Secret, that I soon intended to begin a Newspaper, & might then have Work for him.—My Hopes of Success as I told him were founded on this, that the then only Newspaper, printed by Bradford was a paltry thing, wretchedly manag'd, no way entertaining; and yet was profitable to him.—I therefore thought a good Paper could scarcely fail of good Encouragem! I requested Webb not to mention it, but he told it to Keimer, who immediately, to be beforehand with me, published Proposals for Printing one himself,—on which Webb was to be employ'd.—I resented this, and to counteract them, as I could not yet begin our Paper, I wrote several Pieces of Entertainm' for Bradford's Paper, under the Title of the Busy Body which Breintnal continu'd some Months. By this means the Attention of the Publick was fix'd on that Paper, & Keimers Proposals which we

burlesqu'd & ridicul'd, were disregarded. He began his Paper
however, and after carrying it on three Quarters of a Year,
with at most only 90 Subscribers, he offer'd it to me for a
Trifle, & I having been ready some time to go on with it,
took it in hand directly and it prov'd in a few Years extreamly
profitable to me. —

I perceive that I am apt to speak in the singular Number,
though our Partnership still continu'd. The Reason may be,
that in fact the whole Management of the Business lay upon
me. Meredith was no Compostor, a poor Pressman, & seldom sober. My Friends lamented my Connection with him,
but I was to make the best of it.

Our first Papers made a quite different Appearance from
any before in the Province, a better Type & better printed:
but some spirited Remarks* of my Writing on the Dispute
then going on between Govr Burnet and the Massachusetts
Assembly, struck the principal People, occasion'd the Paper &

*"His Excellency Governor *Burnet* died unexpectedly about two Days after
the Date of this Reply to his last Message: And it was thought the Dispute
would have ended with him, or at least have lain dormant till the Arrival of
a new Governor from *England*, who possibly might, or might not be inclin'd
to enter too rigorously into the Measures of his Predecessor. But our last
Advices by the Post acquaint us, that his Honour the Lieutenant Governour
(on whom the Government immediately devolves upon the Death or Absence of the Commander in Chief) has vigorously renew'd the Struggle on
his own Account; of which the Particulars will be seen in our Next.

"Perhaps some of our Readers may not fully understand the Original or
Ground of this warm Contest between the Governour and Assembly. — It
seems, that People have for these Hundred Years past, enjoyed the Privilege
of Rewarding the Governour for the Time being, according to *their Sense* of
his Merit and Services; and few or none of their Governors have hitherto
complain'd, or had Reason to complain, of a too scanty Allowance. But the
late Gov. *Burnet* brought with him Instructions to demand a *settled Salary* of
1000 *l. per Annum*, Sterling, on him and all his Successors, and the Assembly
were required to fix it immediately. He insisted on it strenuously to the last,
and they as constantly refused it. It appears by their Votes and Proceedings,
that they thought it an Imposition, contrary to their own Charter, and to
Magna Charta; and they judg'd that by the Dictates of Reason there should
be a mutual Dependence between the *Governor* and the *Governed*, and that to
make any Governour independent of his People, would be dangerous, and
destructive of their Liberties, and the ready Way to establish Tyranny: They
thought likewise, that the Province was not the less dependent on the Crown
of *Great-Britain*, by the Governour's depending immediately on them and
his own good Conduct for an ample Support, because all Acts and Laws

the Manager of it to be much talk'd of, & in a few Weeks brought them all to be our Subscribers. Their Example was follow'd by many, and our Number went on growing continually.—This was one of the first good Effects of my having learnt a little to scribble.—Another was, that the leading Men, seeing a News Paper now in the hands of one who could also handle a Pen, thought it convenient to oblige & encourage me.—Bradford still printed the Votes & Laws & other Publick Business. He had printed an Address of the House to the Governor in a coarse blundering manner; We reprinted it elegantly & correctly, and sent one to every Member. They were sensible of the Difference, it strengthen'd the Hands of our Friends in the House, and they voted us their Printers for the Year ensuing.

Among my Friends in the House I must not forget Mr Hamilton before mentioned, who was then returned from England & had a Seat in it. He interested himself for me strongly in that Instance, as he did in many others afterwards,

---

which he might be induc'd to pass, must nevertheless be constantly sent Home for Approbation in Order to continue in Force. Many other Reasons were given and Arguments us'd in the Course of the Controversy, needless to particularize here, because all the material Papers relating to it, have been inserted already in our Public News.

"Much deserved Praise has the deceas'd Governour receiv'd, for his steady Integrity in adhering to his Instructions, notwithstanding the great Difficulty and Opposition he met with, and the strong Temptations offer'd from time to time to induce him to give up the Point.—And yet perhaps something is due to the *Assembly* (as the Love and Zeal of that Country for the present Establishment is too well known to suffer any Suspicion of Want of Loyalty) who continue thus resolutely to Abide by what *they Think* their Right, and that of the People they represent, maugre all the Arts and Menaces of a Governour fam'd for his Cunning and Politicks, back'd with Instructions from Home, and powerfully aided by the great Advantage such an Officer always has of engaging the principal Men of a Place in his Party, by conferring where he pleases so many Posts of Profit and Honour. Their happy Mother Country will perhaps observe with Pleasure, that tho' her gallant Cocks and matchless Dogs abate their native Fire and Intrepidity when transported to a Foreign Clime (as the common Notion is) yet her SONS in the remotest Part of the Earth, and even to the third and fourth Descent, still retain that ardent Spirit of Liberty, and that undaunted Courage in the Defence of it, which has in every Age so gloriously distinguished BRITONS and ENGLISHMEN from all the Rest of Mankind."

continuing his Patronage till his Death.* Mr Vernon about
this time put me in mind of the Debt I ow'd him:—but did
not press me.—I wrote him an ingenuous Letter of Acknowl-
edgments, crav'd his Forbearance a little longer which he allow'd me, & as soon as I was able I paid the Principal with
Interest & many Thanks.—So that *Erratum* was in some degree corrected.—

But now another Difficulty came upon me, which I had
never the least Reason to expect. Mr. Meredith's Father,
who was to have paid for our Printing House according to
the Expectations given me, was able to advance only one
Hundred Pounds, Currency, which had been paid, & a
Hundred more was due to the Merchant; who grew impatient & su'd us all. We gave Bail, but saw that if the Money
could not be rais'd in time, the Suit must come to a Judgment
& Execution, & our hopeful Prospects must with us be
ruined, as the Press & Letters must be sold for Payment, perhaps at half-Price.—In this Distress two true Friends whose
Kindness I have never forgotten nor ever shall forget while I
can remember any thing, came to me separately unknown to
each other, and without any Application from me, offering
each of them to advance me all the Money that should be
necessary to enable me to take the whole Business upon my
self if that should be practicable, but they did not like my
continuing the Partnership with Meredith, who as they said
was often seen drunk in the Streets, & playing at low Games
in Alehouses, much to our Discredit. These two Friends
were *William Coleman* & *Robert Grace*. I told them I could
not propose a Separation while any Prospect remain'd of the
Merediths fulfilling their Part of our Agreement. Because I
thought my self under great Obligations to them for what
they had done & would do if they could. But if they finally
fail'd in their Performance, & our Partnership must be dis-
solv'd, I should then think myself at Liberty to accept the
Assistance of my Friends. Thus the matter rested for some
time. When I said to my Partner, perhaps your Father is dissatisfied at the Part you have undertaken in this Affair of
ours, and is unwilling to advance for you & me what he

*I got his Son once 500£.

would for you alone: If that is the Case, tell me, and I will resign the whole to you & go about my Business. No—says he, my Father has really been disappointed and is really unable; and I am unwilling to distress him farther. I see this is a Business I am not fit for. I was bred a Farmer, and it was a Folly in me to come to Town & put my self at 30 Years of Age an Apprentice to learn a new Trade. Many of our Welsh People are going to settle in North Carolina where Land is cheap: I am inclin'd to go with them, & follow my old Employment. You may find Friends to assist you. If you will take the Debts of the Company upon you, return to my Father the hundred Pound he has advanc'd, pay my little personal Debts, and give me Thirty Pounds & a new Saddle, I will relinquish the Partnership & leave the whole in your Hands. I agreed to this Proposal. It was drawn up in Writing, sign'd & seal'd immediately. I gave him what he demanded & he went soon after to Carolina; from whence he sent me next Year two long Letters, containing the best Account that had been given of that Country, the Climate, Soil, Husbandry, &c. for in those Matters he was very judicious. I printed them in the Papers, and they gave grate Satisfaction to the Publick.

As soon as he was gone, I recurr'd to my two Friends; and because I would not give an unkind Preference to either, I took half what each had offered & I wanted, of one, & half of the other; paid off the Company Debts, and went on with the Business in my own Name, advertising that the Partnership was dissolved. I think this was in or about the Year 1729.—

About this Time there was a Cry among the People for more Paper-Money, only 15,000£ being extant in the Province & that soon to be sunk. The wealthy Inhabitants oppos'd any Addition, being against all Paper Currency, from an Apprehension that it would depreciate as it had done in New England to the Prejudice of all Creditors.—We had discuss'd this Point in our Junto, where I was on the Side of an Addition, being persuaded that the first small Sum struck in 1723 had done much good, by increasing the Trade Employment, & Number of Inhabitants in the Province, since I now saw all the old Houses inhabited, & many new ones building, where as I remember'd well, that when I first walk'd about the Streets of Philadelphia, eating my Roll, I saw most of the Houses in Walnut street between Second & Front streets with Bills on their Doors, to be let; and many likewise in Chesnut Street, & other Streets; which made me then think the Inhabitants of the City were one after another deserting it.—Our Debates possess'd me so fully of the Subject, that I wrote and printed an anonymous Pamphlet on it, entituled, *The Nature & Necessity of a Paper Currency*. It was well receiv'd by the common People in general; but the Rich Men dislik'd it; for it increas'd and strengthen'd the Clamour for more Money; and they happening to have no Writers among them that were able to answer it, their Opposition slacken'd, & the Point was carried by a Majority in the House. My Friends there, who conceiv'd I had been of some Service, thought fit to reward me, by employing me in printing the Money, a very profitable Jobb, and a great Help to me.—This was another Advantage gain'd by my being able to write. The Utility of this Currency became by Time and Experience so evident, as never afterwards to be much disputed, so that it grew soon to 55000,£ and in 1739 to 80,000£ since which it arose during War to upwards of 350,000£. Trade, Building & Inhabitants all the while increasing. Tho' I now think there are Limits beyond which the Quantity may be hurtful.—

I soon after obtain'd, thro' my Friend Hamilton, the Printing of the NewCastle Paper Money, another profitable Jobb, as I then thought it; small Things appearing great to those in small Circumstances. And these to me were really great Advantages, as they were great Encouragements.—He procured me also the Printing of the Laws and Votes of that Government which continu'd in my Hands as long as I follow'd the Business.—

I now open'd a little Stationer's Shop. I had in it Blanks of all Sorts the correctest that ever appear'd among us, being assisted in that by my Friend Brientnal; I had also Paper, Parchment, Chapmen's Books, &c. One Whitemash a Compositor I had known in London, an excellent Workman now came to me & work'd with me constantly & diligently, and I took an Apprentice the Son of Aquila Rose. I began now gradually to pay off the Debt I was under for the Printing-

House.—In order to secure my Credit and Character as a
Tradesmen, I took care not only to be in *Reality* Industrious
& frugal, but to avoid all *Appearances* of the Contrary. I drest
plainly; I was seen at no Places of idle Diversion; I never
went out a-fishing or shooting; a Book, indeed, sometimes
debauch'd me from my Work; but that was seldom, snug, &
gave no Scandal: and to show that I was not above my Business, I sometimes brought home the Paper I purchas'd at the
Stores, thro' the Streets on a Wheelbarrow. Thus being esteem'd an industrious thriving young Man, and paying duly
for what I bought, the Merchants who imported Stationary
solicited my Custom, others propos'd supplying me with
Books, & I went on swimmingly.—In the mean time Keimer's Credit & Business declining daily, he was at last forc'd
to sell his Printing-house to satisfy his Creditors. He went
to Barbadoes, & there lived some Years, in very poor Circumstances.

His Apprentice David Harry, whom I had instructed while
I work'd with him, set up in his Place at Philadelphia having
bought his Materials. I was at first apprehensive of a powerful
Rival in Harry, as his Friends were very able, & had a good
deal of Interest. I therefore propos'd a Partnership to him;
which he, fortunately for me, rejected with Scorn. He was
very proud, dress'd like a Gentleman, liv'd expensively, took
much Diversion & Pleasure abroad, ran in debt, & neglected
his Business, upon which all Business left him; and finding
nothing to do, he follow'd Keimer to Barbadoes; taking the
Printinghouse with him. There this Apprentice employ'd his
former Master as a Journeyman. They quarrel'd often. Harry
went continually behind-hand, and at length was forc'd to sell
his Types, and return to his Country Work in Pensilvania. The
Person that bought them, employ'd Keimer to use them, but
in a few years he died. There remain'd now no Competitor
with me at Philadelphia, but the old one, Bradford, who was
rich & easy, did a little Printing now & then by straggling
Hands, but was not very anxious about the Business. However, as he kept the Post Office, it was imagined he had better
Opportunities of obtaining News, his Paper was thought a
better Distributer of Advertisements than mine, & therefore
had many more, which was a profitable thing to him & a

Disadvantage to me. For tho' I did indeed receive & send Papers by the Post, yet the publick Opinion was otherwise; for what I did send was by Bribing the Riders who took them privately: Bradford being unkind enough to forbid it: which occasion'd some Resentment on my Part; and I thought so meanly of him for it, that when I afterwards came into his Situation, I took care never to imitate it.

I had hitherto continu'd to board with Godfrey who lived in Part of my House with his Wife & Children, & had one Side of the Shop for his Glazier's Business, tho' he work'd little, being always absorb'd in his Mathematics.—Mrs Godfrey projected a Match for me with a Relation's Daughter, took Opportunities of bringing us often together, till a serious Courtship on my Part ensu'd the Girl being in herself very deserving. The old Folks encourag'd me by continual Invitations to Supper, & by leaving us together, till at length it was time to explain. Mrs Godfrey manag'd our little Treaty. I let her know that I expected as much Money with their Daughter as would pay off my Remaining Debt for the Printing-house, which I believe was not then above a Hundred Pounds. She brought me Word they had no such Sum to spare. I said they might mortgage their House in the Loan Office.—The Answer to this after some Days was, that they did not approve the Match; that on Enquiry of Bradford they had been inform'd the Printing Business was not a profitable one, the Types would soon be worn out & more wanted, that S. Keimer & D. Harry had fail'd one after the other, and I should probably soon follow them; and therefore I was forbidden the House, & the Daughter shut up.—Whether this was a real Change of Sentiment, or only Artifice, on a Supposition of our being too far engag'd in Affection to retract, & therefore that we should steal a Marriage, which would leave them at Liberty to give or withold what they pleas'd, I know not: But I suspected the latter, resented it, and went no more. Mrs Godfrey brought me afterwards some more favourable Accounts of their Disposition, & would have drawn me on again: But I declared absolutely my Resolution to have nothing more to do with that Family. This was resented by the Godfreys, we differ'd, and they removed, leaving me the whole House, and I resolved to take no more Inmates. But

this Affair having turn'd my Thoughts to Marriage, I look'd
round me, and made Overtures of Acquaintance in other
Places; but soon found that the Business of a Printer being
generally thought a poor one, I was not to expect Money
with a Wife unless with such a one, as I should not otherwise
think agreable.—In the mean time, that hard-to-be-govern'd
Passion of Youth, had hurried me frequently into Intrigues
with low Women that fell in my Way, which were attended
with some Expence & great Inconvenience, besides a continual Risque to my Health by a Distemper which of all Things
I dreaded, tho' by great good Luck I escaped it.—

A friendly Correspondence as Neighbours & old Acquaintances, had continued between me & Mrs Read's Family who
all had a Regard for me from the time of my first Lodging in
their House. I was often invited there and consulted in their
Affairs, wherein I sometimes was of Service.—I pity'd poor
Miss Read's unfortunate Situation, who was generally de-
jected, seldom chearful, and avoided Company. I consider'd
my Giddiness & Inconstancy when in London as in a great
degree the Cause of her Unhappiness; tho' the Mother was
good enough to think the Fault more her own than mine, as
she had prevented our Marrying before I went thither, and
persuaded the other Match in my Absence. Our mutual Affection was revived, but there were now great Objections to
our Union. That Match was indeed look'd upon as invalid, a
preceding Wife being said to be living in England; but this
could not easily be prov'd, because of the Distance &c. And
tho' there was a Report of his Death, it was not certain.
Then, tho' it should be true, he had left many Debts which
his Successor might be call'd upon to pay. We ventured however, over all these Difficulties, and I took her to Wife Sept.
1. 1730. None of the Inconveniencies happened that we had
apprehended, she prov'd a good & faithful Helpmate, assisted
me much by attending the Shop, we throve together, and
have ever mutually endeavour'd to make each other happy.—
Thus I corrected that great *Erratum* as well as I could.

About this Time our Club meeting, not at a Tavern, but in
a little Room of Mr Grace's set apart for that Purpose; a
Proposition was made by me, that since our Books were often
referr'd to in our Disquisitions upon the Queries, it might be

convenient to us to have them all together where we met, that upon Occasion they might be consulted; and By thus clubbing our Books to a common Library, we should, while we lik'd to keep them together, have each of us the Advantage of using the Books of all the other Members, which would be nearly as beneficial as if each owned the whole. It was lik'd and agreed to, & we fill'd one End of the Room with such Books as we could best spare. The Number was not so great as we expected; and tho' they had been of great Use, yet some Inconveniencies occurring for want of due Care of them, the Collection after about a Year was separated, & each took his Books home again.

And now I set on foot my first Project of a public Nature, that for a Subscription Library. I drew up the Proposals, got them put into Form by our great Scrivener Brockden, and by the help of my Friends in the Junto, procur'd Fifty Subscribers of 40/ each to begin with & 10/ a Year for 50 Years, the Term our Company was to continue. We afterwards obtain'd a Charter, the Company being increas'd to 100. This was the Mother of all the N American Subscription Libraries now so numerous. It is become a great thing itself, & continually increasing.—These Libraries have improv'd the general Conversation of the Americans, made the common Tradesmen & Farmers as intelligent as most Gentlemen from other Countries, and perhaps have contributed in some degree to the Stand so generally made throughout the Colonies in Defence of their Privileges.—

Mem.°

Thus far was written with the Intention express'd in the Beginning and therefore contains several little family Anecdotes of no Importance to others. What follows was written many Years after in compliance with the Advice contain'd in these Letters, and accordingly intended for the Publick. The Affairs of the Revolution occasion'd the Interruption.

Part Two

Letter from Mr. Abel James, with Notes on my Life, (received in Paris.)

My dear & honored Friend.

I have often been desirous of writing to thee, but could not be reconciled to the Thought that the Letter might fall into the Hands of the British, lest some Printer or busy Body should publish some Part of the Contents & give our Friends Pain & myself Censure.

Some Time since there fell into my Hands to my great Joy about 23 Sheets in thy own hand-writing containing an Account of the Parentage & Life of thyself, directed to thy Son ending in the Year 1730 with which there were Notes likewise in thy writing, a Copy of which I inclose in Hopes it may be a means if thou continuedst it up to a later period, that the first & latter part may be put together; & if it is not yet continued, I hope thou wilt not delay it, Life is uncertain as the Preacher tells us, and what will the World say if kind, humane & benevolent Ben Franklin should leave his Friends & the World deprived of so pleasing & profitable a Work, a Work which would be useful & entertaining not only to a few, but to millions.

The Influence Writings under that Class have on the Minds of Youth is very great, and has no where appeared so plain as in our public Friends' Journals. It almost insensibly leads the Youth into the Resolution of endeavouring to become as good and as eminent as the Journalist. Should thine for Instance when published, and I think it could not fail of it, lead the Youth to equal the Industry & Temperance of thy early Youth, what a Blessing with that Class would such a Work be. I know of no Character living nor many of them put together, who has so much in his Power as Thyself to promote a greater Spirit of Industry & early Attention to Business, Frugality and Temperance with the American Youth. Not that I think the Work would have no other Merit & Use in the World, far from it, but the first is of such vast Importance, that I know nothing that can equal it.

———

The foregoing letter and the minutes accompanying it being shewn to a friend, I received from him the following:

LETTER FROM MR. BENJAMIN VAUGHAN.

Paris, January 31, 1783.

MY DEAREST SIR,

When I had read over your sheets of minutes of the principal incidents of your life, recovered for you by your Quaker acquaintance; I told you I would send you a letter expressing my reasons why I thought it would be useful to complete and publish it as he desired. Various concerns have for some time past prevented this letter being written, and I do not know whether it was worth any expectation: happening to be at leisure however at present, I shall by writing at least interest and instruct myself; but as the terms I am inclined to use may tend to offend a person of your manners, I shall only tell you how I would address any other person, who was as good and as great as yourself, but less diffident. I would say to him, Sir, I *solicit* the history of your life from the following motives.

Your history is so remarkable, that if you do not give it, somebody else will certainly give it; and perhaps so as nearly to do as much harm, as your own management of the thing might do good.

It will moreover present a table of the internal circumstances of your country, which will very much tend to invite to it settlers of virtuous and manly minds. And considering the eagerness with which such information is sought by them, and the extent of your reputation, I do not know of a more efficacious advertisement than your Biography would give.

All that has happened to you is also connected with the detail of the manners and situation of *a rising* people; and in this respect I do not think that the writings of Caesar and Tacitus can be more interesting to a true judge of human nature and society.

But these, Sir, are small reasons in my opinion, compared with the chance which your life will give for the forming of future great men; and in conjunction with your *Art of Virtue*, (which you design to publish) of improving the features of private character, and consequently of aiding all happiness both public and domestic.

The two works I allude to, Sir, will in particular give a noble rule and example of *self-education*. School and other education constantly proceed upon false principles, and shew a clumsy apparatus pointed at a false mark; but your apparatus is simple, and the mark a true one; and while parents and young persons are left destitute of other just means of estimating and becoming prepared for a reasonable course in life, your discovery that the thing is in many a man's private power, will be invaluable!

Influence upon the private character late in life, is not only an influence late in life, but a weak influence. It is in *youth* that we plant our chief habits and prejudices; it is in youth that we take our party as to profession, pursuits, and matrimony. In youth therefore the turn is given; in youth the education even of the next generation is given; in youth the private and public character is determined; and the term of life extending but from youth to age, life ought to begin well from youth; and more especially *before* we take our party as to our principal objects.

But your Biography will not merely teach self-education, but the education of *a wise man*; and the wisest man will receive lights and improve his progress, by seeing detailed the conduct of another wise man. And why are weaker men to be deprived of such helps, when we see our race has been blundering on in the dark, almost without a guide in this particular, from the farthest trace of time. Shew then, Sir, how much is to be done, *both to sons and fathers*; and invite all wise men to become like yourself; and other men to become wise.

When we see how cruel statesmen and warriors can be to the humble race, and how absurd distinguished men can be to their acquaintance, it will be instructive to observe the instances multiply of pacific acquiescing manners; and to find how compatible it is to be great and *domestic*; enviable and yet *good-humoured*.

The little private incidents which you will also have to relate, will have considerable use, as we want above all things, *rules of prudence in ordinary affairs*; and it will be curious to see how you have acted in these. It will be so far a sort of key to life, and explain many things that all men ought to have once explained to them, to give them a chance of becoming wise by foresight.

The nearest thing to having experience of one's own, is to have other people's affairs brought before us in a shape that is interesting; this is sure to happen from your pen. Your affairs and management will have an air of simplicity or importance that will not fail to strike; and I am convinced you have conducted them with as much originality as if you had been conducting discussions in politics or philosophy; and what more worthy of experiments and system, (its importance and its errors considered) than human life!

Some men have been virtuous blindly, others have speculated fantastically, and others have been shrewd to bad purposes; but you, Sir, I am sure, will give under your hand, nothing but what is at the same moment, wise, practical, and good.

Your account of yourself (for I suppose the parallel I am drawing for Dr. Franklin, will hold not only in point of character but of private history), will shew that you are ashamed of no origin; a thing the more important, as you prove how little necessary all origin is to happiness, virtue, or greatness.

As no end likewise happens without a means, so we shall find, Sir, that even you yourself framed a plan by which you became considerable; but at the same time we may see that though the event is flattering, the means are as simple as wisdom could make them; that is depending upon nature, virtue, thought, and habit.

Another thing demonstrated will be the propriety of every man's waiting for his time for appearing upon the stage of the world. Our sensations being very much fixed to the moment, we are apt to forget that more moments are to follow the first, and consequently that man should arrange his conduct so as to suit the *whole* of a life. Your attribution appears to have been applied to your *life*, and the passing moments of it have been enlivened with content and enjoyment, instead of being tormented with foolish impatience or regrets. Such a conduct is easy for those who make virtue and themselves their standard, and who try to keep themselves in countenance by examples of other truly great men, of whom patience is so often the characteristic.

Your Quaker correspondent, Sir, (for here again I will suppose the subject of my letter resembling Dr. Franklin,)
praised your frugality, diligence, and temperance, which he
considered as a pattern for all youth: but it is singular that he
should have forgotten your modesty, and your disinterested-
ness, without which you never could have waited for your
advancement, or found your situation in the mean time comfortable; which is a strong lesson to shew the poverty of
glory, and the importance of regulating our minds.

If this correspondent had known the nature of your reputation as well as I do, he would have said; your former writings and measures would secure attention to your Biography,
and Art of Virtue; and your Biography and Art of Virtue, in
return, would secure attention to them. This is an advantage
attendant upon a various character, and which brings all that
belongs to it into greater play; and it is the more useful, as
perhaps more persons are at a loss for the *means* of improving
their minds and characters, than they are for the time or the
inclination to do it.

But there is one concluding reflection, Sir, that will shew
the use of your life as a mere piece of biography. This style
of writing seems a little gone out of vogue, and yet it is a very
useful one; and your specimen of it may be particularly serviceable, as it will make a subject of comparison with the lives
of various public cut-throats and intriguers, and with absurd
monastic self-tormentors, or vain literary triflers. If it encourages more writings of the same kind with your own, and induces more men to spend lives fit to be written; it will be
worth all Plutarch's Lives put together.

But being tired of figuring to myself a character of which
every feature suits only one man in the world, without giving
him the praise of it; I shall end my letter, my dear Dr. Franklin, with a personal application to your proper self.

I am earnestly desirous then, my dear Sir, that you should
let the world into the traits of your genuine character, as civil
broils may otherwise tend to disguise or traduce it. Considering your great age, the caution of your character, and your
peculiar style of thinking, it is not likely that any one besides
yourself can be sufficiently master of the facts of your life, or
the intentions of your mind.

Besides all this, the immense revolution of the present period, will necessarily turn our attention towards the author of it; and when virtuous principles have been pretended in it, it will be highly important to shew that such have really influenced; and, as your own character will be the principal one to receive a scrutiny, it is proper (even for its effects upon your vast and rising country, as well as upon England and upon Europe), that it should stand respectable and eternal. For the furtherance of human happiness, I have always maintained that it is necessary to prove that man is not even at present a vicious and detestable animal; and still more to prove that good management may greatly amend him; and it is for much the same reason, that I am anxious to see the opinion established, that there are fair characters existing among the individuals of the race; for the moment that all men, without exception, shall be conceived abandoned, good people will cease efforts deemed to be hopeless, and perhaps think of taking their share in the scramble of life, or at least of making it comfortable principally for themselves.

Take then, my dear Sir, this work most speedily into hand: shew yourself good as you are good, temperate as you are temperate; and above all things, prove yourself as one who from your infancy have loved justice, liberty, and concord, in a way that has made it natural and consistent for you to have acted, as we have seen you act in the last seventeen years of your life. Let Englishmen be made not only to respect, but even to love you. When they think well of individuals in your native country, they will go nearer to thinking well of your country; and when your countrymen see themselves well thought of by Englishmen, they will go nearer to thinking well of England. Extend your views even further; do not stop at those who speak the English tongue, but after having settled so many points in nature and politics, think of bettering the whole race of men.

As I have not read any part of the life in question, but know only the character that lived it, I write somewhat at hazard. I am sure however, that the life, and the treatise I allude to (on the *Art of Virtue*), will necessarily fulfil the chief of my expectations; and still more so if you take up the measure of suiting these performances to the several views above stated. Should they even prove unsuccessful in all that a sanguine admirer of yours hopes from them, you will at least have framed pieces to interest the human mind; and whoever gives a feeling of pleasure that is innocent to man, has added so much to the fair side of a life otherwise too much darkened by anxiety, and too much injured by pain.

In the hope therefore that you will listen to the prayer addressed to you in this letter, I beg to subscribe myself, my dearest Sir, &c. &c.

Signed   BENJ. VAUGHAN.

Continuation of the Account of my Life.
Begun at Passy 1784

It is some time since I receiv'd the above Letters, but I have been too busy till now to think of complying with the Request they contain. It might too be much better done if I were at home among my Papers, which would aid my Memory, & help to ascertain Dates. But my Return being uncertain, and having just now a little Leisure, I will endeavour to recollect & write what I can; If I live to get home, it may there be corrected and improv'd.

Not having any Copy here of what is already written, I know not whether an Account is given of the means I used to establish the Philadelphia publick Library, which from a small Beginning is now become so considerable, though I remember to have come down to near the Time of that Transaction, 1730. I will therefore begin here, with an Account of it, which may be struck out if found to have been already given.—

At the time I establish'd my self in Pensylvania, there was not a good Bookseller's Shop in any of the Colonies to the Southward of Boston. In New-York & Philadª the Printers were indeed Stationers, they sold only Paper, &c. Almanacks, Ballads, and a few common School Books. Those who lov'd Reading were oblig'd to send for their Books from England.—The Members of the Junto had each a few. We had left the Alehouse where we first met, and hired a Room to hold our Club in. I propos'd that we should all of us bring our Books to that Room, where they would not only be ready to consult in our Conferences, but become a common

Benefit, each of us being at Liberty to borrow such as he wish'd to read at home. This was accordingly done, and for some time contented us. Finding the Advantage of this little Collection, I propos'd to render the Benefit from Books more common by commencing a Public Subscription Library. I drew a Sketch of the Plan and Rules that would be necessary, and got a skilful Conveyancer Mr Charles Brockden to put the whole in Form of Articles of Agreement to be subscribed, by which each Subscriber engag'd to pay a certain Sum down for the first Purchase of Books and an annual Contribution for encreasing them.—So few were the Readers at that time in Philadelphia, and the Majority of us so poor, that I was not able with great Industry to find more than Fifty Persons, mostly young Tradesmen, willing to pay down for this purpose Forty shillings each, & Ten Shillings per Annum. On this little Fund we began. The Books were imported. The Library was open one Day in the Week for lending them to the Subscribers, on their Promisory Notes to pay Double the Value if not duly returned. The Institution soon manifested its Utility, was imitated by other Towns and in other Provinces, the Librarys were augmented by Donations, Reading became fashionable, and our People having no publick Amusements to divert their Attention from Study became better acquainted with Books, and in a few Years were observ'd by Strangers to be better instructed & more intelligent than People of the same Rank generally are in other Countries.—

When we were about to sign the above-mentioned Articles, which were to be binding on us, our Heirs, &c for fifty Years, Mr Brockden, the Scrivener, said to us, "You are young Men, but it is scarce probable that any of you will live to see the Expiration of the Term fix'd in this Instrument." A Number of us, however, are yet living: But the Instrument was after a few Years rendred null by a Charter that incorporated & gave Perpetuity to the Company.—

The Objections, & Reluctances I met with in Soliciting the Subscriptions, made me soon feel the Impropriety of presenting one's self as the Proposer of any useful Project that might be suppos'd to raise one's Reputation in the smallest degree above that of one's Neighbours, when one has need of their

Assistance to accomplish that Project. I therefore put my self as much as I could out of sight, and stated it as a Scheme of *a Number of Friends*, who had requested me to go about and propose it to such as they thought Lovers of Reading. In this way my Affair went on more smoothly, and I ever after practis'd it on such Occasions; and from my frequent Successes, can heartily recommend it. The present little Sacrifice of your Vanity will afterwards be amply repaid. If it remains a while uncertain to whom the Merit belongs, some one more vain than yourself will be encourag'd to claim it, and then even Envy will be dispos'd to do you Justice, by plucking those assum'd Feathers, & restoring them to their right Owner.

This Library afforded me the Means of Improvement by constant Study, for which I set apart an Hour or two each Day; and thus repair'd in some Degree the Loss of the Learned Education my Father once intended for me. Reading was the only Amusement I allow'd my self. I spent no time in Taverns, Games, or Frolicks of any kind. And my Industry in my Business continu'd as indefatigable as it was necessary. I was in debt for my Printing-house, I had a young Family coming on to be educated, and I had to contend with for Business two Printers who were establish'd in the Place before me. My Circumstances however grew daily easier: my original Habits of Frugality continuing. And My Father having among his Instructions to me when a Boy, frequently repeated a Proverb of Solomon, *"Seest thou a Man diligent in his Calling, he shall stand before Kings, he shall not stand before mean Men."* I from thence consider'd Industry as a Means of obtaining Wealth and Distinction, which encourag'd me; tho' I did not think that I should ever literally stand before Kings, which however has since happened.—for I have stood before five, & even had the honour of sitting down with one, the King of Denmark, to Dinner.

We have an English Proverb that says,

> He that would thrive
> Must ask his Wife;

it was lucky for me that I had one as much dispos'd to Industry & Frugality as my self. She assisted me chearfully in my Business, folding & stitching Pamphlets, tending Shop, pur-

chasing old Linen Rags for the Paper-makers, &c &c. We
kept no idle Servants, our Table was plain & simple, our Furniture of the cheapest. For instance my Breakfast was a long
time Bread & Milk, (no Tea,) and I ate it out of a twopenny
earthen Porringer with a Pewter Spoon. But mark how
Luxury will enter Families, and make a Progress, in Spite of
Principle. Being Call'd one Morning to Breakfast, I found it
in a China Bowl with a Spoon of Silver. They had been
bought for me without my Knowledge by my Wife, and had
cost her the enormous Sum of three and twenty Shillings, for
which she had no other Excuse or Apology to make, but that
she thought *her* Husband deserv'd a Silver Spoon & China
Bowl as well as any of his Neighbours. This was the first Appearance of Plate & China in our House, which afterwards in
a Course of Years as our Wealth encreas'd, augmented gradually to several Hundred Pounds in Value.—

I had been religiously educated as a Presbyterian; and tho'
some of the Dogmas of that Persuasion, such as the Eternal
Decrees of God, Election, Reprobation, &c. appear'd to me
unintelligible, others doubtful, & I early absented myself from
the Public Assemblies of the Sect, Sunday being my Study-
ing-Day, I never was without some religious Principles; I
never doubted, for instance, the Existance of the Deity, that
he made the World, & govern'd it by his Providence; that the
most acceptable Service of God was the doing Good to Man;
that our Souls are immortal; and that all Crime will be pun-
ished & Virtue rewarded either here or hereafter; these I esteem'd the Essentials of every Religion, and being to be
found in all the Religions we had in our Country I respected
them all, tho' with different degrees of Respect as I found
them more or less mix'd with other Articles which without
any Tendency to inspire, promote or confirm Morality, serv'd
principally to divide us & make us unfriendly to one another.— This Respect to all, with an Opinion that the worst
had some good Effects, induc'd me to avoid all Discourse that
might tend to lessen the good Opinion another might have
of his own Religion; and as our Province increas'd in People
and new Places of worship were continually wanted, & generally erected by voluntary Contribution, my Mite for such

purpose, whatever might be the Sect, was never refused.—

Tho' I seldom attended any Public Worship, I had still an Opinion of its Propriety, and of its Utility when rightly conducted, and I regularly paid my annual Subscription for the Support of the only Presbyterian Minister or Meeting we had in Philadelphia. He us'd to visit me sometimes as a Friend, and admonish me to attend his Administrations, and I was now and then prevail'd on to do so, once for five Sundays successively. Had he been, *in my Opinion*, a good Preacher perhaps I might have continued, notwithstanding the occasion I had for the Sunday's Leisure in my Course of Study: But his Discourses were chiefly either polemic Arguments, or Explications of the peculiar Doctrines of our Sect, and were all to me very dry, uninteresting and unedifying, since not a single moral Principle was inculcated or enforc'd, their Aim seeming to be rather to make us Presbyterians than good Citizens. At length he took for his Text that Verse of the 4th Chapter of Philippians, *Finally, Brethren, Whatsoever Things are true, honest, just, pure, lovely, or of good report, if there be any virtue, or any praise, think on these Things*; & I imagin'd in a Sermon on such a Text, we could not miss of having some Morality: But he confin'd himself to five Points only as meant by the Apostle, viz. 1. Keeping holy the Sabbath Day. 2. Being diligent in Reading the Holy Scriptures. 3. Attending duly the Publick Worship. 4. Partaking of the Sacrament. 5. Paying a due Respect to God's Ministers.—These might be all good Things, but as they were not the kind of good Things that I expected from that Text, I despaired of ever meeting with them from any other, was disgusted, and attended his Preaching no more.—I had some Years before compos'd a little Liturgy or Form of Prayer for my own private Use, viz, in 1728. entitled, *Articles of Belief & Acts of Religion*. I return'd to the Use of this, and went no more to the public Assemblies.—My Conduct might be blameable, but I leave it without attempting farther to excuse it, my present purpose being to relate Facts, and not to make Apologies for them.—

It was about this time that I conceiv'd the bold and arduous Project of arriving at moral Perfection. I wish'd to live without committing any Fault at any time; I would conquer all that either Natural Inclination, Custom, or Company might lead me into. As I knew, or thought I knew, what was right and wrong, I did not see why I might not *always* do the one and avoid the other. But I soon found I had undertaken a Task of more Difficulty than I had imagined: While my Care was employ'd in guarding against one Fault, I was often surpriz'd by another. Habit took the Advantage of Inattention. Inclination was sometimes too strong for Reason. I concluded at length, that the mere speculative Conviction that it was our Interest to be compleatly virtuous, was not sufficient to prevent our Slipping, and that the contrary Habits must be broken and good Ones acquired and established, before we can have any Dependance on a steady uniform Rectitude of Conduct. For this purpose I therefore contriv'd the following Method.—

In the various Enumerations of the moral Virtues I had met with in my Reading, I found the Catalogue more or less numerous, as different Writers included more or fewer Ideas under the same Name. Temperance, for Example, was by some confin'd to Eating & Drinking, while by others it was extended to mean the moderating every other Pleasure, Appetite, Inclination or Passion, bodily or mental, even to our Avarice & Ambition. I propos'd to myself, for the sake of Clearness, to use rather more Names with fewer Ideas annex'd to each, than a few Names with more Ideas; and I included under Thirteen Names of Virtues all that at that time occurr'd to me as necessary or desirable, and annex'd to each a short Precept, which fully express'd the Extent I gave to its Meaning.—

These Names of Virtues with their Precepts were

1. TEMPERANCE.

Eat not to Dulness
Drink not to Elevation.

2. SILENCE.

Speak not but what may benefit others or your self. Avoid trifling Conversation.

3. ORDER.

Let all your Things have their Places. Let each Part of your Business have its Time.

4. RESOLUTION.

Resolve to perform what you ought. Perform without fail what you resolve.

5. FRUGALITY.

Make no Expence but to do good to others or yourself: i.e. Waste nothing.

6. INDUSTRY.

Lose no Time.—Be always employ'd in something useful.—Cut off all unnecessary Actions.—

7. SINCERITY.

Use no hurtful Deceit.

Think innocently and justly; and, if you speak; speak accordingly.

8. JUSTICE.

Wrong none, by doing Injuries or omitting the Benefits that are your Duty.

9. MODERATION.

Avoid Extreams. Forbear resenting Injuries so much as you think they deserve.

10. CLEANLINESS

Tolerate no Uncleanness in Body, Cloaths or Habitation.—

11. TRANQUILITY

Be not disturbed at Trifles, or at Accidents common or unavoidable.

12. CHASTITY.

Rarely use Venery but for Health or Offspring; Never to Dulness, Weakness, or the Injury of your own or another's Peace or Reputation.—

13. HUMILITY.

Imitate Jesus and Socrates.—

My intention being to acquire the *Habitude* of all these Virtues, I judg'd it would be well not to distract my Attention by attempting the whole at once, but to fix it on one of them at a time, and when I should be Master of that, then to proceed to another, and so on till I should have gone thro' the thirteen. And as the previous Acquisition of some might facilitate the Acquisition of certain others, I arrang'd them with that View as they stand above. *Temperance* first, as it tends to procure that Coolness & Clearness of Head, which is so necessary where constant Vigilance was to be kept up, and Guard maintained, against the unremitting Attraction of ancient Habits, and the Force of perpetual Temptations. This being acquir'd & establish'd, *Silence* would be more easy, and my Desire being to gain Knowledge at the same time that I improv'd in Virtue, and considering that in Conversation it was obtain'd rather by the Use of the Ears than of the Tongue, & therefore wishing to break a Habit I was getting into of Prattling, Punning & Joking, which only made me acceptable to trifling Company, I gave *Silence* the second Place. This, and the next, *Order*, I expected would allow me more Time for attending to my Project and my Studies; RESOLUTION once become habitual, would keep me firm in my Endeavours to obtain all the subsequent Virtues; *Frugality* & *Industry*, by freeing me from my remaining Debt, & producing Affluence & Independance would make more easy the Practice of *Sincerity* and *Justice*, &c. &c.. Conceiving then that agreeable to the Advice of Pythagoras in his Golden Verses,* daily Examination would be necessary, I contriv'd the following Method for conducting that Examination.

I made a little Book in which I allotted a Page for each of the Virtues. I rul'd each Page with red Ink so as to have seven Columns, one for each Day of the Week, marking each Column with a Letter for the Day. I cross'd these Columns with thirteen red Lines, marking the Beginning of each Line with

*Let not the stealing God of Sleep surprize,
 Nor creep in Slumbers on thy weary Eyes,
 Ere ev'ry Action of the former Day,
 Strictly *thou dost, and* righteously *survey.*
 With Rev'rence at thy own Tribunal stand,
 And answer justly to thy own Demand.
 Where have I been? In what have I transgrest?
 What Good or Ill has this Day's Life exprest?
 Where have I fail'd in what I ought to do?
 In what to GOD, to Man, or to myself I owe?
 Inquire severe whate'er from first to last,
 From Morning's Dawn till Ev'nings Gloom has past.
 If Evil were thy Deeds, repenting mourn,
 And let thy Soul with strong Remorse be torn:
 If Good, the Good with Peace of Mind repay, ⎫
 And to thy secret Self with Pleasure say, ⎬
 Rejoice, my Heart, for all went well to Day. ⎭

the first Letter of one of the Virtues, on which Line & in its proper Column I might mark by a little black Spot every Fault I found upon Examination, to have been committed respecting that Virtue upon that Day.

Form of the Pages

TEMPERANCE.						
Eat not to Dulness. *Drink not to Elevation.*						
S	M	T	W	T	F	S
T						
S ●●	●		●	●		
O ●	●	●		●	●	●
R		●		●		
F	●			●		
I		●				
S						
J						
M						
Cl.						
T						
Ch						
H						

I determined to give a Week's strict Attention to each of the Virtues successively. Thus in the first Week my great Guard was to avoid every the least Offence against Temperance, leaving the other Virtues to their ordinary Chance, only marking every Evening the Faults of the Day. Thus if in the first Week I could keep my first Line marked T clear of Spots, I suppos'd the Habit of that Virtue so much strengthen'd and its opposite weaken'd, that I might venture extending my Attention to include the next, and for the following Week keep both Lines clear of Spots. Proceeding thus to the last, I could go thro' a Course compleat in Thirteen Weeks, and four Courses in a Year.—And like him who having a Garden to weed, does not attempt to eradicate all the bad Herbs at once, which would exceed his Reach and his Strength, but works on one of the Beds at a time, & having accomplish'd the first proceeds to a second; so I should have, (I hoped) the encouraging Pleasure of seeing on my Pages the Progress I made in Virtue, by clearing successively my Lines of their Spots, till in the End by a Number of Courses, I should be happy in viewing a clean Book after a thirteen Weeks daily Examination.

This my little Book had for its Motto these Lines from *Addison's Cato*;

> *Here will I hold: If there is a Pow'r above us,*
> *(And that there is, all Nature cries aloud*
> *Thro' all her Works) he must delight in Virtue,*
> *And that which he delights in must be happy.*

Another from *Cicero*.

O Vitæ Philosophia Dux! O Virtutum indagatrix, expultrixque vitiorum! Unus dies bene, & ex preceptis tuis actus, peccanti imm rtalitati est anteponendus.

Another from the Proverbs of Solomon speaking of Wisdom or Virtue;

Length of Days is in her right hand, and in her Left Hand Riches and Honours; Her Ways are Ways of Pleasantness, and all her Paths are Peace.   III, 16, 17.

And conceiving God to be the Fountain of Wisdom, I thought it right and necessary to solicit his Assistance for obtaining it; to this End I form'd the following little Prayer, which was prefix'd to my Tables of Examination; for daily Use.

O Powerful Goodness! bountiful Father! merciful Guide! Increase in me that Wisdom which discovers my truest Interests; Strengthen my Resolutions to perform what that Wisdom dictates. Accept my kind Offices to thy other Children, as the only Return in my Power for thy continual Favours to me.

I us'd also sometimes a little Prayer which I took from *Thomson's* Poems. viz

> *Father of Light and Life, thou Good supreme,*
> *O teach me what is good, teach me thy self!*
> *Save me from Folly, Vanity and Vice,*
> *From every low Pursuit, and fill my Soul*
> *With Knowledge, conscious Peace, & Virtue pure,*
> *Sacred, substantial, neverfading Bliss!*

The Precept of *Order* requiring that *every Part of my Business should have its allotted Time*, one Page in my little Book contain'd the following Scheme of Employment for the Twenty-four Hours of a natural Day,

The Morning Ques-tion, What Good shall I do this Day?	5	Rise, wash, and address *Powerful Good-ness;* contrive Day's Business and take the Resolution of the Day; prosecute the present Study: and breakfast?—
	6	
	7	
	8	
	9	Work.
	10	
	11	
	12	Read, or overlook my Accounts, and dine.
	1	
	2	
	3	Work.
	4	
	5	
	6	Put Things in their Places, Supper, Musick, or Diversion, or Con-versation, Examination of the Day.
	7	
Evening Question, What Good have I done to day?	8	
	9	
	10	
	11	
	12	
	1	Sleep.—
	2	
	3	
	4	

I enter'd upon the Execution of this Plan for Self Examination, and continu'd it with occasional Intermissions for some time. I was surpriz'd to find myself so much fuller of Faults than I had imagined, but I had the Satisfaction of seeing them diminish. To avoid the Trouble of renewing now & then my little Book, which by scraping out the Marks on the Paper of old Faults to make room for new Ones in a new Course, became full of Holes: I transferr'd my Tables & Precepts to the Ivory Leaves of a Memorandum Book, on which the Lines were drawn with red Ink that made a durable Stain, and on those Lines I mark'd my Faults with a black Lead Pencil, which Marks I could easily wipe out with a wet Sponge. After a while I went thro' one Course only in a Year, and afterwards only one in several Years; till at length I

omitted them entirely, being employ'd in Voyages & Business
abroad with a Multiplicity of Affairs, that interfered. But I
always carried my little Book with me. My Scheme of OR-
DER, gave me the most Trouble, and I found, that tho' it
might be practicable where a Man's Business was such as to
leave him the Disposition of his Time, that of a Journey-man
Printer for instance, it was not possible to be exactly observ'd
by a Master, who must mix with the World, and often receive
People of Business at their own Hours.— *Order* too, with regard to Places for Things, Papers, &c. I found extreamly difficult to acquire. I had not been early accustomed to it, &
having an exceeding good Memory, I was not so sensible of
the Inconvenience attending Want of Method. This Article
therefore cost me so much painful Attention & my Faults in
it vex'd me so much, and I made so little Progress in Amendment, & had such frequent Relapses, that I was almost ready
to give up the Attempt, and content my self with a faulty
Character in that respect. Like the Man who in buying an Ax
of a Smith my Neighbour, desired to have the whole of its
Surface as bright as the Edge; the Smith consented to grind
it bright for him if he would turn the Wheel. He turn'd while
the Smith press'd the broad Face of the Ax hard & heavily on
the Stone, which made the Turning of it very fatiguing. The
Man came every now & then from the Wheel to see how the
Work went on; and at length would take his Ax as it was
without farther Grinding. No, says the Smith, Turn on, turn
on; we shall have it bright by and by; as yet 'tis only speckled.
Yes, says the Man; but— *I think I like a speckled Ax best.* —
And I believe this may have been the Case with many who
having for want of some such Means as I employ'd found the
Difficulty of obtaining good, & breaking bad Habits, in other
Points of Vice & Virtue, have given up the Struggle, & concluded that *a speckled Ax was best.* For something that pretended to be Reason was every now and then suggesting to
me, that such extream Nicety as I exacted of my self might be
a kind of Foppery in Morals, which if it were known would
make me ridiculous; that a perfect Character might be attended with the Inconvenience of being envied and hated;
and that a benevolent Man should allow a few Faults in himself, to keep his Friends in Countenance. In Truth I found

myself incorrigible with respect to *Order*; and now I am grown old, and my Memory bad, I feel very sensibly the want of it. But on the whole, tho' I never arrived at the Perfection I had been so ambitious of obtaining, but fell far short of it, yet I was by the Endeavour made a better and a happier Man than I otherwise should have been, if I had not attempted it; As those who aim at perfect Writing by imitating the engraved Copies, tho' they never reach the wish'd for Excellence of those Copies, their Hand is mended by the Endeavour, and is tolerable while it continues fair & legible. —

And it may be well my Posterity should be informed, that to this little Artifice, with the Blessing of God, their Ancestor ow'd the constant Felicity of his Life down to his 79th Year in which this is written. What Reverses may attend the Remainder is in the Hand of Providence: But if they arrive the Reflection on past Happiness enjoy'd ought to help his Bearing them with more Resignation. To *Temperance* he ascribes his long-continu'd Health, & what is still left to him of a good Constitution. To *Industry* and *Frugality* the early Easiness of his Circumstances, & Acquisition of his Fortune, with all that Knowledge which enabled him to be an useful Citizen, and obtain'd for him some Degree of Reputation among the Learned. To *Sincerity* & *Justice* the Confidence of his Country, and the honourable Employs it conferr'd upon him. And to the joint Influence of the whole Mass of the Virtues, even in their imperfect State he was able to acquire them, all that Evenness of Temper, & that Chearfulness in Conversation which makes his Company still sought for, & agreable even to his younger Acquaintance. I hope therefore that some of my Descendants may follow the Example & reap the Benefit. —

It will be remark'd that, tho' my Scheme was not wholly without Religion there was in it no Mark of any of the distinguishing Tenets of any particular Sect. — I had purposely avoided them; for being fully persuaded of the Utility and Excellency of my Method, and that it might be serviceable to People in all Religions, and intending some time or other to publish it, I would not have any thing in it that should prejudice any one of any Sect against it. — I purposed writing a little Comment on each Virtue, in which I would have shown

the Advantages of possessing it, & the Mischiefs attending its
opposite Vice; and I should have called my Book the ART *of
Virtue*, because it would have shown the *Means & Manner* of
obtaining Virtue; which would have distinguish'd it from the
mere Exhortation to be good, that does not instruct & indicate the Means; but is like the Apostle's Man of verbal Charity, who only, without showing to the Naked & the Hungry
how or where they might get Cloaths or Victuals, exhorted
them to be fed & clothed. *James* II, 15, 16. —

But it so happened that my Intention of writing & publishing this Comment was never fulfilled. I did indeed, from time
to time put down short Hints of the Sentiments, Reasonings,
&c. to be made use of in it; some of which I have still by me:
But the necessary close Attention to private Business in the
earlier part of Life, and public Business since, have occasioned
my postponing it. For it being connected in my Mind with a
great and extensive Project that required the whole Man to
execute, and which an unforeseen Succession of Employs prevented my attending to, it has hitherto remain'd unfinish'd. —

In this Piece it was my Design to explain and enforce this
Doctrine, that vicious Actions are not hurtful because they are
forbidden, but forbidden because they are hurtful, the Nature
of Man alone consider'd: That it was therefore every ones
Interest to be virtuous, who wish'd to be happy even in this
World. And I should from this Circumstance, there being always in the World a Number of rich Merchants, Nobility,
States and Princes, who have need of honest Instruments for
the Management of their Affairs, and such being so rare, have
endeavoured to convince young Persons, that no Qualities
were so likely to make a poor Man's Fortune as those of
Probity & Integrity.

My List of Virtues contain'd at first but twelve: But a
Quaker Friend having kindly inform'd me that I was gener-
ally thought proud; that my Pride show'd itself frequently in
Conversation; that I was not content with being in the right
when discussing any Point, but was overbearing & rather
insolent; of which he convinc'd me by mentioning several
Instances; — I determined endeavouring to cure myself if
I could of this Vice or Folly among the rest, and I added

Humility to my List, giving an extensive Meaning to the Word.—I cannot boast of much Success in acquiring the *Reality* of this Virtue; but I had a good deal with regard to the *Appearance* of it.—I made it a Rule to forbear all direct Contradiction to the Sentiments of others, and all positive Assertion of my own. I even forbid myself agreable to the old Laws of our Junto, the Use of every Word or Expression in the Language that imported a fix'd Opinion; such as *certainly*, *undoubtedly*, &c. and I adopted instead of them, *I conceive*, *I apprehend*, or *I imagine* a thing to be so or so, or it so appears to me at present.—When another asserted something that I thought an Error, I deny'd my self the Pleasure of contradicting him abruptly, and of showing immediately some Absurdity in his Proposition; and in answering I began by observing that in certain Cases or Circumstances his Opinion would be right, but that in the present case there *appear'd* or *seem'd* to me some Difference, &c. I soon found the Advantage of this Change in my Manners. The Conversations I engag'd in went on more pleasantly. The modest way in which I propos'd my Opinions, procur'd them a readier Reception and less Contradiction; I had less Mortification when I was found to be in the wrong, and I more easily prevail'd with others to give up their Mistakes & join with me when I happen'd to be in the right. And this Mode, which I at first put on, with some violence to natural Inclination, became at length so easy & so habitual to me, that perhaps for these Fifty Years past no one has ever heard a dogmatical Expression escape me. And to this Habit (after my Character of Integrity) I think it principally owing, that I had early so much Weight with my Fellow Citizens, when I proposed new Institutions, or Alterations in the old; and so much Influence in public Councils when I became a Member. For I was but a bad Speaker, never eloquent, subject to much Hesitation in my choice of Words, hardly correct in Language, and yet I generally carried my Points.—

In reality there is perhaps no one of our natural Passions so hard to subdue as *Pride*. Disguise it, struggle with it, beat it down, stifle it, mortify it as much as one pleases, it is still alive, and will every now and then peep out and show itself.

You will see it perhaps often in this History. For even if I could conceive that I had compleatly overcome it, I should probably be proud of my Humility.—

Thus far written at Passy 1784

Part Three

I am now about to write at home, Aug^r 1788.—but cannot have the help expected from my Papers, many of them being lost in the War. I have however found the following.

Having mentioned *a great & extensive Project* which I had conceiv'd, it seems proper that some Account should be here given of that Project and its Object. Its first Rise in my Mind appears in the following little Paper, accidentally preserv'd, viz.

OBSERVATIONS on my Reading History in Library, May 9. 1731.

"That the great Affairs of the World, the Wars, Revolutions, &c. are carried on and effected by Parties.—

"That the View of these Parties is their present general Interest, or what they take to be such.—

"That the different Views of these different Parties, occasion all Confusion.

"That while a Party is carrying on a general Design, each Man has his particular private Interest in View.

"That as soon as a Party has gain'd its general Point, each Member becomes intent upon his particular Interest, which thwarting others, breaks that Party into Divisions, and occasions more Confusion.

"That few in Public Affairs act from a meer View of the Good of their Country, whatever they may pretend; and tho' their Actings bring real Good to their Country, yet Men primarily consider'd that their own and their Country's Interest was united, and did not act from a Principle of Benevolence.

"That fewer still in public Affairs act with a View to the Good of Mankind.

"There seems to me at present to be great Occasion for raising an united Party for Virtue, by forming the Virtuous and good Men of all Nations into a regular Body, to be govern'd by suitable good and wise Rules, which good and wise Men may probably be more unanimous in their Obedience to, than common People are to common Laws.

"I at present think, that whoever attempts this aright, and is well qualified, cannot fail of pleasing God, & of meeting with Success.— B F."—

Revolving this Project in my Mind, as to be undertaken hereafter when my Circumstances should afford me the necessary Leisure, I put down from time to time on Pieces of Paper such Thoughts as occur'd to me respecting it. Most of these are lost; but I find one purporting to be the Substance of an intended Creed, containing as I thought the Essentials of every known Religion, and being free of every thing that might shock the Professors of any Religion. It is express'd in these Words. viz.

"That there is one God who made all things.

"That he governs the World by his Providence.—

"That he ought to be worshipped by Adoration, Prayer & Thanksgiving.

"But that the most acceptable Service of God is doing Good to Man.

"That the Soul is immortal.

"And that God will certainly reward Virtue and punish Vice either here or hereafter."—

My Ideas at that time were, that the Sect should be begun & spread at first among young and single Men only; that each Person to be initiated should not only declare his Assent to such Creed, but should have exercis'd himself with the Thirteen Weeks Examination and Practice of the Virtues as in the before-mention'd Model; that the Existence of such a Society should be kept a Secret till it was become considerable, to prevent Solicitations for the Admission of improper Persons; but that the Members should each of them search among his Acquaintance for ingenuous well-disposed Youths, to whom with prudent Caution the Scheme should be gradually communicated: That the Members should engage to afford their Advice Assistance and Support to each other in promoting one another's Interest Business and Advancement in Life: That for Distinction we should be call'd the Society of the *Free and Easy*; Free, as being by the general Practice and Habit of the Virtues, free from the Dominion of Vice, and particularly by the Practice of Industry & Frugality, free from Debt, which exposes a Man to Confinement and a Species of Slavery to his Creditors. This is as much as I can now recollect of the Project, except that I communicated it in part to two young Men, who adopted it with some Enthusiasm. But my then narrow Circumstances, and the Necessity I was under of sticking close to my Business, occasion'd my Postponing the farther Prosecution of it at that time, and my multifarious Occupations public & private induc'd me to continue postponing, so that it has been omitted till I have no longer Strength or Activity left sufficient for such an Enterprize: Tho' I am still of Opinion that it was a practicable Scheme, and might have been very useful, by forming a great Number of good Citizens: And I was not discourag'd by the seeming Magnitude of the Undertaking, as I have always thought that one Man of tolerable Abilities may work great Changes, & accomplish great Affairs among Mankind, if he first forms a good Plan, and, cutting off all Amusements or other Employments that would divert his Attention, makes the Execution of that same Plan his sole Study and Business.—

In 1732 I first published my Almanack, under the Name of *Richard Saunders*; it was continu'd by me about 25 Years, commonly call'd *Poor Richard*'s Almanack. I endeavour'd to make it both entertaining and useful, and it accordingly came to be in such Demand that I reap'd considerable Profit from it, vending annually near ten Thousand. And observing that it was generally read, scarce any Neighbourhood in the Province being without it, I consider'd it as a proper Vehicle for conveying Instruction among the common People, who bought scarce any other Books. I therefore filled all the little Spaces that occurr'd between the Remarkable Days in the Calendar, with Proverbial Sentences, chiefly such as inculcated Industry and Frugality, as the Means of procuring Wealth and thereby securing Virtue, it being more difficult for a Man in Want to act always honestly, as (to use here one of those Proverbs) *it is hard for an empty Sack to stand upright*. These Proverbs, which contained the Wisdom of many Ages and Nations, I assembled and form'd into a connected Discourse prefix'd to the Almanack of 1757, as the Harangue of a wise old Man to the People attending an Auction. The bringing all these scatter'd Counsels thus into a Focus, enabled them to make greater Impression. The Piece being universally approv'd was copied in all the Newspapers of the Continent, reprinted in Britain on a Broadside to be stuck up in Houses, two Translations were made of it in French, and great Numbers bought by the Clergy & Gentry to distribute gratis among their poor Parishioners and Tenants. In Pennsylvania, as it discouraged useless Expence in foreign Superfluities, some thought it had its share of Influence in producing that growing Plenty of Money which was observable for several Years after its Publication.—

I consider'd my Newspaper also as another Means of communicating Instruction, & in that View frequently reprinted in it Extracts from the Spectator and other moral Writers, and sometimes publish'd little Pieces of my own which had been first compos'd for Reading in our Junto. Of these are a Socratic Dialogue tending to prove, that, whatever might be his Parts and Abilities, a vicious Man could not properly be called a Man of Sense. And a Discourse on Self denial, showing that Virtue was not Secure, till its Practice became a Habitude, & was free from the Opposition of contrary Inclinations.—These may be found in the Papers about the beginning of 1735.—In the Conduct of my Newspaper I carefully excluded all Libelling and Personal Abuse, which is of late Years become so disgraceful to our Country. Whenever I was solicited to insert any thing of that kind, and the Writers pleaded as they generally did, the Liberty of the Press, and that a Newspaper was like a Stage Coach in which any one who would pay had a Right to a Place, my Answer was, that I would print the Piece separately if desired, and the Author might have as many Copies as he pleased to distribute himself, but that I would not take upon me to spread his Detraction, and that having contracted with my Subscribers to furnish them with what might be either useful or entertaining, I could not fill their Papers with private Altercation in which they had no Concern without doing them manifest Injustice. Now many of our Printers make no scruple of gratifying the Malice of Individuals by false Accusations of the fairest Characters among ourselves, augmenting Animosity even to the producing of Duels, and are moreover so indiscreet as to print scurrilous Reflections on the Government of neighbouring States, and even on the Conduct of our best national Allies, which may be attended with the most pernicious Consequences.— These Things I mention as a Caution to young Printers, &

that they may be encouraged not to pollute their Presses and disgrace their Profession by such infamous Practices, but refuse steadily; as they may see by my Example, that such a Course of Conduct will not on the whole be injurious to their Interests. —

In 1733, I sent one of my Journeymen to Charleston South Carolina where a Printer was wanting. I furnish'd him with a Press and Letters, on an Agreement of Partnership, by which I was to receive One Third of the Profits of the Business, paying One Third of the Expence. He was a Man of Learning and honest, but ignorant in Matters of Account; and tho' he sometimes made me Remittances, I could get no Account from him, nor any satisfactory State of our Partnership while he lived. On his Decease, the Business was continued by his Widow, who being born & bred in Holland, where as I have been inform'd the Knowledge of Accompts makes a Part of Female Education, she not only sent me as clear a State as she could find of the Transactions past, but continu'd to account with the greatest Regularity & Exactitude every Quarter afterwards; and manag'd the Business with such Success that she not only brought up reputably a Family of Children, but at the Expiration of the Term was able to purchase of me the Printing-House and establish her Son in it. I mention this Affair chiefly for the Sake of recommending that Branch of Education for our young Females, as likely to be of more Use to them & their Children in Case of Widowhood than either Music or Dancing, by preserving them from Losses by Imposition of crafty Men, and enabling them to continue perhaps a profitable mercantile House with establish'd Correspondence till a Son is grown up fit to undertake and go on with it, to the lasting Advantage and enriching of the Family. —

About the Year 1734. there arrived among us from Ireland, a young Presbyterian Preacher named Hemphill, who delivered with a good Voice, & apparently extempore, most excellent Discourses, which drew together considerable Numbers of different Persuasions, who join'd in admiring them. Among the rest I became one of his constant Hearers, his Sermons pleasing me as they had little of the dogmatical kind, but inculcated strongly the Practice of Virtue, or what in the

religious Stile are called Good Works. Those however, of our
Congregation, who considered themselves as orthodox Presbyterians, disapprov'd his Doctrine, and were join'd by most
of the old Clergy, who arraign'd him of Heterodoxy before
the Synod, in order to have him silenc'd. I became his zealous
Partisan, and contributed all I could to raise a Party in his
Favour; and we combated for him a while with some Hopes
of Success. There was much Scribbling pro & con upon the
Occasion; and finding that tho' an elegant Preacher he was
but a poor Writer, I lent him my Pen and wrote for him two
or three Pamphlets, and one Piece in the Gazette of April 1735.
Those Pamphlets, as is generally the Case with controversial
Writings, tho' eagerly read at the time, were soon out of
Vogue, and I question whether a single Copy of them now
exists. During the Contest an unlucky Occurrence hurt his
Cause exceedingly. One of our Adversaries having heard him
preach a Sermon that was much admired, thought he had
somewhere read that Sermon before, or at least a part of it.
On Search he found that Part quoted at length in one of the
British Reviews, from a Discourse of Dr Forster's. This De-
tection gave many of our Party Disgust, who accordingly
abandoned his Cause, and occasion'd our more speedy Dis-
comfiture in the Synod. I stuck by him, however, as I rather
approv'd his giving us good Sermons compos'd by others,
than bad ones of his own Manufacture; tho' the latter was the
Practice of our common Teachers. He afterwards acknowledg'd to me that none of those he preach'd were his own;
adding that his Memory was such as enabled him to retain
and repeat any Sermon after one Reading only.—On our Defeat he left us, in search elsewhere of better Fortune, and I
quitted the Congregation, never joining it after, tho' I continu'd many Years my Subscription for the Support of its
Ministers.—

I had begun in 1733 to study Languages. I soon made myself so much a Master of the French as to be able to read the
Books with Ease. I then undertook the Italian. An Acquaintance who was also learning it, us'd often to tempt me to play
Chess with him. Finding this took up too much of the Time
I had to spare for Study, I at length refus'd to play any more,
unless on this Condition, that the Victor in every Game,

should have a Right to impose a Task, either in Parts of the Grammar to be got by heart, or in Translation, &c. which Tasks the Vanquish'd was to perform upon Honour before our next Meeting. As we play'd pretty equally we thus beat one another into that Language.—I afterwards with a little Pains-taking acquir'd as much of the Spanish as to read their Books also. I have already mention'd that I had only one Years Instruction in a Latin School, and that when very young, after which I neglected that Language entirely.—But when I had attained an Acquaintance with the French, Italian and Spanish, I was surpriz'd to find, on looking over a Latin Testament, that I understood so much more of that Language than I had imagined; which encouraged me to apply my self again to the Study of it, & I met with the more Success, as those preceding Languages had greatly smooth'd my Way. From these Circumstances I have thought, that there is some Inconsistency in our common Mode of Teaching Languages. We are told that it is proper to begin first with the Latin, and having acquir'd that it will be more easy to attain those modern Languages which are deriv'd from it; and yet we do not begin with the Greek in order more easily to acquire the Latin. It is true, that if you can clamber & get to the Top of a Stair-Case without using the Steps, you will more easily gain them in descending: but certainly if you begin with the lowest you will with more Ease ascend to the Top. And I would therefore offer it to the Consideration of those who superintend the Educating of our Youth, whether, since many of those who begin with the Latin, quit the same after spending some Years, without having made any great Proficiency, and what they have learnt becomes almost useless, so that their time has been lost, it would not have been better to have begun them with the French, proceeding to the Italian &c. for tho' after spending the same time they should quit the Study of Languages, & never arrive at the Latin, they would however have acquir'd another Tongue or two that being in modern Use might be serviceable to them in common Life.

    After ten Years Absence from Boston, and having become more easy in my Circumstances, I made a Journey thither to visit my Relations, which I could not sooner well afford. In returning I call'd at Newport, to see my Brother then settled there with his Printing-House. Our former Differences were forgotten, and our Meeting was very cordial and affectionate. He was fast declining in his Health, and requested of me that in case of his Death which he apprehended not far distant, I would take home his Son, then but 10 Years of Age, and bring him up to the Printing Business. This I accordingly perform'd, sending him a few Years to School before I took him into the Office. His Mother carry'd on the Business till he was grown up, when I assisted him with an Assortment of new Types, those of his Father being in a Manner worn out.—Thus it was that I made my Brother ample Amends for the Service I had depriv'd him of by leaving him so early.—

In 1736 I lost one of my Sons a fine Boy of 4 Years old, by the Small Pox taken in the common way. I long regretted bitterly & still regret that I had not given it to him by Inoculation; This I mention for the Sake of Parents, who omit that Operation on the Supposition that they should never forgive themselves if a Child died under it; my Example showing that the Regret may be the same either way, and that therefore the safer should be chosen.—

Our Club, the Junto, was found so useful, & afforded such Satisfaction to the Members, that several were desirous of introducing their Friends, which could not well be done without exceeding what we had settled as a convenient Number, viz. Twelve. We had from the Beginning made it a Rule to keep our Institution a Secret, which was pretty well observ'd. The Intention was, to avoid Applications of improper Persons for Admittance, some of whom perhaps we might find it difficult to refuse. I was one of those who were against any Addition to our Number, but instead of it made in Writing a Proposal, that every Member separately should endeavour to form a subordinate Club, with the same Rules respecting Queries, &c. and without informing them of the Connexion with the Junto. The Advantages propos'd were the Improvement of so many more young Citizens by the Use of our Institutions; Our better Acquaintance with the general Sentiments of the Inhabitants on any Occasion, as the Junto-Member might propose what Queries we should desire, and was to report to Junto what pass'd in his separate Club; the Promotion of our particular Interests in Business by more

extensive Recommendations; and the Increase of our Influence in public Affairs & our Power of doing Good by spread-
ing thro' the several Clubs the Sentiments of the Junto. The
Project was approv'd, and every Member undertook to form
his Club: but they did not all succeed. Five or six only were
compleated, which were call'd by different Names, as the
Vine, the Union, the Band, &c. they were useful to themselves, & afforded us a good deal of Amusement, Information
& Instruction, besides answering in some considerable Degree our Views of influencing the public Opinion on particular Occasions, of which I shall give some Instances in course
of time as they happened. —

My first Promotion was my being chosen in 1736 Clerk of
the General Assembly. The Choice was made that Year without Opposition; but the Year following when I was again
propos'd (the Choice, like that of the Members being annual)
a new Member made a long Speech against me in order to
favour some other Candidate. I was however chosen; which
was the more agreable to me, as besides the Pay for immediate Service as Clerk, the Place gave me a better Opportunity
of keeping up an Interest among the Members, which secur'd
to me the Business of Printing the Votes, Laws, Paper
Money, and other occasional Jobbs for the Public, that on the
whole were very profitable. I therefore did not like the Opposition of this new Member, who was a Gentleman of Fortune, & Education, with Talents that were likely to give him
in time great Influence in the House, which indeed afterwards
happened. I did not however aim at gaining his Favour by
paying any servile Respect to him, but after some time took
this other Method. Having heard that he had in his Library a
certain very scarce & curious Book, I wrote a Note to him
expressing my Desire of perusing that Book, and requesting
he would do me the Favour of lending it to me for a few
Days. He sent it immediately; and I return'd it in about a
Week, with another Note expressing strongly my Sense of the
Favour. When we next met in the House he spoke to me,
(which he had never done before) and with great Civility.
And he ever afterwards manifested a Readiness to serve me
on all Occasions, so that we became great Friends, & our
Friendship continu'd to his Death. This is another Instance

of the Truth of an old Maxim I had learnt, which says, *He that has once done you a Kindness will be more ready to do you another, than he whom you yourself have obliged*. And it shows how much more profitable it is prudently to remove, than to resent, return & continue inimical Proceedings.—

In 1737, Col. Spotswood, late Governor of Virginia, & then Post-master, General, being dissatisfied with the Conduct of his Deputy at Philadelphia, respecting some Negligence in rendering, & Inexactitude of his Accounts, took from him the Commission & offered it to me. I accepted it readily, and found it of great Advantage; for tho' the Salary was small, it facilitated the Correspondence that improv'd my Newspaper, encreas'd the Number demanded, as well as the Advertisements to be inserted, so that it came to afford me a very considerable Income. My old Competitor's Newspaper declin'd proportionably, and I was satisfy'd without retaliating his Refusal, while Postmaster, to permit my Papers being carried by the Riders. Thus He suffer'd greatly from his Neglect in due Accounting; and I mention it as a Lesson to those young Men who may be employ'd in managing Affairs for others that they should always render Accounts & make Remittances, with great Clearness and Punctuality.—The Character of observing Such a Conduct is the most powerful of all Recommendations to new Employments & Increase of Business.

I began now to turn my Thoughts a little to public Affairs, beginning however with small Matters. The City Watch was one of the first Things that I conceiv'd to want Regulation. It was managed by the Constables of the respective Wards in Turn. The Constable warn'd a Number of Housekeepers to attend him for the Night. Those who chose never to attend paid him Six Shillings a Year to be excus'd, which was suppos'd to be for hiring Substitutes; but was in Reality much more than was necessary for that purpose, and made the Constableship a Place of Profit. And the Constable for a little Drink often got such Ragamuffins about him as a Watch, that reputable Housekeepers did not chuse to mix with. Walking the Rounds too was often neglected, and most of the Night spent in Tippling. I thereupon wrote a Paper to be read in Junto, representing these Irregularities, but insisting more particularly on the Inequality of this Six Shilling Tax of the

Constables, respecting the Circumstances of those who paid it, since a poor Widow Housekeeper, all whose Property to be guarded by the Watch did not perhaps exceed the Value of Fifty Pounds, paid as much as the wealthiest Merchant who had Thousands of Pounds-worth of Goods in his Stores. On the whole I proposed as a more effectual Watch, the Hiring of proper Men to serve constantly in that Business; and as a more equitable Way of supporting the Charge, the levying a Tax that should be proportion'd to Property. This Idea being approv'd by the Junto, was communicated to the other Clubs, but as arising in each of them. And tho' the Plan was not immediately carried into Execution, yet by preparing the Minds of People for the Change, it paved the Way for the Law obtain'd a few Years after, when the Members of our Clubs were grown into more Influence.—

About this time I wrote a Paper, (first to be read in Junto but it was afterwards publish'd) on the different Accidents and Carelessnesses by which Houses were set on fire, with Cautions against them, and Means proposed of avoiding them. This was much spoken of as a useful Piece, and gave rise to a Project, which soon followed it, of forming a Company for the more ready Extinguishing of Fires, and mutual Assistance in Removing & Securing of Goods when in Danger. Associates in this Scheme were presently found amounting to Thirty. Our Articles of Agreement oblig'd every Member to keep always in good Order and fit for Use, a certain Number of Leather Buckets, with strong Bags & Baskets (for packing & transporting of Goods), which were to be brought to every Fire; and we agreed to meet once a Month & spend a social Evening together, in discoursing, and communicating such Ideas as occur'd to us upon the Subject of Fires as might be useful in our Conduct on such Occasions. The Utility of this Institution soon appeard, and many more desiring to be admitted than we thought convenient for one Company, they were advised to form another; which was accordingly done. And this went on, one new Company being formed after another, till they became so numerous as to include most of the Inhabitants who were Men of Property; and now at the time of my Writing this, tho' upwards of Fifty Years since its Establishment, that which I first formed, called the Union Fire Company, still subsists and flourishes, tho' the first Members are all deceas'd but myself & one who is older by a Year than I am.—The small Fines that have been paid by Members for Absence at the Monthly Meetings, have been apply'd to the Purchase of Fire Engines, Ladders, Firehooks, and other useful Implements for each Company, so that I question whether there is a City in the World better provided with the Means of putting a Stop to beginning Conflagrations; and in fact since these Institutions, the City has never lost by Fire more than one or two Houses at a time, and the Flames have often been extinguish'd before the House in which they began has been half-consumed.—

In 1739 arriv'd among us from England the Rev. Mr Whitefiel, who had made himself remarkable there as an itinerant Preacher. He was at first permitted to preach in some of our Churches; but the Clergy taking a Dislike to him, soon refus'd him their Pulpits and he was oblig'd to preach in the Fields. The Multitudes of all Sects and Denominations that attended his Sermons were enormous and it was matter of Speculation to me who was one of the Number, to observe the extraordinary Influence of his Oratory on his Hearers, and how much they admir'd & respected him, notwithstanding his common Abuse of them, by assuring them they were naturally *half Beasts and half Devils*. It was wonderful to see the Change soon made in the Manners of our Inhabitants; from being thoughtless or indifferent about Religion, it seem'd as if all the World were growing Religious; so that one could not walk thro' the Town in an Evening without Hearing Psalms sung in different Families of every Street. And it being found inconvenient to assemble in the open Air, subject to its Inclemencies, the Building of a House to meet-in was no sooner propos'd and Persons appointed to receive Contributions, but sufficient Sums were soon receiv'd to procure the Ground and erect the Building which was 100 feet long & 70 broad, about the Size of Westminster-hall; and the Work was carried on with such Spirit as to be finished in a much shorter time than could have been expected. Both House and Ground were vested in Trustees, expressly for the Use of any Preacher of any religious Persuasion who might desire to say something to the People of Philadelphia, the Design in building not being to accommodate any particular Sect, but the Inhabitants in general, so that even if the Mufti of Constantinople were to send a Missionary to preach Mahometanism to us, he would find a Pulpit at his Service.—

Mr Whitfield, in leaving us, went preaching all the Way thro' the Colonies to Georgia. The Settlement of that Province had lately been begun; but instead of being made with hardy industrious Husbandmen accustomed to Labour, the only People fit for such an Enterprise, it was with Families of broken Shopkeepers and other insolvent Debtors, many of indolent & idle habits, taken out of the Goals, who being set down in the Woods, unqualified for clearing Land, & unable to endure the Hardships of a new Settlement, perished in Numbers, leaving many helpless Children unprovided for. The Sight of their miserable Situation inspired the benevolent Heart of Mr Whitefield with the Idea of building an Orphan House there, in which they might be supported and educated. Returning northward he preach'd up this Charity, & made large Collections;—for his Eloquence had a wonderful Power over the Hearts & Purses of his Hearers, of which I myself was an Instance. I did not disapprove of the Design, but as Georgia was then destitute of Materials & Workmen, and it was propos'd to send them from Philadelphia at a great Expence, I thought it would have been better to have built the House here & brought the Children to it. This I advis'd, but he was resolute in his first Project, and rejected my Counsel, and I thereupon refus'd to contribute. I happened soon after to attend one of his Sermons, in the Course of which I perceived he intended to finish with a Collection, & I silently resolved he should get nothing from me. I had in my Pocket a Handful of Copper, Money, three or four silver Dollars, and five Pistoles in Gold. As he proceeded I began to soften, and concluded to give the Coppers. Another Stroke of his Oratory made me asham'd of that, and determin'd me to give the Silver; & he finish'd so admirably, that I empty'd my Pocket wholly into the Collector's Dish, Gold and all. At this Sermon there was also one of our Club, who being of my Sentiments respecting the Building in Georgia, and suspecting a Collection might be intended, had by Precaution emptied his Pockets before he came from home; towards the

Conclusion of the Discourse however, he felt a strong Desire to give, and apply'd to a Neighbour who stood near him to borrow some Money for the Purpose. The Application was unfortunately to perhaps the only Man in the Company who had the firmness not to be affected by the Preacher. His Answer was, *At any other time, Friend Hopkinson, I would lend to thee freely; but not now; for thee seems to be out of thy right Senses.*—

Some of Mr Whitfield's Enemies affected to suppose that he would apply these Collections to his own private Emolument; but I, who was intimately acquainted with him, (being employ'd in printing his Sermons and Journals, &c.) never had the least Suspicion of his Integrity, but am to this day decidedly of Opinion that he was in all his Conduct, a perfectly *honest Man.* And methinks my Testimony in his Favour ought to have the more Weight, as we had no religious Connection. He us'd indeed sometimes to pray for my Conversion, but never had the Satisfaction of believing that his Prayers were heard. Ours was a mere civil Friendship, sincere on both Sides, and lasted to his Death.

The following Instance will show something of the Terms on which we stood. Upon one of his Arrivals from England at Boston, he wrote to me that he should come soon to Philadelphia, but knew not where he could lodge when there, as he understood his old kind Host Mr Benezet was remov'd to Germantown. My Answer was; You know my House, if you can make shift with its scanty Accommodations you will be most heartily welcome. He reply'd, that if I made that kind Offer for Christ's sake, I should not miss of a Reward.—And I return'd, *Don't let me be mistaken; it was not for Christ's sake, but for your sake.* One of our common Acquaintance jocosely remark'd, that knowing it to be the Custom of the Saints, when they receiv'd any favour, to shift the Burthen of the Obligation from off their own Shoulders, and place it in Heaven, I had contriv'd to fix it on Earth.—

The last time I saw Mr Whitefield was in London, when he consulted me about his Orphan House Concern, and his Purpose of appropriating it to the Establishment of a College.

He had a loud and clear Voice, and articulated his Words & Sentences so perfectly that he might be heard and understood at a great Distance, especially as his Auditories, how-ever numerous, observ'd the most exact Silence. He preach'd one Evening from the Top of the Court House Steps, which are in the Middle of Market Street, and on the West Side of Second Street which crosses it at right angles. Both Streets were fill'd with his Hearers to a considerable Distance. Being among the hindmost in Market Street, I had the Curiosity to learn how far he could be heard, by retiring backwards down the Street towards the River, and I found his Voice distinct till I came near Front-Street, when some Noise in that Street, obscur'd it. Imagining then a Semi-Circle, of which my Dis-tance should be the Radius, and that it were fill'd with Audi-tors, to each of whom I allow'd two square feet, I computed that he might well be heard by more than Thirty-Thousand. This reconcil'd me to the Newspaper Accounts of his having preach'd to 25000 People in the Fields, and to the antient Histories of Generals haranguing whole Armies, of which I had sometimes doubted.—

By hearing him often I came to distinguish easily between Sermons newly compos'd, & those which he had often preach'd in the Course of his Travels. His Delivery of the latter was so improv'd by frequent Repetitions, that every Accent, every Emphasis, every Modulation of Voice, was so perfectly well turn'd and well plac'd, that without being interested in the Subject, one could not help being pleas'd with the Discourse, a Pleasure of much the same kind with that receiv'd from an excellent Piece of Musick. This is an Advantage itinerant Preachers have over those who are sta-tionary: as the latter cannot well improve their Delivery of a Sermon by so many Rehearsals.—

His Writing and Printing from time to time gave great Advantage to his Enemies. Unguarded Expressions and even erroneous Opinions del^d in Preaching might have been afterwards explain'd, or qualify'd by supposing others that might have accompany'd them; or they might have been deny'd; But *litera scripta manet.* Critics attack'd his Writings violently, and with so much Appearance of Reason as to di-minish the Number of his Votaries, and prevent their En-crease: So that I am of Opinion, if he had never written any thing he would have left behind him a much more numerous and important Sect. And his Reputation might in that case have been still growing, even after his Death; as there being nothing of his Writing on which to found a Censure; and give him a lower Character, his Proselites would be left at Liberty to feign for him as great a Variety of Excellencies, as their enthusiastic Admiration might wish him to have possessed.

My Business was now continually augmenting, and my Circumstances growing daily easier, my Newspaper having become very profitable, as being for a time almost the only one in this and the neighbouring Provinces.—I experienc'd too the Truth of the Observation, that *after getting the first hundred Pound, it is more easy to get the second*: Money itself being of a prolific Nature: The Partnership at Carolina having succeeded, I was encourag'd to engage in others, and to promote several of my Workmen who had behaved well, by establishing them with Printing-Houses in different Colonies, on the same Terms with that in Carolina. Most of them did well, being enabled at the End of our Term, Six Years, to purchase the Types of me; and go on working for themselves, by which means several Families were raised. Partnerships often finish in Quarrels, but I was happy in this, that mine were all carry'd on and ended amicably; owing I think a good deal to the Precaution of having very explicitly settled in our Articles every thing to be done by or expected from each Partner, so that there was nothing to dispute, which Precaution I would therefore recommend to all who enter into Partnerships, for whatever Esteem Partners may have for & Confidence in each other at the time of the Contract, little Jealousies and Disgusts may arise, with Ideas of Inequality in the Care & Burthen of the Business, &c. which are attended often with Breach of Friendship & of the Connection, perhaps with Lawsuits and other disagreable Consequences.

I had on the whole abundant Reason to be satisfied with my being established in Pennsylvania. There were however two things that I regretted: There being no Provision for Defence, nor for a compleat Education of Youth. No Militia nor any College. I therefore in 1743, drew up a Proposal for establishing an Academy; & at that time thinking the Rev^d Mr Peters, who was out of Employ, a fit Person to superin-

tend such an Institution, I communicated the Project to him.
But he having more profitable Views in the Service of the
Proprietor, which succeeded, declin'd the Undertaking. And
not knowing another at that time suitable for such a Trust, I
let the Scheme lie a while dormant.—I succeeded better the
next Year, 1744, in proposing and establishing a Philosophical
Society. The Paper I wrote for that purpose will be found
among my Writings when collected.—

    With respect to Defence, Spain having been several Years
at War against Britain, and being at length join'd by France,
which brought us into greater Danger; and the laboured &
long-continued Endeavours of our Governor Thomas to prevail with our Quaker Assembly to pass a Militia Law, & make
other Provisions for the Security of the Province having
proved abortive, I determined to try what might be done by
a voluntary Association of the People. To promote this I first
wrote & published a Pamphlet, intitled, PLAIN TRUTH, in
which I stated our defenceless Situation in strong Lights,
with the Necessity of Union & Discipline for our Defence,
and promis'd to propose in a few Days an Association to be
generally signed for that purpose. The Pamphlet had a sudden
& surprizing Effect. I was call'd upon for the Instrument of
Association: And having settled the Draft of it with a few
Friends, I appointed a Meeting of the Citizens in the large
Building before mentioned. The House was pretty full. I had
prepared a Number of printed Copies, and provided Pens and
Ink dispers'd all over the Room. I harangu'd them a little on
the Subject, read the Paper & explain'd it, and then distrib-
uted the Copies which were eagerly signed, not the least
Objection being made. When the Company separated, & the
Papers were collected we found above Twelve hundred
Hands; and other Copies being dispers'd in the Country the
Subscribers amounted at length to upwards of Ten Thousand.
These all furnish'd themselves as soon as they could with
Arms; form'd themselves into Companies, and Regiments,
chose their own Officers, & met every Week to be instructed
in the manual Exercise, and other Parts of military Discipline.
The Women, by Subscriptions among themselves, provided
Silk Colours, which they presented to the Companies, painted
with different Devices and Motto's which I supplied. The

Officers of the Companies composing the Philadelphia Regiment, being met, chose me for their Colonel; but conceiving myself unfit, I declin'd that Station, & recommended Mr Lawrence, a fine Person and Man of Influence, who was accordingly appointed. I then propos'd a Lottery to defray the Expence of Building a Battery below the Town, and furnishing it with Cannon. It filled expeditiously and the Battery was soon erected, the Merlons being fram'd of Logs & fill'd with Earth. We bought some old Cannon from Boston, but these not being sufficient, we wrote to England for more, soliciting at the same Time our Proprietaries for some Assistance, tho' without much Expectation of obtaining it. Mean while Colonel Lawrence, William Allen, Abraham Taylor, Esquires, and myself were sent to New York by the Associators, commission'd to borrow some Cannon of Governor Clinton. He at first refus'd us peremptorily: but at a Dinner with his Council where there was great Drinking of Madeira Wine, as the Custom at that Place then was, he soften'd by degrees, and said he would lend us Six. After a few more Bumpers he advanc'd to Ten. And at length he very good-naturedly conceded Eighteen. They were fine Cannon, 18 pounders, with their Carriages, which we soon transported and mounted on our Battery, where the Associators kept a nightly Guard while the War lasted: And among the rest I regularly took my Turn of Duty there as a common Soldier.—

My Activity in these Operations was agreable to the Governor and Council; they took me into Confidence, & I was consulted by them in every Measure wherein their Concurrence was thought useful to the Association. Calling in the Aid of Religion, I propos'd to them the Proclaiming a Fast, to promote Reformation, & implore the Blessing of Heaven on our Undertaking. They embrac'd the Motion, but as it was the first Fast ever thought of in the Province, the Secretary had no Precedent from which to draw the Proclamation. My Education in New England, where a Fast is proclaim'd every Year, was here of some Advantage. I drew it in the accustomed Stile, it was translated into German, printed in both Languages and divulg'd thro' the Province. This gave the Clergy of the different Sects an Opportunity of Influencing their Congregations to join in the Association; and it would probably have been general among all but Quakers if the Peace had not soon interven'd.

It was thought by some of my Friends that by my Activity in these Affairs, I should offend that Sect, and thereby lose my Interest in the Assembly where they were a great Majority. A young Gentleman who had likewise some Friends in the House, and wish'd to succeed me as their Clerk, acquainted me that it was decided to displace me at the next Election, and he therefore in good Will advis'd me to resign, as more consistent with my Honour than being turn'd out. My Answer to him was, that I had read or heard of some Public Man, who made it a Rule never to ask for an Office, and never to refuse one when offer'd to him. I approve, says I, of his Rule, and will practise it with a small Addition; I shall never *ask*, never *refuse*, nor ever *resign* an Office. If they will have my Office of Clerk to dispose of to another, they shall take it from me. I will not by giving it up, lose my Right of some time or other making Reprisals on my Adversaries. I heard however no more of this. I was chosen again, unanimously as usual, at the next Election. Possibly as they dislik'd my late Intimacy with the Members of Council, who had join'd the Governors in all the Disputes about military Preparations with which the House had long been harass'd, they might have been pleas'd if I would voluntarily have left them; but they did not care to displace me on Account merely of my Zeal for the Association; and they could not well give another Reason.—Indeed I had some Cause to believe, that the Defence of the Country was not disagreeable to any of them, provided they were not requir'd to assist in it. And I found that a much greater Number of them than I could have imagined, tho' against offensive War, were clearly for the defensive. Many Pamphlets *pro & con*. were publish'd on the Subject, and some by good Quakers in favour of Defence, which I believe convinc'd most of their younger People. A Transaction in our Fire Company gave me some Insight into their prevailing Sentiments. It had been propos'd that we should encourage the Scheme for building a Battery by laying out the present Stock, then about Sixty Pounds, in Tickets of the Lottery. By our Rules no Money could be dispos'd of but at the next Meeting after the Proposal. The Company consisted of Thirty Members, of which Twenty-two were Quakers, & Eight only of other Persuasions. We eight punctually attended the Meeting; but tho' we thought that some of the Quakers would join us, we were by no means sure of a Majority. Only one Quaker, Mr James Morris, appear'd to oppose the Measure: He express'd much Sorrow that it had ever been propos'd, as he said *Friends* were all against it, and it would create such Discord as might break up the Company. We told him, that we saw no Reason for that; we were the Minority, and if *Friends* were against the Measure and outvoted us, we must and should, agreable to the Usage of all Societies, submit. When the Hour for Business arriv'd, it was mov'd to put the Vote. He allow'd we might then do it by the Rules, but as he could assure us that a Number of Members intended to be present for the purpose of opposing it, it would be but candid to allow a little time for their appearing. While we were disputing this, a Waiter came to tell me two Gentlemen below desir'd to speak with me. I went down, and found they were two of our Quaker Members. They told me there were eight of them assembled at a Tavern just by; that they were determin'd to come and vote with us if there should be occasion, which they hop'd would not be the Case; and desir'd we would not call for their Assistance if we could do without it, as their Voting for such a Measure might embroil them with their Elders & Friends; Being thus secure of a Majority, I went up, and after a little seeming Hesitation, agreed to a Delay of another Hour. This Mr Morris allow'd to be extreamly fair. Not one of his opposing Friends appear'd, at which he express'd great Surprize; and at the Expiration of the Hour, we carry'd the Resolution Eight to one; And as of the 22 Quakers, Eight were ready to vote with us and, Thirteen by their Absence manifested that they were not inclin'd to oppose the Measure, I afterwards estimated the Proportion of Quakers sincerely against Defence as one to twenty one only. For these were all regular Members, of that Society, and in good Reputation among them, and had due Notice of what was propos'd at that Meeting.

The honourable & learned Mr Logan, who had always been of that Sect, was one who wrote an Address to them, declaring his Approbation of defensive War, and supporting his Opinion by many strong Arguments: He put into my Hands Sixty Pounds, to be laid out in Lottery Tickets for the Battery, with Directions to apply what Prizes might be drawn wholly to that Service. He told me the following Anecdote of his old Master Wm Penn respecting Defence. He came over from England, when a young Man, with that Proprietary, and as his Secretary. It was War Time, and their Ship was chas'd by an armed Vessel suppos'd to be an Enemy. Their Captain prepar'd for Defence, but told Wm Penn and his Company of Quakers, that he did not expect their Assistance, and they might retire into the Cabin; which they did, except James Logan, who chose to stay upon Deck, and was quarter'd to a Gun. The suppos'd Enemy prov'd a Friend; so there was no Fighting. But when the Secretary went down to communicate the Intelligence, Wm Penn rebuk'd him severely for staying upon Deck and undertaking to assist in defending the Vessel, contrary to the Principles of *Friends*, especially as it had not been required by the Captain. This Reproof being before all the Company, piqu'd the Secretary, who answer'd, *I being thy Servant, why did thee not order me to come down: but thee was willing enough that I should stay and help to fight the Ship when thee thought there was Danger.*

My being many Years in the Assembly, the Majority of which were constantly Quakers, gave me frequent Opportunities of seeing the Embarassment given them by their Principle against War, whenever Application was made to them by Order of the Crown to grant Aids for military Purposes. They were unwilling to offend Government on the one hand, by a direct Refusal, and their Friends the Body of Quakers on the other, by a Compliance contrary to their Principles. Hence a Variety of Evasions to avoid Complying, and Modes of disguising the Compliance when it became unavoidable. The common Mode at last was to grant Money under the Phrase of its being *for the King's Use*, and never to enquire how it was applied. But if the Demand was not directly from the Crown, that Phrase was found not so proper, and some other was to be invented. As when Powder was wanting, (I think it was for the Garrison at Louisburg,) and the Government of New England solicited a Grant of some from Pensilvania, which was much urg'd on the House by Governor

Thomas, they could not grant Money to buy Powder, because that was an Ingredient of War, but they voted an Aid to New England, of Three Thousand Pounds, to be put into the hands of the Governor, and appropriated it for the Purchasing of Bread, Flour, Wheat, *or other Grain*. Some of the Council desirous of giving the House still farther Embarassment, advis'd the Governor not to accept Provision, as not being the Thing he had demanded. But he reply'd, "I shall take the Money, for I understand very well their Meaning; *Other Grain*, is Gunpowder;" which he accordingly bought; and they never objected to it. It was in Allusion to this Fact, that when in our Fire Company we feared the Success of our Proposal in favour of the Lottery, & I had said to my Friend Mr Syng, one of our Members, if we fail, let us move the Purchase of a Fire Engine with the Money; the Quakers can have no Objection to that: and then if you nominate me, and I you, as a Committee for that purpose, we will buy a great Gun, which is certainly a *Fire-Engine*: I see, says he, you have improv'd by being so long in the Assembly; your equivocal Project would be just a Match for their Wheat *or other Grain*.

These Embarassments that the Quakers suffer'd from having establish'd & published it as one of their Principles, that no kind of War was lawful, and which being once published, they could not afterwards, however they might change their minds, easily get rid of, reminds me of what I think a more prudent Conduct in another Sect among us; that of the Dunkers. I was acquainted with one of its Founders, Michael Welfare, soon after it appear'd.—He complain'd to me that they were grievously calumniated by the Zealots of other Persuasions, and charg'd with abominable Principles and Practices to which they were utter Strangers. I told him this had always been the case with new Sects; and that to put a Stop to such Abuse, I imagin'd it might be well to publish the Articles of their Belief and the Rules of their Discipline. He said that it had been propos'd among them, but not agreed to, for this Reason; "When we were first drawn together as a Society, says he, it had pleased God to inlighten our Minds so far, as to see that some Doctrines which we once esteemed Truths were Errors, & that others which we had esteemed Errors were real Truths. From time to time he has been

pleased to afford us farther Light, and our Principles have
been improving, & our Errors diminishing. Now we are not
sure that we are arriv'd at the End of this Progression, and at
the Perfection of Spiritual or Theological Knowledge; and we
fear that if we should once print our Confession of Faith, we
should feel ourselves as if bound & confin'd by it, and perhaps be unwilling to receive farther Improvement; and our
Successors still more so, as conceiving what we their Elders
& Founders had done, to be something sacred, never to be
departed from."—This Modesty in a Sect is perhaps a singular
Instance in the History of Mankind, every other Sect supposing itself in Possession of all Truth, and that those who differ
are so far in the Wrong: Like a Man travelling in foggy
Weather: Those at some Distance before him on the Road he
sees wrapt up in the Fog, as well as those behind him, and
also the People in the Fields on each side; but neer him all
appears clear.—Tho' in truth he is as much in the Fog as any
of them. To avoid this kind of Embarrassment the Quakers
have of late Years been gradually declining the public Service
in the Assembly & in the Magistracy. Chusing rather to quit
their Power than their Principle.

In Order of Time I should have mentioned before, that
having in 1742 invented an open Stove, for the better warming of Rooms and at the same time saving Fuel, as the fresh
Air admitted was warmed in Entring, I made a Present of the
Model to Mr Robert Grace, one of my early Friends, who
having an Iron Furnace, found the Casting of the Plates for
these Stoves a profitable Thing, as they were growing in Demand. To promote that Demand I wrote and published a
Pamphlet Intitled, *An Account of the New-Invented* PENNSYL-
VANIA FIRE PLACES: *Wherein their Construction & manner of
Operation is particularly explained; their Advantages above every
other Method of warming Rooms demonstrated; and all Objections
that have been raised against the Use of them answered &
obviated, &c.* This Pamphlet had a good Effect, Gov.' Thomas
was so pleas'd with the Construction of this Stove, as des-
crib'd in it that he offer'd to give me a Patent for the sole
Vending of them for a Term of Years; but I declin'd it from a
Principle which has ever weigh'd with me on such Occasions,
viz. *That as we enjoy great Advantages from the Inventions of*

others, we should be glad of an Opportunity to serve others by any Invention of ours, and this we should do freely and generously. An Ironmonger in London, however, after assuming a good deal of my Pamphlet & working it up into his own, and making some small Changes in the Machine, which rather hurt its Operation, got a Patent for it there, and made as I was told a little Fortune by it.—And this is not the only Instance of Patents taken out for my Inventions by others, tho' not always with the same Success:—which I never contested, as having no Desire of profiting by Patents my self, and hating Disputes.—The Use of these Fireplaces in very many Houses both of this and the neighbouring Colonies, has been and is a great Saving of Wood to the Inhabitants.—

Peace being concluded, and the Association Business therefore at an End, I turn'd my Thoughts again to the Affair of establishing an Academy. The first Step I took was to associate in the Design a Number of active Friends, of whom the Junto furnished a good Part; the next was to write and publish a Pamphlet intitled, *Proposals relating to the Education of Youth in Pennsylvania.*—This I distributed among the principal Inhabitants gratis; and as soon as I could suppose their Minds a little prepared by the Perusal of it, I set on foot a Subscription for Opening and Supporting an Academy; it was to be paid in Quotas yearly for Five Years; by so dividing it I judg'd the Subscription might be larger, and I believe it was so, amounting to no less (if I remember right) than Five thousand Pounds.—In the Introduction to these Proposals, I stated their Publication not as an Act of mine, but of some *publick-spirited Gentlemen*; avoiding as much as I could, according to my usual Rule, the presenting myself to the Publick as the Author of any Scheme for their Benefit.—

The Subscribers, to carry the Project into immediate Execution chose out of their Number Twenty-four Trustees, and appointed Mr Francis, then Attorney General, and myself, to draw up Constitutions for the Government of the Academy, which being done and signed, an House was hired, Masters engag'd and the Schools opened I think in the same Year 1749. The Scholars encreasing fast, the House was soon found too small, and we were looking out for a Piece of Ground properly situated, with Intention to build, when

Providence threw into our way a large House ready built, which with a few Alterations might well serve our purpose, this was the Building before mentioned erected by the Hearers of Mr Whitefield, and was obtain'd for us in the following Manner.

It is to be noted, that the Contributions to this Building being made by People of different Sects, Care was taken in the Nomination of Trustees, in whom the Building & Ground was to be vested, that a Predominancy should not be given to any Sect, lest in time that Predominancy might be a means of appropriating the whole to the Use of such Sect, contrary to the original Intention; it was therefore that one of each Sect was appointed, viz. one Church-of-England-man, one Presbyterian, one Baptist, one Moravian, &c. Those in case of Vacancy by Death were to fill it by Election from among the Contributors. The Moravian happen'd not to please his Colleagues, and on his Death, they resolved to have no other of that Sect. The Difficulty then was, how to avoid having two of some other Sect, by means of the new Choice. Several Persons were named and for that Reason not agreed to. At length one mention'd me, with the Observation that I was merely an honest Man, & of no Sect at all; which prevail'd with them to chuse me. The Enthusiasm which existed when the House was built, had long since abated, and its Trustees had not been able to procure fresh Contributions for paying the Ground Rent, and discharging some other Debts the Building had occasion'd, which embarrass'd them greatly. Being now a Member of both Sets of Trustees, that for the Building & that for the Academy, I had good Opportunity of negociating with both, & brought them finally to an Agreement, by which the Trustees for the Building were to cede it to those of the Academy, the latter undertaking to discharge the Debt, to keep forever open in the Building a large Hall for occasional Preachers according to the original Intention, and maintain a Free School for the Instruction of poor Children. Writings were accordingly drawn, and on paying the Debts the Trustees of the Academy were put in Possession of the Premises, and by dividing the great & lofty Hall into Stories, and different Rooms above & below for the several Schools, and purchasing some additional Ground, the whole was soon made fit for our purpose, and the Scholars remov'd into the Building. The Care and Trouble of agreeing with the Workmen, purchasing Materials, and superintending the Work fell upon me, and I went thro' it the more chearfully, as it did not then interfere with my private Business, having the Year before taken a very able, industrious & honest Partner, Mr David Hall, with whose Character I was well acquainted, as he had work'd for me four Years. He took off my Hands all Care of the Printing-Office, paying me punctually my Share of the Profits. This Partnership continued Eighteen Years, successfully for us both.—

The Trustees of the Academy after a while were incorporated by a Charter from the Governor; their Funds were increas'd by Contributions in Britain, and Grants of Land from the Proprietaries, to which the Assembly has since made considerable Addition, and thus was established the present University of Philadelphia. I have been continued one of its Trustees from the Beginning, now near forty Years, and have had the very great Pleasure of seeing a Number of the Youth who have receiv'd their Education in it, distinguish'd by their improv'd Abilities, serviceable in public Stations, and Ornaments to their Country.

When I disengag'd myself as above mentioned from private Business, I flatter'd myself that, by the sufficient tho' moderate Fortune I had acquir'd, I had secur'd Leisure during the rest of my Life, for Philosophical Studies and Amusements; I purchas'd all Dr Spence's Apparatus, who had come from England to lecture here; and I proceeded in my Electrical Experiments with great Alacrity; but the Publick now considering me as a Man of Leisure, laid hold of me for their Purposes; every Part of our Civil Government, and almost at the same time, imposing some Duty upon me. The Governor put me into the Commission of the Peace; the Corporation of the City chose me of the Common Council, and soon after an Alderman; and the Citizens at large chose me a Burgess to represent them in Assembly. This latter Station was the more agreable to me, as I was at length tired with sitting there to hear Debates in which as Clerk I could take no part, and which were often so unentertaining, that I was induc'd to amuse myself with making magic Squares, or Circles, or any thing to avoid Weariness. And I conceiv'd my becoming a Member would enlarge my Power of doing Good. I would not however insinuate that my Ambition was not flatter'd by all these Promotions. It certainly was. For considering my low Beginning they were great Things to me. And they were still more pleasing, as being so many spontaneous Testimonies of the public's good Opinion, and by me entirely unsolicited.

The Office of Justice of the Peace I try'd a little, by attending a few Courts, and sitting on the Bench to hear Causes. But finding that more Knowledge of the Common Law than I possess'd, was necessary to act in that Station with Credit, I gradually withdrew from it, excusing myself by my being oblig'd to attend the higher Dutys of a Legislator in the Assembly. My Election to this Trust was repeated every Year for Ten Years, without my ever asking any Elector for his Vote, or signifying either directly or indirectly any Desire of being chosen.—On taking my Seat in the House, my Son was appointed their Clerk.

The Year following, a Treaty being to be held with the Indians at Carlisle, the Governor sent a Message to the House, proposing that they should nominate some of their Members to be join'd with some Members of Council as Commissioners for that purpose. The House nam'd the Speaker (Mr Norris) and my self; and being commission'd we went to Carlisle, and met the Indians accordingly.—As those People are extreamly apt to get drunk, and when so are very quarrelsome & disorderly, we strictly forbad the selling any Liquor to them; and when they complain'd of this Restriction, we told them that if they would continue sober during the Treaty, we would give them Plenty of Rum when Business was over. They promis'd this; and they kept their Promise—because they could get no Liquor—and the Treaty was conducted very orderly, and concluded to mutual Satisfaction. They then claim'd and receiv'd the Rum. This was in the Afternoon. They were near 100 Men, Women & Children, and were lodg'd in temporary Cabins built in the Form of a Square just without the Town. In the Evening, hearing a great Noise among them, the Commission.^{rs} walk'd out to see what was the Matter. We found they had made a great Bonfire in the Middle of the Square. They were all drunk Men and Women, quarrelling and fighting. Their dark-colour'd Bodies, half naked, seen only by the gloomy Light of the Bonfire, running after and beating one another with Fire-brands, accompanied by their horrid Yellings, form'd a Scene the most resembling our Ideas of Hell that could well be imagin'd. There was no appeasing the Tumult, and we retired to our Lodging. At Midnight a Number of them came thundering at our Door, demanding more Rum; of which we took no Notice. The next Day, sensible they had misbehav'd in giving us that Disturbance, they sent three of their old Counsellors to make their Apology. The Orator acknowledg'd the Fault, but laid it upon the Rum; and then endeavour'd to excuse the Rum, by saying, *"The great Spirit who made all things made every thing for some Use, and whatever Use he design'd any thing for, that Use it should always be put to; Now, when he made Rum, he said,* LET THIS BE FOR INDIANS TO GET DRUNK WITH. *And it must be so."*—And indeed if it be the Design of Providence to extirpate these Savages in order to make room for Cultivators of the Earth, it seems not improbable that Rum may be the appointed Means. It has already annihilated all the Tribes who formerly inhabited the Seacoast.—

In 1751. Dr Thomas Bond, a particular Friend of mine, conceiv'd the Idea of establishing a Hospital in Philadelphia for the Reception and Cure of poor sick Persons, whether Inhabitants of the Province or Strangers. A very beneficent Design, which has been ascrib'd to me, but was originally his. He was zealous & active in endeavouring to procure Subscriptions for it; but the Proposal being a Novelty in America, and at first not well understood, he met with small Success. At length he came to me, with the Compliment that he found there was no such thing as carrying a public Spirited Project through, without my being concern'd in it; "for, says he, I am often ask'd by those to whom I propose Subscribing, Have you consulted Franklin upon this Business? and what does he think of it?—And when I tell them that I have not, (supposing it rather out of your Line,) they do not subscribe, but say they will consider of it." I enquir'd into the Nature, & probable Utility of his Scheme, and receiving from him a very satisfactory Explanation, I not only subscrib'd to it myself, but engag'd heartily in the Design of Procuring Subscriptions from others. Previous however to the Solicitation, I endeavoured to prepare the Minds of the People by writing on the Subject in the Newspapers, which was my usual Custom in such Cases, but which he had omitted. The Subscriptions afterwards were more free and generous, but beginning to flag, I saw they would be insufficient without some Assistance from the Assembly, and therefore propos'd to petition for it, which was done. The Country Members did not at first relish the Project. They objected that it could only be serviceable to the City, and therefore the Citizens should alone be at the Expence of it; and they doubted whether the Citizens themselves generally approv'd of it: My Allegation on the contrary, that it met with such Approbation as to leave no doubt of our being able to raise 2000£ by voluntary Donations, they considered as a most extravagant Supposition, and utterly impossible. On this I form'd my Plan; and asking Leave to bring in a Bill, for incorporating the Contributors, according to the Prayers of their Petition, and granting them a blank Sum of Money, which Leave was obtain'd chiefly on the Consideration that the House could throw the Bill out if they did not like it, I drew it so as to make the important Clause a conditional One, viz. "And be it enacted by the Authority aforesaid That when the said Contributors shall have met and chosen their Managers and Treasurer, *and shall have raised by their Contributions a Capital Stock of 2000£ Value*, (the yearly Interest of which is to be applied to the Accommodating of the Sick Poor in the said Hospital, free of Charge for Diet, Attendance, Advice and Medicines) and *shall make the same appear to the Satisfaction of the Speaker of the Assembly* for the time being; that *then* it shall and may be lawful for the said Speaker, and he is hereby required to sign an Order on the Provincial Treasurer for the Payment of Two Thousand Pounds in two yearly Payments, to the Treasurer of the said Hospital, to be applied to the Founding, Building and Finishing of the same."—This Condition carried the Bill through; for the Members who had oppos'd the Grant, and now conceiv'd they might have the Credit of being charitable without the Expence, agreed to its Passage; And then in soliciting Subscriptions among the People we urg'd the conditional

Promise of the Law as an additional Motive to give, since every Man's Donation would be doubled. Thus the Clause work'd both ways. The Subscriptions accordingly soon exceeded the requisite Sum, and we claim'd and receiv'd the Public Gift, which enabled us to carry the Design into Execution. A convenient and handsome Building was soon erected, the Institution has by constant Experience been found useful, and flourishes to this Day.—And I do not remember any of my political Maneuvres, the Success of which gave me at the time more Pleasure. Or that in after-thinking of it, I more easily excus'd my-self for having made some Use of Cunning.—

It was about this time that another Projector, the Revd Gilbert Tennent, came to me, with a Request that I would assist him in procuring a Subscription for erecting a new Meeting-house. It was to be for the Use of a Congregation he had gathered among the Presbyterians who were originally Disciples of Mr Whitefield. Unwilling to make myself disagreable to my fellow Citizens, by too frequently soliciting their Contributions, I absolutely refus'd. He then desir'd I would furnish him with a List of the Names of Persons I knew by Experience to be generous and public-spirited. I thought it would be unbecoming in me, after their kind Compliance with my Solicitations, to mark them out to be worried by other Beggars, and therefore refus'd also to give such a List.—He then desir'd I would at least give him my Advice. That I will readily do, said I; and, in the first Place, I advise you to apply to all those whom you know will give something; next to those whom you are uncertain whether they will give any thing or not; and show them the List of those who have given: and lastly, do not neglect those who you are sure will give nothing; for in some of them you may be mistaken.—He laugh'd, and thank'd me, and said he would take my Advice. He did so, for he ask'd of *every body*; and he obtain'd a much larger Sum than he expected, with which he erected the capacious and very elegant Meeting-house that stands in Arch street.—

Our City, tho' laid out with a beautifull Regularity, the Streets large, strait, and crossing each other at right Angles, had the Disgrace of suffering those Streets to remain long unpav'd, and in wet Weather the Wheels of heavy Carriages plough'd them into a Quagmire, so that it was difficult to cross them. And in dry Weather the Dust was offensive. I had liv'd near what was call'd the Jersey Market, and saw with Pain the Inhabitants wading in Mud while purchasing their Provisions. A Strip of Ground down the middle of that Market was at length pav'd with Brick, so that being once in the Market they had firm Footing, but were often over Shoes in Dirt to get there.—By talking and writing on the Subject, I was at length instrumental in getting the Street pav'd with Stone between the Market and the brick'd Foot-Pavement that was on each Side next the Houses. This for some time gave an easy Access to the Market, dry-shod. But the rest of the Street not being pav'd, whenever a Carriage came out of the Mud upon this Pavement, it shook off and left its Dirt on it, and it was soon cover'd with Mire, which was not remov'd, the City as yet having no Scavengers.—After some Enquiry I found a poor industrious Man, who was willing to undertake keeping the Pavement clean, by sweeping it twice a week & carrying off the Dirt from before all the Neighbours Doors, for the Sum of Sixpence per Month, to be paid by each House. I then wrote and printed a Paper, setting forth the Advantages to the Neighbourhood that might be obtain'd by this small Expence; the greater Ease in keeping our Houses clean, so much Dirt not being brought in by People's Feet; the Benefit to the Shops by more Custom, as Buyers could more easily get at them, and by not having in windy Weather the Dust blown in upon their Goods, &c. &c. I sent one of these Papers to each House, and in a Day or two went round to see who would subscribe an Agreement to pay these Sixpences. It was unanimously sign'd, and for a time well executed. All the Inhabitants of the City were delighted with the Cleanliness of the Pavement that surrounded the Market; it being a Convenience to all; and this rais'd a general Desire to have all the Streets paved; & made the People more willing to submit to a Tax for that purpose. After some time I drew a Bill for Paving the City, and brought it into the Assembly. It was just before I went to England in 1757. and did not pass till I was gone, and then with an Alteration in the Mode of Assessment, which I thought not for the better, but with an additional Provision for lighting as well as Paving the Streets, which was a great Improvement.—It was by a private Person, the late Mr John Clifton, his giving a Sample of the Utility of Lamps by placing one at his Door, that the People were first impress'd with the Idea of enlightning all the City. The Honour of this public Benefit has also been ascrib'd to me, but it belongs truly to that Gentleman. I did but follow his Example; and have only some Merit to claim respecting the Form of our Lamps as differing from the Globe Lamps we at first were supply'd with from London. Those we found inconvenient in these respects; they admitted no Air below, the Smoke therefore did not readily go out above, but circulated in the Globe, lodg'd on its Inside, and soon obstructed the Light they were intended to afford; giving, besides, the daily Trouble of wiping them clean: and an accidental Stroke on one of them would demolish it, & render it totally useless. I therefore suggested the composing them of four flat Panes, with a long Funnel above to draw up the Smoke, and Crevices admitting Air below, to facilitate the Ascent of the Smoke. By this means they were kept clean, and did not grow dark in a few Hours as the London Lamps do, but continu'd bright till Morning; and an accidental Stroke would generally break but a single Pane, easily repair'd. I have sometimes wonder'd that the Londoners did not, from the Effect Holes in the Bottom of the Globe Lamps us'd at Vauxhall, have in keeping them clean, learn to have such Holes in their Street Lamps. But those Holes being made for another purpose, viz. to communicate Flame more suddenly to the Wick, by a little Flax hanging down thro' them, the other Use of letting in Air seems not to have been thought of.—And therefore, after the Lamps have been lit a few Hours, the Streets of London are very poorly illuminated.—

The Mention of these Improvements puts me in mind of one I propos'd when in London, to Dr Fothergill, who was among the best Men I have known, and a great Promoter of useful Projects. I had observ'd that the Streets when dry were never swept and the light Dust carried away, but it was suffer'd to accumulate till wet Weather reduc'd it to Mud, and then after lying some Days so deep on the Pavement that there was no Crossing but in Paths kept clean by poor People with Brooms, it was with great Labour rak'd together & thrown up into Carts open above, the Sides of which suffer'd some of the Slush at every jolt on the Pavement to shake out and fall, some times to the Annoyance of Foot-Passengers. The Reason given for not sweeping the dusty Streets was, that the Dust would fly into the Windows of Shops and Houses. An accidental Occurrence had instructed me how much Sweeping might be done in a little Time. I found at my Door in Craven Street one Morning a poor Woman sweeping my Pavement with a birch Broom. She appeared very pale & feeble as just come out of a Fit of Sickness. I ask'd who employ'd her to sweep there. She said, "Nobody; but I am very poor and in Distress, and I sweeps before Gentlefolkeses Doors, and hopes they will give me something." I bid her sweep the whole Street clean and I would give her a Shilling. This was at 9 aClock. At 12 she came for the Shilling. From the Slowness I saw at first in her Working, I could scarce believe that the Work was done so soon, and sent my Servant to examine it, who reported that the whole Street was swept perfectly clean, and all the Dust plac'd in the Gutter which was in the Middle. And the next Rain wash'd it quite away, so that the Pavement & even the Kennel were perfectly clean.— I then judg'd that if that feeble Woman could sweep such a Street in 3 Hours, a strong active Man might have done it in half the time. And here let me remark the Convenience of having but one Gutter in such a narrow Street, running down its Middle, instead of two, one on each Side near the Footway. For Where all the Rain that falls on a Street runs from the Sides and meets in the middle, it forms there a Current strong enough to wash away all the Mud it meets with: But when divided into two Channels, it is often too weak to cleanse either, and only makes the Mud it finds more fluid, so that the Wheels of Carriages and Feet of Horses throw and dash it up on the Foot Pavement which is thereby rendred foul and slippery, and sometimes splash it upon those who are walking.—My Proposal communicated to the good Doctor, was as follows.

"For the more effectual cleaning and keeping clean the Streets of London and Westminster, it is proposed,

"That the several Watchmen be contracted with to have the

Dust swept up in dry Seasons, and the Mud rak'd up at other Times, each in the several Streets & Lanes of his Round.

"That they be furnish'd with Brooms and other proper Instruments for these purposes, to be kept at their respective Stands, ready to furnish the poor People they may employ in the Service.

"That in the dry Summer Months the Dust be all swept up into Heaps at proper Distances, before the Shops and Windows of Houses are usually opened: when the Scavengers with close-covered Carts shall also carry it all away.—

"That the Mud when rak'd up be not left in Heaps to be spread abroad again by the Wheels of Carriages & Trampling of Horses; but that the Scavengers be provided with Bodies of Carts, not plac'd high upon Wheels, but low upon Sliders; with Lattice Bottoms, which being cover'd with Straw, will retain the Mud thrown into them, and permit the Water to drain from it, whereby it will become much lighter, Water making the greatest Part of its Weight. These Bodies of Carts to be plac'd at convenient Distances, and the Mud brought to them in Wheelbarrows, they remaining where plac'd till the Mud is drain'd, and then Horses brought to draw them away."—

I have since had Doubts of the Practicability of the latter Part of this Proposal, on Account of the Narrowness of some Streets, and the Difficulty of placing the Draining Sleds so as not to encumber too much the Passage: But I am still of Opinion that the former, requiring the Dust, to be swept up & carry'd away before the Shops are open, is very practicable in the Summer, when the Days are long. For in walking thro' the Strand and Fleet street one Morning at 7 aClock I observ'd there was not one shop open tho' it had been Day-light & the Sun up above three Hours. The Inhabitants of London chusing voluntarily to live much by Candle Light, and sleep by Sunshine; and yet often complain a little absurdly, of the Duty on Candles and the high Price of Tallow.—

Some may think these trifling Matters not worth minding or relating: But when they consider, that tho' Dust blown into the Eyes of a single Person or into a single Shop on a windy Day, is but of small Importance, yet the great Number of the Instances in a populous City, and its frequent Repetitions give it Weight & Consequence; perhaps they will not censure very severely those who bestow some of Attention to Affairs of this seemingly low Nature. Human Felicity is produc'd not so much by great Pieces of good Fortune that seldom happen, as by little Advantages that occur every Day. Thus if you teach a poor young Man to shave himself and keep his Razor in order, you may contribute more to the Happiness of his Life than in giving him a 1000 Guineas. The Money may be soon spent, and the Regret only remaining of having foolishly consum'd it. But in the other Case he escapes the frequent Vexation of waiting for Barbers, & of their sometimes, dirty Fingers, offensive Breaths and dull Razors. He shaves when most convenient to him, and enjoys daily the Pleasure of its being done with a good Instrument.—With these Sentiments I have hazarded the few preceding Pages, hoping they may afford Hints which some time or other may be useful to a City I love, having lived many Years in it very happily; and perhaps to some of our Towns in America.—

Having been for some time employed by the Postmaster General of America, as his Comptroller, in regulating the several Offices, and bringing the Officers to account, I was upon his Death in 1753 appointed jointly with Mr William Hunter to succeed him by a Commission from the Postmaster General in England. The American Office had never hitherto paid any thing to that of Britain. We were to have 600£ a Year between us if we could make that Sum out of the Profits of the Office. To do this, a Variety of Improvements were necessary; some of these were inevitably at first expensive; so that in the first four Years the Office became above 900£ in debt to us.—But it soon after began to repay us, and before I was displac'd, by a Freak of the Minister's, of which I shall speak hereafter, we had brought it to yield *three times* as much clear Revenue to the Crown as the Post-Office of Ireland. Since that imprudent Transaction, they have receiv'd from it,—Not one Farthing.—

The Business of the Post-Office occasion'd my taking a Journey this Year to New England, where the College of Cambridge of their own Motion, presented me with the Degree of Master of Arts. Yale College in Connecticut, had before made me a similar Compliment. Thus without studying in any College I came to partake of their Honours. They were confer'd in Consideration of my Improvements & Discoveries in the electric Branch of Natural Philosophy.—

In 1754, War with France being again apprehended, a Congress of Commissioners from the different Colonies, was by an Order of the Lords of Trade, to be assembled at Albany, there to confer with the Chiefs of the Six Nations, concerning the Means of defending both their Country and ours. Governor Hamilton, having receiv'd this Order, acquainted the House with it, requesting they would furnish proper Presents for the Indians to be given on this Occasion; and naming the Speaker (Mr Norris) and my self, to join Mr Thomas Penn & Mr Secretary Peters, as Commissioners to act for Pennsylvania. The House approv'd the Nomination, and provided the Goods for the Present, tho' they did not much like treating out of the Province, and we met the other Commissioners and met at Albany about the Middle of June. In our Way thither, I projected and drew up a Plan for the Union of all the Colonies, under one Government so far as might be necessary for Defence, and other important general Purposes. As we pass'd thro' New York, I had there shown my Project to Mr James Alexander & Mr Kennedy, two Gentlemen of great Knowledge in public Affairs, and being fortified by their Approbation I ventur'd to lay it before the Congress. It then appear'd that several of the Commissioners had form'd Plans of the same kind. A previous Question was first taken whether a Union should be established, which pass'd in the Affirmative unanimously. A Committee was then appointed. One Member from each Colony, to consider the several Plans and report. Mine happen'd to be prefer'd, and with a few Amendments was accordingly reported. By this Plan, the general Government was to be administred by a President General appointed and supported by the Crown, and a Grand Council to be chosen by the Representatives of the People of the several Colonies met in their respective Assemblies. The Debates upon it in Congress went on daily hand in hand with the Indian Business. Many Objections and Difficulties were started, but at length they were all overcome, and the Plan was unanimously agreed to, and Copies ordered to be transmitted to the Board of Trade and to the Assemblies of the several Provinces. Its Fate was singular. The Assemblies did not adopt it, as they all thought there was too much *Prerogative* in it; and in England it was judg'd to have too much of the *Democratic*: The Board of Trade therefore did not approve of it; nor recommend it for the Approbation of his Majesty; but another Scheme was form'd (suppos'd better to answer the same Purpose) whereby the Governors of the Provinces with some Members of their respective Councils were to meet and order the raising of Troops, building of Forts, &c. &c to draw on the Treasury of Great Britain for the Expence, which was afterwards to be refunded by an Act of Parliament laying a Tax on America. My Plan, with my Reasons in support of it, is to be found among my political Papers that are printed. Being the Winter following in Boston, I had much Conversation with Gov' Shirley upon both the Plans. Part of what pass'd between us on the Occasion may also be seen among those Papers.—The different & contrary Reasons of dislike to my Plan, makes me suspect that it was really the true Medium; & I am still of Opinion it would have been happy for both Sides the Water if it had been adopted. The Colonies so united would have been sufficiently strong to have defended themselves; there would then have been no need of Troops from England; of course the subsequent Pretence for Taxing America, and the bloody Contest it occasioned, would have been avoided. But such Mistakes are not new; History is full of the Errors of States & Princes.

"Look round the habitable World, how few
Know their own Good, or knowing it pursue."

Those who govern, having much Business on their hands, do not generally like to take the Trouble of considering and carrying into Execution new Projects. The best public Measures are therefore seldom *adopted from previous Wisdom*, but *forc'd by the Occasion.*

The Governor of Pennsylvania in sending it down to the Assembly, express'd his Approbation of the Plan "as appearing to him to be drawn up with great Clearness & Strength of Judgment, and therefore recommended it as well worthy their closest & most serious Attention." The House however, by the Managem' of a certain Member, took it up when I happen'd to be absent, which I thought not very fair, and reprobated it without paying any Attention to it at all, to my no small Mortification.

In my Journey to Boston this Year I met at New York with our new Governor, Mr Morris, just arriv'd there from England, with whom I had been before intimately acquainted. He brought a Commission to supersede Mr Hamilton, who, tir'd with the Disputes his Proprietary Instructions subjected him to, had resigned. Mr Morris ask'd me, if I thought he must expect as uncomfortable an Administration. I said, No; you may on the contrary have a very comfortable one, if you will only take care not to enter into any Dispute with the Assembly; "My dear Friend, says he, pleasantly, how can you advise my avoiding Disputes. You know I love Disputing; it is one of my greatest Pleasures: However, to show the Regard I have for your Counsel, I promise you I will if possible avoid them." He had some Reason for loving to dispute, being eloquent, an acute Sophister, and therefore generally successful in argumentative Conversation. He had been brought up to it from a Boy, his Father (as I have heard) accustoming his Children to dispute with one another for his Diversion while sitting at Table after Dinner. But I think the Practice was not wise, for in the Course of my Observation, these disputing, contradicting & confuting People are generally unfortunate in their Affairs. They get Victory sometimes, but they never get Good Will, which would be of more use to them. We parted, he going to Philadelphia, and I to Boston. In returning, I met at New York with the Votes of the Assembly, by which it appear'd that notwithstanding his Promise to me, he and the House were already in high Contention, and it was a continual Battle between them, as long as he retain'd the Government. I had my Share of it; for as soon as I got back to my Seat in the Assembly, I was put on every Committee for answering his Speeches and Messages, and by the Committees always desired to make the Drafts. Our Answers as well as his Messages were often tart, and sometimes indecently abusive. And as he knew I wrote for the Assembly, one might have imagined that when we met we could hardly avoid cutting Throats. But he was so good-natur'd a Man, that no personal Difference between him and me was occasion'd by the Contest, and we often din'd together. One Afternoon in the height of this public Quarrel, we met in the Street. "Franklin, says he, you must go home with me and spend the Evening. I am to have some Company that you will like;" and taking me by the Arm he led me to his House. In gay Conversation over our Wine after Supper he told us Jokingly that he much admir'd the Idea of Sancho Panza, who when it was propos'd to give him a Government, requested it might be a Government of *Blacks*, as then, if he could not agree with his People he might sell them. One of his Friends who sat next me, says, "Franklin, why do you continue to side with these damn'd Quakers? had not you better sell them? the Proprietor would give you a good Price." The Governor, says I, has not yet *black'd* them enough. He had indeed labour'd hard to blacken the Assembly in all his Messages, but they wip'd off his Colouring as fast as he laid it on, and plac'd it in return thick upon his own Face; so that finding he was likely to be negrify'd himself, he as well as Mr Hamilton, grew tir'd of the Contest, and quitted the Government.

These public Quarrels were all at bottom owing to the Proprietaries, our hereditary Governors; who when any Expence was to be incurr'd for the Defence of their Province, with incredible Meanness instructed their Deputies to pass no Act for levying the necessary Taxes, unless their vast Estates were in the same Act expresly excused; and they had even taken Bonds of those Deputies to observe such Instructions. The Assemblies for three Years held out against this Injustice, Tho' constrain'd to bend at last. At length Capt. Denny, who was Governor Morris's Successor, ventur'd to disobey those Instructions; how that was brought about I shall show hereafter.

But I am got forward too fast with my Story; there are still some Transactions to be mentioned that happened during the Administration of Governor Morris.—

War being, in a manner, commenced with France, the Government of Massachusets Bay projected an Attack upon Crown Point, and sent Mr Quincy to Pennsylvania, and Mr Pownall, afterwards Govr Pownall, to N. York to sollicit Assistance. As I was in the Assembly, knew its Temper, & was Mr Quincy's Countryman, he apply'd to me for my Influence & Assistance. I dictated his Address to them which was well receiv'd. They voted an Aid of Ten Thousand Pounds, to be laid out in Provisions. But the Governor refusing his Assent to their Bill, (which included this with other Sums granted for the Use of the Crown) unless a Clause were inserted exempting the Proprietary Estate from bearing any Part of the Tax that would be necessary, the Assembly, tho' very desirous of making their Grant to New England effectual, were at a Loss how to accomplish it. Mr Quincy laboured hard with the Governor to obtain his Assent, but he was obstinate. I then suggested a Method of doing the Business without the Governor, by Orders on the Trustees of the Loan-Office, which by Law the Assembly had the Right of Drawing. There was indeed little or no Money at that time in the Office, and therefor I propos'd that the Orders should be payable in a Year and to bear an Interest of Five percent. With these Orders I suppos'd the Provisions might easily be purchas'd. The Assembly with very little Hesitation adopted the Proposal. The Orders were immediately printed, and I was one of the Committee directed to sign and dispose of them. The Fund for Paying them was the Interest of all the Paper Currency then extant in the Province upon Loan, together with the Revenue arising from the Excise which being known to be more than sufficient, they obtain'd instant Credit, and were not only receiv'd in Payment for the Provisions, but many money'd People who had Cash lying by them, vested it in those Orders, which they found advantageous, as they bore Interest while upon hand, and might on any Occasion be used as Money: So that they were eagerly all bought up, and in a few Weeks none of them were to be seen. Thus this important Affair was by my means compleated, Mr Quincy return'd Thanks to the Assembly in a handsome Memorial, went home highly pleas'd with the Success of his Embassy, and ever after bore for me the most cordial and affectionate Friendship.—

The British Government not chusing to permit the Union of the Colonies, as propos'd at Albany, and to trust that Union with their Defence, lest they should thereby grow too military, and feel their own Strength, Suspicions & Jealousies

at this time being entertain'd of them; sent over General
Braddock with two Regiments of Regular English Troops for
that purpose. He landed at Alexandria in Virginia, and thence
march'd to Frederic Town in Maryland, where he halted for
Carriages. Our Assembly apprehending, from some Information, that he had conceived violent Prejudices against them,
as averse to the Service, wish'd me to wait upon him, not as
from them, but as Postmaster General, under the guise of
proposing to settle with him the Mode of conducting with
most Celerity and Certainty the Dispatches between him and
the Governors of the several Provinces, with whom he must
necessarily have continual Correspondence, and of which they
propos'd to pay the Expence. My Son accompanied me on
this Journey. We found the General at Frederic Town, waiting
impatiently for the Return of those he had sent thro' the back
Parts of Maryland & Virginia to collect Waggons. I staid with
him several Days, Din'd with him daily, and had full Opportunity of removing all his Prejudices, by the Information of
what the Assembly had before his Arrival actually done and
were still willing to do to facilitate his Operations. When I
was about to depart, the Returns of Waggons to be obtain'd
were brought in, by which it appear'd that they amounted
only to twenty-five, and not all of those were in serviceable
Condition. The General and all the Officers were surpriz'd,
declar'd the Expedition was then at an End, being impossible,
and exclaim'd against the Ministers for ignorantly landing
them in a Country destitute of the Means of conveying their
Stores, Baggage, &c. not less than 150 Waggons being necessary. I happen'd to say, I thought it was pity they had not
been landed rather in Pennsylvania, as in that Country almost
every Farmer had his Waggon. The General eagerly laid hold
of my Words, and said, "Then you, Sir, who are a Man of
Interest there, can probably procure them for us; and I beg
you will undertake it." I ask'd what Terms were to be offer'd
the Owners of the Waggons; and I was desir'd to put on
Paper the Terms that appear'd to me necessary. This I did,
and they were agreed to, and a Commission and Instructions
accordingly prepar'd immediately. What those Terms were
will appear in the Advertisement I publish'd as soon as I arriv'd at Lancaster; which being, from the great and sudden

Effect it produc'd, a Piece of some Curiosity, I shall insert at length, as follows.

ADVERTISEMENT.

Lancaster, April 26, 1755.

WHEREAS 150 Waggons, with 4 Horses to each Waggon, and 1500 Saddle or Pack-Horses are wanted for the Service of his Majesty's Forces now about to rendezvous at *Wills*'s Creek; and his Excellency General *Braddock* hath been pleased to impower me to contract for the Hire of the same; I hereby give Notice, that I shall attend for that Purpose at *Lancaster* from this Time till next *Wednesday* Evening; and at *York* from next *Thursday* Morning 'till *Friday* Evening; where I shall be ready to agree for Waggons and Teams, or single Horses, on the following Terms, *viz.*

1*st*. That there shall be paid for each Waggon with 4 good Horses and a Driver, *Fifteen Shillings* per *Diem*: And for each able Horse with a Pack-Saddle or other Saddle and Furniture, *Two Shillings* per *Diem*. And for each able Horse without a Saddle, *Eighteen Pence* per *Diem*.

2*dly*, That the Pay commence from the Time of their joining the Forces at *Wills*'s Creek (which must be on or before the twentieth of *May* ensuing) and that a reasonable Allowance be made over and above for the Time necessary for their travelling to *Wills*'s Creek and home again after their Discharge.

3*dly*, Each Waggon and Team, and every Saddle or Pack Horse is to be valued by indifferent Persons, chosen between me and the Owner, and in Case of the Loss of any Waggon, Team or other Horse in the Service, the Price according to such Valuation, is to be allowed and paid.

4*thly*, Seven Days Pay is to be advanced and paid in hand by me to the Owner of each Waggon and Team, or Horse, at the Time of contracting, if required; and the Remainder to be paid by General *Braddock*, or by the Paymaster of the Army, at the Time of their Discharge, or from time to time as it shall be demanded.

5*thly*, No Drivers of Waggons, or Persons taking care of the hired Horses, are on any Account to be called upon to do the Duty of Soldiers, or be otherwise employ'd than in conducting or taking Care of their Carriages and Horses.

6*thly*, All Oats, Indian Corn or other Forage, that Waggons or Horses bring to the Camp more than is necessary for the Subsistence of the Horses, is to be taken for the Use of the Army, and a reasonable Price paid for it.

Note. My Son *William Franklin*, is impowered to enter into like Contracts with any Person in *Cumberland* County.

B. FRANKLIN.

To the Inhabitants of the Counties of
Lancaster, York, *and* Cumberland.

Friends and Countrymen,

BEING occasionally at the Camp at *Frederic* a few Days since, I found the General and Officers of the Army extreamly exasperated, on Account of their not being supply'd with Horses and Carriages, which had been expected from this Province as most able to furnish them; but thro' the Dissensions between our Governor and Assembly, Money had not been provided nor any Steps taken for that Purpose.

It was proposed to send an armed Force immediately into these Counties, to seize as many of the best Carriages and Horses as should be wanted, and compel as many Persons into the Service as would be necessary to drive and take care of them.

I apprehended that the Progress of a Body of Soldiers thro' these Counties on such an Occasion, especially considering the Temper they are in, and their Resentment against us, would be attended with many and great Inconveniencies to the Inhabitants; and therefore more willingly undertook the Trouble of trying first what might be done by fair and equitable Means.

The People of these back Counties have lately complained to the Assembly that a sufficient Currency was wanting; you have now an Opportunity of receiving and dividing among you a very considerable Sum; for if the Service of this Expedition should continue (as it's more than probable it will) for 120 Days, the Hire of these Waggons and Horses will amount to upwards of *Thirty thousand Pounds*, which will be paid you in Silver and Gold of the King's Money.

The Service will be light and easy, for the Army will scarce march above 12 Miles per Day, and the Waggons and Baggage

Horses, as they carry those Things that are absolutely necessary to the Welfare of the Army, must march with the Army and no faster, and are, for the Army's sake, always plac'd where they can be most secure, whether on a March or in Camp.

If you are really, as I believe you are, good and loyal Subjects to His Majesty, you may now do a most acceptable Service, and make it easy to yourselves; for three or four of such as cannot separately spare from the Business of their Plantations a Waggon and four Horses and a Driver, may do it together, one furnishing the Waggon, another one or two Horses, and another the Driver, and divide the Pay proportionably between you. But if you do not this Service to your King and Country voluntarily, when such good Pay and reasonable Terms are offered you, your Loyalty will be strongly suspected; the King's Business must be done; so many brave Troops, come so far for your Defence, must not stand idle, thro' your backwardness to do what may be reasonably expected from you; Waggons and Horses must be had; violent Measures will probably be used; and you will be to seek for a Recompence where you can find it, and your Case perhaps be little pitied or regarded.

I have no particular Interest in this Affair; as (except the Satisfaction of endeavouring to do Good and prevent Mischief) I shall have only my Labour for my Pains. If this Method of obtaining the Waggons and Horses is not like to succeed, I am oblig'd to send Word to the General in fourteen Days; and I suppose Sir *John St. Clair* the Hussar, with a Body of Soldiers, will immediately enter the Province, for the Purpose aforesaid, of which I shall be sorry to hear, because

I am,   *very sincerely and truly*
your Friend and Well-wisher,

B. FRANKLIN

I receiv'd of the General about 800£ to be disburs'd in Advance-money to the Waggon-Owners &c: but that Sum being insufficient, I advanc'd upwards of 200£ more, and in two Weeks, the 150 Waggons with 259 carrying Horses were on their March for the Camp.—The Advertisement promised Payment according to the Valuation, in case any Waggon or

Horse should be lost. The Owners however, alledging they did not know General Braddock, or what Dependance might be had on his Promise, insisted on my Bond for the Performance, which I accordingly gave them.

While I was at the Camp, supping one Evening with the Officers of Col. Dunbar's Regiment, he represented to me his Concern for the Subalterns, who he said were generally not in Affluence, and could ill afford in this dear Country to lay in the Stores that might be necessary in so long a March thro' a Wilderness where nothing was to be purchas'd. I commiserated their Case, and resolved to endeavour procuring them some Relief. I said nothing however to him of my Intention, but wrote the next Morning to the Committee of Assembly, who had the Disposition of some public Money, warmly recommending the Case of these Officers to their Consideration, and proposing that a Present should be sent them of Necessaries & Refreshments. My Son, who had had some Experience of a Camp Life, and of its Wants, drew up a List for me, which I inclos'd in my Letter. The Committee approv'd, and used such Diligence, that conducted by my Son, the Stores arrived at the Camp as soon as the Waggons. They consisted of 20 Parcels, each containing

6 lb Loaf Sugar
6 lb good Muscovado D°—
1 lb good Green Tea
1 lb good Bohea D°
6 lb good ground Coffee
6 lb Chocolate
1/2 C.^{wt} best white Biscuit
1/2 lb Pepper
1 Quart best white Wine Vinegar
1 Gloucester Cheese
1 Kegg cont.^{g} 20 lb good Butter
2 Doz. old Madeira Wine
2 Gallons Jamaica Spirits
1 Bottle Flour of Mustard
2 well-cur'd Hams
1/2 Doz dry'd Tongues
6 lb Rice
6 lb Raisins.

These 20 Parcels well pack'd were plac'd on as many Horses, each Parcel with the Horse, being intended as a Present for one Officer. They were very thankfully receiv'd, and the Kindness acknowledg'd by Letters to me from the Colonels of both Regiments in the most grateful Terms. The General too was highly satisfied with my Conduct in procuring him the Waggons, &c. and readily paid my Acc^t of Disbursements; thanking me repeatedly and requesting my farther Assistance in sending Provisions after him. I undertook this also, and was busily employ'd in it till we heard of his Defeat, advancing, for the Service, of my own Money, upwards of 1000£ Sterling, of which I sent him an Account. It came to his Hands luckily for me a few Days before the Battle, and he return'd me immediately an Order on the Paymaster for the round Sum of 1000£ leaving the Remainder to the next Account. I consider this Payment as good Luck; having never been able to obtain that Remainder; of which more hereafter.

This General was I think a brave Man, and might probably have made a Figure as a good Officer in some European War. But he had too much self-confidence, too high an Opinion of the Validity of Regular Troops, and too mean a One of both Americans and Indians. George Croghan, our Indian Interpreter, join'd him on his March with 100 of those People, who might have been of great Use to his Army as Guides, Scouts, &c. if he had treated them kindly;—but he slighted & neglected them, and they gradually left him. In Conversation with him one day, he was giving me some Account of his intended Progress. "After taking Fort Du Quesne, says he, I am to proceed to Niagara; and having taken that, to Frontenac, if the Season will allow time; and I suppose it will; for Duquesne can hardly detain me above three or four Days; and then I see nothing that can obstruct my March to Niagara."—Having before revolv'd in my Mind the long Line his Army must make in their March, by a very narrow Road to be cut for them thro' the Woods & Bushes; & also what I had read of a former Defeat of 1500 French who invaded the Iroquois Country, I had conceiv'd some Doubts,— & some Fears for the Event of the Campaign. But I ventur'd only to say, To be sure, Sir, if you arrive well before Duquesne, with these fine Troops so well provided with Artillery, that Place, not yet compleatly fortified, and as we hear with no very strong Garrison, can probably make but a short Resistance. The only Danger I apprehend of Obstruction to your March, is from Ambuscades of Indians, who by constant Practice are dextrous in laying & executing them. And the slender Line near four Miles long, which your Army must make, may expose it to be attack'd by Surprize in its Flanks, and to be cut like a Thread into several Pieces, which from their Distance cannot come up in time to support each other. He smil'd at my Ignorance, & reply'd, "These Savages may indeed be a formidable Enemy to your raw American Militia; but, upon the King's regular & disciplin'd Troops, Sir, it is impossible they should make any Impression." I was conscious of an Impropriety in my Disputing with a military Man in Matters of his Profession, and said no more.—The Enemy however did not take the Advantage of his Army which I apprehended its long Line of March expos'd it to, but let it advance without Interruption till within 9 Miles of the Place; and then when more in a Body, (for it had just pass'd a River, where the Front had halted till all were come over) & in a more open Part of the Woods than any it had pass'd, attack'd its advanc'd Guard, by a heavy Fire from behind Trees & Bushes; which was the first Intelligence the General had of an Enemy's being near him. This Guard being disordered, the General hurried the Troops up to their Assistance, which was done in great Confusion thro' Waggons, Baggage and Cattle; and presently the Fire came upon their Flank; the Officers being on Horseback were more easily distinguish'd, pick'd out as Marks, and fell very fast; and the Soldiers were crowded together in a Huddle, having or hearing no Orders, and standing to be shot at till two thirds of them were killed, and then being seiz'd with a Pannick the whole fled with Precipitation. The Waggoners took each a Horse out of his Team, and scamper'd; their Example was immediately follow'd by others, so that all the Waggons, Provisions, Artillery and Stores were left to the Enemy. The General being wounded was brought off with Difficulty, his Secretary Mr Shirley was killed by his Side, and out of 86 Officers 63 were killed or wounded, and 714 Men killed out of 1100. These 1100 had been picked Men, from the whole Army, the Rest had been left behind with

Col. Dunbar, who was to follow with the heavier Part of the Stores, Provisions and Baggage. The Flyers, not being pursu'd, arriv'd at Dunbar's Camp, and the Pannick they brought with them instantly seiz'd him and all his People. And tho' he had now above 1000 Men, and the Enemy who had beaten Braddock did not at most exceed 400, Indians and French together; instead of Proceeding and endeavouring to recover some of the lost Honour, he order'd all the Stores Ammunition, &c to be destroy'd, that he might have more Horses to assist his Flight towards the Settlements and less Lumber to remove. He was there met with Requests from the Governor's of Virginia, Maryland and Pennsylvania, that he would post his Troops on the Frontiers so as to afford some Protection to the Inhabitants; but he continu'd his hasty March thro' all the Country, not thinking himself safe till he arriv'd at Philadelphia, where the Inhabitants could protect him. This whole Transaction gave us Americans the first Suspicion that our exalted Ideas of the Prowess of British Regulars had not been well founded.—

In their first March too, from their Landing till they got beyond the Settlements, they had plundered and stript the Inhabitants, totally ruining some poor Families, besides insulting, abusing & confining the People if they remonstrated. —This was enough to put us out of Conceit of such Defenders if we had really wanted any. How different was the Conduct of our French Friends in 1781, who during a March thro' the most inhabited Part of our Country, from Rhodeisland to Virginia, near 700 Miles, occasion'd not the smallest Complaint, for the Loss of a Pig, a Chicken, or even an Apple!

Capt. Orme, who was one of the General's Aid de Camps, and being grievously wounded was brought off with him, and continu'd with him to his Death, which happen'd in a few Days, told me, that he was totally silent, all the first Day, and at Night only said, *Who'd have thought it?* that he was silent again the following Days, only saying at last, *We shall better know how to deal with them another time*; and dy'd a few Minutes after.

The Secretary's Papers with all the General's Orders, Instructions and Correspondence falling into the Enemy's Hands, they selected and translated into French a Number of the Articles, which they printed to prove the hostile Intentions of the British Court before the Declaration of War. Among these I saw some Letters of the General to the Ministry speaking highly of the great Service I had rendred the Army, & recommending me to their Notice. David Hume too, who was some Years after Secretary to Lord Harcourt when Minister in France, and afterwards to Gen.ˡ Conway when Secretary of State, told me he had seen among the Papers in that Office Letters from Braddock highly recommending me. But the Expedition having been unfortunate, my Service it seems was not thought of much Value, for those Recommendations were never of any Use to me.—

As to Rewards from himself, I ask'd only one, which was, that he would give Orders to his Officers not to enlist any more of our bought Servants, and that he would discharge such as had been already enlisted. This he readily granted, and several were accordingly return'd to their Masters on my Application.—Dunbar, when the Command devolv'd on him, was not so generous. He Being at Philadelphia on his Retreat, or rather Flight, I apply'd to him for the Discharge of the Servants of three poor Farmers of Lancaster County that he had inlisted, reminding him of the late General's Orders on that head. He promis'd me, that if the Masters would come to him at Trenton, where he should be in a few Days on his March to New York, he would there deliver their Men to them. They accordingly were at the Expence & Trouble of going to Trenton,—and there he refus'd to perform his Promise, to their great Loss & Disappointment.—

As soon as the Loss of the Waggons and Horses was generally known, all the Owners came upon me for the Valuation wᶜʰ I had given Bond to pay. Their Demands gave me a great deal of Trouble, my acquainting them that the Money was ready in the Paymaster's Hands, but that Orders for payᵍ it must first be obtained from General Shirley, and my assuring them that I had apply'd to that General by Letter, but he being at a Distance an Answer could not soon be receiv'd, and they must have Patience; all this was not sufficient to satisfy, and some began to sue me. General Shirley at length reliev'd me from this terrible Situation, by appointing Commissioners to examine the Claims and ordering Payment.

They amounted to near twenty Thousand Pound, which to pay would have ruined me.

Before we had the News of this Defeat, the two Doctors Bond came to me with a Subscription Paper, for raising Money to defray the Expence of a grand Fire Work, which it was intended to exhibit at a Rejoicing on receipt of the News of our Taking Fort Duquesne. I looked grave and said, "it would, I thought, be time enough to prepare for the Rejoicing when we knew we should have occasion to rejoice."— They seem'd surpriz'd that I did not immediately comply with their Proposal. "Why, the D——l, says one of them, you surely don't suppose that the Fort will not be taken?" "I don't know that it will not be taken; but I know that the Events of War are subject to great Uncertainty."—I gave them the Reasons of my doubting. The Subscription was dropt, and the Projectors thereby miss'd that Mortification they would have undergone if the Firework had been prepared.—Dr Bond on some other Occasions afterwards said, that he did not like Franklin's forebodings.—

Governor Morris who had continually worried the Assembly w.th Message after Message before the Defeat of Braddock, to beat them into the making of Acts to raise Money for the Defence of the Province without Taxing among others the Proprietary Estates, and had rejected all their Bills for not having such an exempting Clause, now redoubled his Attacks, with more hope of Success, the Danger & Necessity being greater. The Assembly however continu'd firm, believing they had Justice on their side, and that it would be giving up an essential Right, if they suffered the Governor to amend their Money-Bills. In one of the last, indeed, which was for granting 50,000£ his propos'd Amendment was only of a single Word; the Bill express'd that all Estates real and personal were to be taxed, those of the Proprietaries *not* excepted. His Amendment was; For *not* read *only*. A small but very material Alteration!—However, when the News of this Disaster reach'd England, our Friends there whom we had taken care to furnish with all the Assembly's Answers to the Governor's Messages, rais'd a Clamour against the Proprietaries for their Meanness & Injustice in giving their Governor such Instructions, some going so far as to say that by obstructing the

Defence of their Province, they forfeited their Right to it. They were intimidated by this, and sent Orders to their Receiver General to add 5000£ of their Money to whatever Sum might be given by the Assembly, for such Purpose. This being notified to the House, was accepted in Lieu of their Share of a general Tax, and a new Bill was form'd with an exempting Clause which pass'd accordingly. By this Act I was appointed one of the Commissioners for disposing of the Money, 60,000£. I had been active in modelling it, and procuring its Passage: and had at the same time drawn a Bill for establishing and disciplining a voluntary Militia, which I carried thro' the House without much Difficulty, as Care was taken in it, to leave the Quakers at their Liberty. To promote the Association necessary to form the Militia, I wrote a Dialogue,* stating and answering all the Objections I could think of to such a Militia, which was printed & had as I thought great Effect. While the several Companies in the City & Country were forming and learning their Exercise, the Governor prevail'd with me to take Charge of our Northwestern Frontier, which was infested by the Enemy, and provide for the Defence of the Inhabitants by raising Troops, & building a Line of Forts. I undertook this military Business, tho' I did not conceive myself well-qualified for it. He gave me a Commission with full Powers and a Parcel of blank Commissions for Officers to be given to whom I thought fit. I had but little Difficulty in raising Men, having soon 560 under my Command. My Son who had in the preceding War been an Officer in the Army rais'd against Canada, was my Aid de Camp, and of great Use to me. The Indians had burnt Gnadenhut, a Village settled by the Moravians, and massacred the Inhabitants, but the Place was thought a good Situation for one of the Forts. In order to march thither, I assembled the Companies at Bethlehem, the chief Establishment of those People. I was surprized to find it in so good a Posture of Defence. The Destruction of Gnadenhut had made them apprehend Danger. The principal Buildings were defended by a Stockade: They had purchased a Quantity of Arms & Ammunition from New York, and had even plac'd Quantities of small Paving

*This Dialogue and the Militia Act, are in the Gent Magazine for Feb.^y & March 1756—

Stones between the Windows of their high Stone Houses, for their Women to throw down upon the Heads of any Indians that should attempt to force into them. The armed Bretheren too, kept Watch, and reliev'd as methodically as in any Garrison Town. In Conversation with Bishop Spangenberg, I mention'd this my Surprize; for knowing they had obtain'd an Act of Parliament exempting them from military Duties in the Colonies, I had suppos'd they were conscienciously scrupulous of bearing Arms. He answer'd me, "That it was not one of their establish'd Principles; but that at the time of their obtaining that Act, it was thought to be a Principle with many of their People. On this Occasion, however, they to their Surprize found it adopted by but a few." It seems they were either deceiv'd in themselves, or deceiv'd the Parliament. But Common Sense aided by present Danger, will sometimes be too strong for whimsicall Opinions.

It was the Beginning of January when we set out upon this Business of Building Forts. I sent one Detachment towards the Minisinks, with Instructions to erect one for the Security of that upper Part of the Country; and another to the lower Part, with similar Instructions. And I concluded to go myself with the rest of my Force to Gnadenhut, where a Fort was tho't more immediately necessary. The Moravians procur'd me five Waggons for our Tools, Stores, Baggage, &c. Just before we left Bethlehem, Eleven Farmers who had been driven from their Plantations by the Indians, came to me, requesting a supply of Fire Arms, that they might go back and fetch off their Cattle. I gave them each a Gun with suitable Ammunition. We had not march'd many Miles before it began to rain, and it continu'd raining all Day. There were no Habitations on the Road, to shelter us, till we arriv'd near Night, at the House of a German, where and in his Barn we were all huddled together as wet as Water could make us. It was well we were not attack'd in our March, for Our Arms were of the most ordinary Sort, and our Men could not keep their Gunlocks dry. The Indians are dextrous in Contrivances for that purpose, which we had not. They met that Day the eleven poor Farmers above-mentioned & kill'd Ten of them. The one who escap'd inform'd that his & his Companions Guns would not go off, the Priming being wet with the Rain. The

next Day being fair, we continu'd our March and arriv'd at
the desolated Gnadenhut. There was a Saw Mill near, round
which were left several Piles of Boards, with which we soon
hutted ourselves; an Operation the more necessary at that in-
clement Season, as we had no Tents. Our first Work was to
bury more effectually the Dead we found there, who had
been half interr'd by the Country People. The next Morning
our Fort was plann'd and mark'd out, the Circumference
measuring 455 feet, which would require as many Palisades to
be made of Trees one with another of a Foot Diameter each.
Our Axes, of which we had 70 were immediately set to work,
to cut down Trees; and our Men being dextrous in the Use
of them, great Dispatch was made. Seeing the Trees fall so
fast, I had the Curiosity to look at my Watch when two Men
began to cut at a Pine. In 6 Minutes they had it upon the
Ground; and I found it of 14 Inches Diameter. Each Pine
made three Palisades of 18 Feet long, pointed at one End.
While these were preparing, our other Men, dug a Trench all
round of three feet deep in which the Palisades were to be
planted, and our Waggons, the Body being taken off, and the
fore and hind Wheels separated by taking out the Pin which
united the two Parts of the Perch, we had 10 Carriages with
two Horses each, to bring the Palisades from the Woods to
the Spot. When they were set up, our Carpenters built a
Stage of Boards all round within, about 6 Feet high, for the
Men to stand on when to fire thro' the Loopholes. We had
one swivel Gun which we mounted on one of the Angles;
and fired it as soon as fix'd, to let the Indians know, if any
were within hearing, that we had such Pieces. And thus our
Fort, (if such a magnificent Name may be given to so miserable a Stockade) was finished in a Week, tho' it rain'd so hard
every other Day that the Men could not work.

This gave me occasion to observe, that when Men are employ'd they are best contented. For on the Days they work'd
they were good-natur'd and chearful; and with the conscious-
ness of having done a good Days work they spent the Evenings jollily; but on the idle Days they were mutinous and
quarrelsome, finding fault with their Pork, the Bread, &c. and
in continual ill-humour: which put me in mind of a Sea-
Captain, whose Rule it was to keep his Men constantly at

Work; and when his Mate once told him that they had done every thing, and there was nothing farther to employ them about; O, says he, *make them scour the Anchor.*

This kind of Fort, however contemptible, is a sufficient Defence against Indians who have no Cannon. Finding our selves now posted securely, and having a Place to retreat to on Occasion, we ventur'd out in Parties to scour the adjacent Country. We met with no Indians, but we found the Places on the neighbouring Hills where they had lain to watch our Proceedings. There was an Art in their Contrivance of these Places that seems worth mention. It being Winter, a Fire was necessary for them. But a common Fire on the Surface of the Ground would by its Light have discover'd their Position at a Distance. They had therefore dug Holes in the Ground about three feet Diameter, and some what deeper. We saw where they had with their Hatchets cut off the Charcoal from the Sides of burnt Logs lying in the Woods. With these Coals they had made small Fires in the Bottom of the Holes, and we observ'd among the Weeds & Grass the Prints of their Bodies made by their laying all round with their Legs hanging down in the Holes to keep their Feet warm, which with them is an essential Point. This kind of Fire, so manag'd, could not discover them either by its Light, Flame; Sparks or even Smoke. It appear'd that their Number was not great, and it seems they saw we were too many to be attack'd by them with Prospect of Advantage.

We had for our Chaplain a zealous Presbyterian Minister, Mr Beatty, who complain'd to me that the Men did not generally attend his Prayers & Exhortations. When they enlisted, they were promis'd, besides Pay & Provisions, a Gill of Rum a Day, which was punctually serv'd out to them half in the Morning and the other half in the Evening, and I observ'd they were as punctual in attending to receive it. Upon which I said to Mr. Beatty, "It is perhaps below the Dignity of your Profession to act as Steward of the Rum. But if you were to deal it out, and only just after Prayers, you would have them all about you." He lik'd the Thought, undertook the Office, and with the help of a few hands to measure out the Liquor executed it to Satisfaction; and never were Prayers more generally & more punctually attended. So that I thought this

PART THREE 145

Method preferable to the Punishments inflicted by some military Laws for Non-Attendance on Divine Service.

I had hardly finish'd this Business, and got my Fort well stor'd with Provisions, when I receiv'd a Letter from the Governor, acquainting me that he had called the Assembly, and wish'd my Attendance there, if the Posture of Affairs on the Frontiers was such that my remaining there was no longer necessary. My Friends too of the Assembly pressing me by their Letters to be if possible at the Meeting, and my three intended Forts being now compleated, and the Inhabitants contented to remain on their Farms under that Protection, I resolved to return. The more willingly as a New England Officer, Col. Clapham, experienc'd in Indian War, being on a Visit to our Establishment, consented to accept the Command. I gave him a Commission, and parading the Garrison had it read before them, and introduc'd him to them as an Officer who from his Skill in Military Affairs, was much more fit to command them than myself; and giving them a little Exhortation took my Leave. I was escorted as far as Bethlehem, where I rested a few Days, to recover from the Fatigue I had undergone. The first Night being in a good Bed, I could hardly sleep, it was so different from my hard Lodging on the Floor of our Hut at Gnaden, wrapt only in a Blanket or two.—

While at Bethlehem, I enquir'd a little into the Practices of the Moravians. Some of them had accompanied me, and all were very kind to me. I found they work'd for a common Stock, eat at common Tables, and slept in common Dormitorys, great Numbers together. In the Dormitories I observ'd Loopholes at certain Distances all along just under the Cieling, which I thought judiciously plac'd for Change of Air. I was at their Church, where I was entertain'd with good Musick, the Organ being accompanied with Violins, Hautboys, Flutes, Clarinets, &c. I understood that their Sermons were not usually preached to mix'd Congregations; of Men Women and Children, as is our common Practice; but that they assembled sometimes the married Men, at other times their Wives, then the Young Men, the young Women, and the little Children, each Division by itself. The Sermon I heard was to the latter, who came in and were plac'd in Rows on Benches,

the Boys under the Conduct of a young Man their Tutor, and
the Girls conducted by a young Woman. The Discourse
seem'd well adapted to their Capacities, and was delivered in
a pleasing familiar Manner, coaxing them as it were to be
good. They behav'd very orderly, but look'd pale and un-
healthy, which made me suspect they were kept too much
within-doors, or not allow'd sufficient Exercise. I enquir'd
concerning the Moravian Marriages, whether the Report was
true that they were by Lot? I was told that Lots were us'd
only in particular Cases. That generally when a young Man
found himself dispos'd to marry, he inform'd the Elders of
his Class, who consulted the Elder Ladies that govern'd the
young Women. As these Elders of the different Sexes were
well acquainted with the Tempers & Dispositions of their respective Pupils, they could best judge what Matches were
suitable, and their Judgments were generally acquiesc'd in.
But if for example it should happen that two or three young
Women were found to be *equally* proper for the young Man,
the Lot was then recurr'd to. I objected, If the Matches are
not made by the mutual Choice of the Parties, some of them
may chance to be very unhappy. And so they may, answer'd
my Informer, if you let the Parties chuse for themselves.—
Which indeed I could not deny.

Being return'd to Philadelphia, I found the Association
went on swimmingly, the Inhabitants that were not Quakers
having pretty generally come into it, form'd themselves into
Companies, and chosen their Captains, Lieutenants and En-
signs according to the new Law. Dr B. visited me, and gave
me an Account of the Pains he had taken to spread a general
good Liking to the Law, and ascrib'd much to those Endeavours. I had had the Vanity to ascribe all to my Dialogue;
However, not knowing but that he might be in the right, I
let him enjoy his Opinion, which I take to be generally the
best way in such Cases.—The Officers meeting chose me to
be Colonel of the Regiment;—which I this time accepted. I
forget how many Companies we had, but We paraded about
1200 well-looking Men, with a Company of Artillery who had
been furnish'd with 6 brass Field Pieces, which they had
become so expert in the Use of as to fire twelve times in a
Minute. The first Time I review'd my Regiment, they

accompanied me to my House, and would salute me with some Rounds fired before my Door, which shook down and broke several Glasses of my Electrical Apparatus. And my new Honour prov'd not much less brittle; for all our Commissions were soon after broke by a Repeal of the Law in England.—

During the short time of my Colonelship, being about to set out on a Journey to Virginia, the Officers of my Regiment took it into their heads that it would be proper for them to escort me out of town as far as the Lower Ferry. Just as I was getting on Horseback, they came to my door, between 30 & 40, mounted, and all in their Uniforms. I had not been previously acquainted with the Project, or I should have prevented it, being naturally averse to the assuming of State on any Occasion, & I was a good deal chagrin'd at their Appearance, as I could not avoid their accompanying me. What made it worse, was, that as soon as we began to move, they drew their Swords, and rode with them naked all the way. Somebody wrote an Account of this to our Proprietor, and it gave him great Offence. No such Honour had been paid him when in the Province; nor to any of his Governors; and he said it was only proper to Princes of the Blood Royal; which may be true for aught I know, who was, and still am, ignorant of the Etiquette, in such Cases. This silly Affair, however greatly increas'd his Rancour against me, which was before considerable, not a little, on account of my Conduct in the Assembly, respecting the Exemption of his Estate from Taxation, which I had always oppos'd very warmly, & not without severe Reflections on his Meanness & Injustice in contending for it. He accus'd me to the Ministry as being the great Obstacle to the King's Service, preventing by my Influence in the House the proper Forming of the Bills for raising Money; and he instanc'd this Parade with my Officers as a Proof of my having an Intention to take the Government of the Province out of his Hands by Force. He also apply'd to Sir Everard Fauckener, then Post Master General, to deprive me of my Office. But this had no other Effect, than to procure from Sir Everard a gentle Admonition.

Notwithstanding the continual Wrangle between the Governor and the House, in which I as a Member had so large a

Share, there still subsisted a civil Intercourse between that Gentleman & myself, and we never had any personal Difference. I have sometimes since thought that his little or no Resentment against me for the Answers it was known I drew up to his Messages, might be the Effect of professional Habit, and that, being bred a Lawyer, he might consider us both as merely Advocates for contending Clients in a Suit, he for the Proprietaries & I for the Assembly, He would therefore sometimes call in a friendly way to advise with me on difficult Points, and sometimes, tho' not often, take my Advice. We acted in Concert to supply Braddock's Army with Provisions, and When the shocking News arriv'd of his Defeat, the Govern.ᵗ sent in haste for me, to consult with him on Measures for preventing the Desertion of the back Counties. I forget now the Advice I gave, but I think it was, that Dunbar should be written to and prevail'd with if possible to post his Troops on the Frontiers for their Protection, till by Reinforcements from the Colonies he might be able to proceed on the Expedition.—And after my Return from the Frontier, he would have had me undertake the Conduct of such an Expedition with Provincial Troops, for the Reduction of Fort Duquesne, Dunbar & his Men being otherwise employ'd; and he propos'd to commission me as General. I had not so good an Opinion of my military Abilities as he profess'd to have; and I believe his Professions must have exceeded his real Sentiments: but probably he might think that my Popularity would facilitate the Raising of the Men, and my Influence in Assembly the Grant of Money to pay them;—and that perhaps without taxing the Proprietary Estate. Finding me not so forward to engage as he expected, the Project was dropt: and he soon after left the Government, being superseded by Capt. Denny.—

Before I proceed in relating the Part I had in public Affairs under this new Governor's Administration, it may not be amiss here to give some Account of the Rise & Progress of my Philosophical Reputation.—

In 1746 being at Boston, I met there with a Dr Spence, who was lately arrived from Scotland, and show'd me some electric Experiments. They were imperfectly perform'd, as he was not very expert; but being on a Subject quite new to me, they equally surpriz'd and pleas'd me. Soon after my Return to Philadelphia, our Library Company receiv'd from Mr Peter Colinson, F.R.S. of London a Present of a Glass Tube, with some Account of the Use of it in making such Experiments. I eagerly seiz'd the Opportunity of repeating what I had seen at Boston, and by much Practice acquir'd great Readiness in performing those also which we had an Account of from England, adding a Number of new Ones.—I say much Practice, for my House was continually full for some time, with People who came to see these new Wonders. To divide a little this Incumbrance among my Friends, I caused a Number of similar Tubes to be blown at our Glass-House, with which they furnish'd themselves, so that we had at length several Performers. Among these the principal was Mr Kinnersley, an ingenious Neighbour, who being out of Business, I encouraged to undertake showing the Experiments for Money, and drew up for him two Lectures, in which the Experiments were rang'd in such Order and accompanied with Explanations, in such Method, as that the foregoing should assist in Comprehending the following. He procur'd an elegant Apparatus for the purpose, in which all the little Machines that I had roughly made for myself, were nicely form'd by Instrument-makers. His Lectures were well attended and gave great Satisfaction; and after some time he went thro' the Colonies exhibiting them in every capital Town, and pick'd up some Money. In the West India Islands indeed it was with Difficulty the Experim.^{ts} could be made, from the general Moisture of the Air.

Oblig'd as we were to Mr Colinson for his Present of the Tube, &c. I thought it right he should be inform'd of our Success in using it, and wrote him several Letters containing Accounts of our Experiments. He got them read in the Royal Society, where they were not at first thought worth so much Notice as to be printed in their Transactions. One Paper which I wrote for Mr. Kinnersley, on the Sameness of Lightning with Electricity, I sent to Dr. Mitchel, an Acquaintance of mine, and one of the Members also of that Society; who wrote me word that it had been read but was laught at by the Connoisseurs: The Papers however being shown to Dr Fothergill, he thought them of too much value to be stifled, and advis'd the Printing of them. Mr Collinson then gave them to *Cave* for publication in his Gentleman's Magazine; but he chose to print them separately in a Pamphlet, and Dr Fothergill wrote the Preface. *Cave* it seems judg'd rightly for his Profit; for by the Additions that arriv'd afterwards they swell'd to a Quarto Volume, which has had five Editions, and cost him nothing for Copy-money.

It was however some time before those Papers were much taken Notice of in England. A Copy of them happening to fall into the Hands of the Count de Buffon, a Philosopher deservedly of great Reputation in France, and indeed all over Europe he prevail'd with M. Dalibard to translate them into French; and they were printed at Paris. The Publication offended the Abbé Nollet, Preceptor in Natural Philosophy to the Royal Family, and an able Experimenter, who had form'd and publish'd a Theory of Electricity, which then had the general Vogue. He could not at first believe that such a Work came from America, & said it must have been fabricated by his Enemies at Paris, to decry his System. Afterwards having been assur'd that there really existed such a Person as Franklin of Philadelphia, which he had doubted, he wrote and published a Volume of Letters, chiefly address'd to me, defending his Theory, & denying the Verity of my Experiments and of the Positions deduc'd from them. I once purpos'd answering the Abbé, and actually began the Answer. But on Consideration that my Writings contain'd only a Description of Experiments, which any one might repeat & verify, and if not to be verify'd could not be defended; or of Observations, offer'd as Conjectures, & not deliverd dogmatically, therefore not laying me under any Obligation to defend them; and reflecting that a Dispute between two Persons writing in different Languages might be lengthend greatly by mis-translations, and thence misconceptions of one anothers Meaning, much of one of the Abbe's Letters being founded on an Error in the Translation; I concluded to let my Papers shift for themselves; believing it was better to spend what time I could spare from public Business in making new Experiments, than in Disputing about those already made. I therefore never answer'd M. Nollet; and the Event gave me no Cause to repent my Silence; for my friend M. le Roy of the Royal Academy of Sciences took up my Cause & refuted him, my Book was translated into the Italian, German and Latin Languages, and the Doctrine it contain'd was by degrees universally adopted by the Philosophers of Europe in preference to that of the Abbé, so that he liv'd to see himself the last of his Sect: except Mr B—— his Eleve & immediate Disciple.

What gave my Book the more sudden and general Celebrity, was the Success of one of its propos'd Experiments, made by Messrs Dalibard & Delor, at Marly; for drawing Lightning from the Clouds. This engag'd the public Attention every where. M. Delor, who had an Apparatus for experimental Philosophy, and lectur'd in that Branch of Science, undertook to repeat what he call'd the *Philadelphia Experiments*, and after they were performed before the King & Court, all the Curious of Paris flock'd to see them. I will not swell this Narrative with an Account of that capital Experiment, nor of the infinite Pleasure I receiv'd in the Success of a similar one I made soon after with a Kite at Philadelphia, as both are to be found in the Histories of Electricity.—Dr Wright, an English Physician then at Paris, wrote to a Friend who was of the Royal Society an Account of the high Esteem my Experiments were in among the Learned abroad, and of their Wonder that my Writings had been so little noticed in England. The Society on this resum'd the Consideration of the Letters that had been read to them, and the celebrated Dr Watson drew up a summary Acc^t of them, & of all I had afterwards sent to England on the Subject, which he accompanied with some Praise of the Writer. This Summary was then printed in their Transactions: And some Members of the Society in London, particularly the very ingenious Mr Canton, having verified the Experiment of procuring Lightnin from the Clouds by a Pointed Rod, and acquainting them with the Success, they soon made me more than Amends for the Slight with which they had before treated me. Without my having made any Application for that Honour, they chose me a Member, and voted that I should be excus'd the customary Payments, which would have amounted to twenty-five Guineas, and ever since have given me their Transactions gratis.—They also presented me with the Gold Medal of Sir Godfrey Copley for the Year 1753, the Delivery of which was accompanied by a very handsome Speech of the President Lord Macclesfield, wherein I was highly honoured.—

Our new Governor, Capt. Denny, brought over for me the before mentioned Medal from the Royal Society, which he presented to me at an Entertainment given him by the City. He accompanied it with very polite Expressions of his Esteem for me, having, as he said been long acquainted with my Character. After Dinner, when the Company as was customary at that time, were engag'd in Drinking, he took me aside into another Room, and acquainted me that he had been advis'd by his Friends in England to cultivate a Friendship with me, as one who was capable of giving him the best Advice, & of contributing most effectually to the making his Administration easy. That he therefore desired of all things to have a good Understanding with me; and he begg'd me to be assur'd of his Readiness on all Occasions to render me every Service that might be in his Power. He said much to me also of the Proprietor's good Dispositions towards the Province, and of the Advantage it might be to us all, and to me in particular, if the Opposition that had been so long continu'd to his Measures, were dropt, and Harmony restor'd between him and the People, in effecting which it was thought no one could be more serviceable than my self, and I might depend on adequate Acknowledgements & Recompences, &c. &c. The Drinkers finding we did not return immediately to the Table, sent us a Decanter of Madeira, which the Governor made liberal Use of, and in proportion became more profuse of his Solicitations and Promises. My Answers were to this purpose, that my Circumstances, Thanks to God, were such as to make Proprietary Favours unnecessary to me; and that being a Member of the Assembly I could not possibly accept of any; that however I had no personal Enmity to the Proprietary, and that whenever the public Measures he propos'd should appear to be for the Good of the People, no one should espouse and forward them more zealously than myself, my past Opposition having been founded on this, that the Measures which had been urg'd were evidently intended to serve the Proprietary Interest with great Prejudice to that of the People. That I was much obliged to him (the Governor) for his Professions of Regard to me, and that he might rely on every thing in my Power to make his Administration as easy to him as possible, hoping at the same time that he had not brought with him the same unfortunate Instructions his Predecessor had been hamper'd with. On this he did not then explain himself. But when he afterwards came to do Business with the Assembly they appear'd again, the Disputes were renewed, and I was as active as ever in the Opposition, being the Penman first of the Request to have a Communication of the Instructions, and then of the Remarks upon them, which may be found in the Votes of the Time, and in the Historical Review I afterwards publish'd; but between us personally no Enmity arose; we were often together, he was a Man of Letters, had seen much of the World, and was very entertaining & pleasing in Conversation. He gave me the first Information that my old Friend Ja⁵ Ralph was still alive, that he was esteem'd one of the best political Writers in England, had been employ'd in the Dispute between Prince Frederic and the King, and had obtain'd a Pension of Three Hundred a Year; that his Reputation was indeed small as a Poet, *Pope* having damn'd his Poetry in the Dunciad, but his Prose was thought as good as any Man's.—

The Assembly finally, finding the Proprietaries obstinately persisted in manacling their Deputies with Instructions inconsistent not only with the Privileges of the People, but with the Service of the Crown, resolv'd to petition the King against them, and appointed me their Agent to go over to England to present & support the Petition. The House had sent up a Bill to the Governor granting a Sum of Sixty Thousand Pounds for the King's Use, (10,000£ of which was subjected to the Orders of the then General Lord Loudon,) which the Governor absolutely refus'd to pass in Compliance with his Instructions. I had agreed with Captain Morris of the Packet at New York for my Passage, and my Stores were put on board, when Lord Loudon arriv'd at Philadelphia, expresly, as he told me to endeavour an Accomodation between the Governor and Assembly, that his Majesty's Service might not be obstructed by their Dissensions: Accordingly he desir'd the Governor & myself to meet him, that he might hear what was to be said on both sides. We met and discuss'd the Business. In behalf of the Assembly I urg'd all the Arguments that may be found in the publick Papers of that Time, which were of my Writing, and are printed with the Minutes of the Assembly & the Governor pleaded his Instructions, the Bond he had given to observ them, and his Ruin if he disobey'd: Yet seem'd not unwilling to hazard himself if Lord Loudon would advise it. This his Lordship did not chuse to do, tho' I once thought I had nearly prevail'd with him to do it; but finally he rather chose to urge the Compliance of the Assembly; and he intreated me to use my Endeavours with them for that purpose; declaring he could spare none of the King's Troops for the Defence of our Frontiers, and that if we did not continue to provide for that Defence ourselves they must remain expos'd to the Enemy. I acquainted the House with what had pass'd, and presenting them with a Set of Resolutions I had drawn up, declaring our Rights, & that we did not relinquish our Claim to those Rights but only suspended the Exercise of them on this Occasion thro' *Force*, against which we protested, they at length agreed to drop that Bill and frame another conformable to the Proprietary Instructions. This of course the Governor pass'd, and I was then at Liberty to proceed on my Voyage: but in the meantime the Pacquet had sail'd with my Sea-Stores, which was some Loss to me, and my only Recompence was his Lordship's Thanks for my Service, all the Credit of obtaining the Accommodation falling to his Share.

He set out for New York before me; and as the Time for dispatching the Pacquet Boats, was in his Disposition, and there were two then remaining there, one of which he said was to sail very soon, I requested to know the precise time, that I might not miss her by any Delay of mine. His Answer was, I have given out that she is to sail on Saturday next, but I may let you know *entre nous*, that if you are there by Monday morning you will be in time, but do not delay longer. By some Accidental Hindrance at a Ferry, it was Monday Noon before I arrived, and I was much afraid she might have sailed as the Wind was fair, but I was soon made easy by the Information that she was still in the Harbour, and would not move till the next Day.—

One would imagine that I was now on the very point of Departing for Europe. I thought so; but I was not then so well acquainted with his Lordship's Character, of which *In-decision* was one of the Strongest Features. I shall give some Instances. It was about the Beginning of April that I came to New York, and I think it was near the End of June before we sail'd. There were then two of the Pacquet Boats which had been long in Port, but were detain'd for the General's Letters, which were always to be ready to-morrow. Another Pacquet arriv'd, and she too was detain'd, and before we sail'd a fourth was expected. Ours was the first to be dispatch'd, as having been there longest. Passengers were engag'd in all, & some extreamly impatient to be gone, and the Merchants uneasy about their Letters, & the Orders they had given for Insurance (it being War-time) & for Fall Goods, But their Anxiety avail'd nothing; his Lordships Letters were not ready. And yet whoever waited on him found him always at his Desk, Pen in hand, and concluded he must needs write abundantly. Going my self one Morning to pay my Respects, I found in his Antechamber one Innis, a Messenger of Philadelphia, who had come from thence express, with a Pacquet from Governor Denny for the General. He deliver'd to me some Letters from my Friends there, which occasion'd my enquiring when he was to return & where he lodg'd, that I might send some Letters by him. He told me he was order'd to call to-morrow at nine for the General's Answer to the Governor, and should set off immediately. I put my Letters into his Hands the same Day. A Fortnight after I met him again in the same Place. So you are soon return'd, Innis! *Return'd*; No, I am not *gone* yet.—How so?—I have call'd here by Order every Morning these two Weeks past for his Lordship's Letter, and it is not yet ready.—Is it possible, when he is so great a Writer, for I see him constantly at his Scritore. Yes, says Innis, but he is like St. George on the Signs, *always on horseback, and never rides on*. This Observation of the Messenger was it seems well founded; for when in England, I understood that Mr Pitt gave it as one Reason for Removing this General, and sending Amherst & Wolf, *that the Ministers never heard from him, and could not know what he was doing*.

This daily Expectation of Sailing, and all the three Packets going down Sandy hook, to join the Fleet there the Passengers, thought it best to be on board, lest by a sudden Order

the Ships should sail, and they be left behind. There if I remember right we were about Six Weeks, consuming our Sea
Stores, and oblig'd to procure more. At length the Fleet
sail'd, the General and all his Army on board, bound to
Lewisburg with Intent to besiege and take that Fortress; all
the Packet-Boats in Company, ordered to attend the General's
Ship, ready to receive his Dispatches when those should be
ready. We were out 5 Days before we got a Letter with Leave
to part; and then our Ship quitted the Fleet and steered for
England. The other two Packets he still detain'd, carry'd them
with him to Halifax, where he staid some time to exercise the
Men in sham Attacks upon sham Forts, then alter'd his Mind
as to besieging Louisburg, and return'd to New York with all
his Troops, together with the two Packets abovementioned
and all their Passengers. During his Absence the French and
Savages had taken Fort George on the Frontier of that Province, and the Savages had massacred many of the Garrison
after Capitulation. I saw afterwards in London, Capt. Bon-
nell, who commanded one of those Packets. He told me, that
when he had been detain'd a Month, he acquainted his Lordship that his Ship was grown foul, to a degree that must necessarily hinder her fast Sailing, a Point of consequence for a
Packet Boat, and requested an Allowance of Time to heave
her down and clean her Bottom. He was ask'd how long time
that would require. He answer'd Three Days. The General
reply'd, If you can do it in one Day, I give leave; otherwise
not; for you must certainly sail the Day after to-morrow. So
he never obtain'd leave tho' detain'd afterwards from day to
day during full three Months. I saw also in London one of
Bonell's Passengers, who was so enrag'd against his Lordship
for deceiving and detaining him so long at New-York, and
then carrying him to Halifax, and back again, that he swore
he would sue him for Damages. Whether he did or not I
never heard; but as he represented the Injury to his Affairs it
was very considerable. On the whole I then wonder'd much,
how such a Man came to be entrusted with so important a
Business as the Conduct of a great Army: but having since
seen more of the great World, and the means of obtaining &
Motives for giving Places, & Employments my Wonder is di-
minished. General Shirley, on whom the Command of the

Army devolved upon the Death of Braddock, would in my Opinion if continued in Place, have made a much better Campaign than that of Loudon in 1757, which was frivolous, expensive and disgraceful to our Nation beyond Conception: For tho' Shirley was not a bred Soldier, he was sensible and sagacious in himself, and attentive to good Advice from others, capable of forming judicious Plans, quick and active in carrying them into Execution. Loudon, instead of defending the Colonies with his great Army, left them totally expos'd while he paraded it idly at Halifax, by which means Fort George was lost;—besides he derang'd all our mercantile Operations, & distress'd our Trade by a long Embargo on the Exportation of Provisions, on pretence of keeping Supplies from being obtain'd by the Enemy, but in Reality for beating down their Price in Favour of the Contractors, in whose Profits it was said, perhaps from Suspicion only, he had a Share. And when at length the Embargo was taken off, by neglecting to send Notice of it to Charlestown, the Carolina Fleet was detain'd near three Months longer, whereby their Bottoms were so much damag'd by the Worm, that a great Part of them founder'd in the Passage home. Shirley was I believe sincerely glad of being reliev'd from so burthensom a Charge as the Conduct of an Army must be to a Man unacquainted with military Business. I was at the Entertainment given by the City of New York, to Lord Loudon on his taking upon him the Command. Shirley, tho' thereby superseded, was present also. There was a great Company of Officers, Citizens and Strangers, and some Chairs having been borrowed in the Neighbourhood, there was one among them very low which fell to the Lot of Mr Shirley. Perceiving it as I sat by him, I said, they have given you, Sir, too low a Seat.—No Matter, says he; Mr Franklin; I find *a low Seat* the easiest!

While I was, as aforemention'd, detain'd at New York, I receiv'd all the Accounts of the Provisions, &c. that I had furnish'd to Braddock, some of which Acc^{ts} could not sooner be obtain'd from the different Persons I had employ'd to assist in the Business. I presented them to Lord Loudon, desiring to be paid the Ballance. He caus'd them to be regularly examin'd by the proper Officer, who, after comparing every Article with its Voucher, certified them to be right, and the

Ballance due, for which his Lordship promis'd to give me an Order on the Paymaster. This, however, was put off from time to time, and tho' I called often for it by Appointment, I did not get it. At length, just before my Departure, he told me he had on better Consideration concluded not to mix his Accounts with those of his Predecessors. And you, says he, when in England, have only to exhibit your Accounts at the Treasury, and you will be paid immediately. I mention'd, but without Effect, the great & unexpected Expence I had been put to by being detain'd so long at N York, as a Reason for my desiring to be presently paid; and On my observing that it was not right I should be put to any farther Trouble or Delay in obtaining the Money I had advanc'd, as I charg'd no Commissions for my Service. O, Sir, says he, you must not think of persuading us that you are no Gainer. We understand better those Affairs, and know that every one concern'd in supplying the Army finds means in the doing it to fill his own Pockets. I assur'd him that was not my Case, and that I had not pocketed a Farthing: but he appear'd clearly not to believe me; and indeed I have since learnt that immense Fortunes are often made in such Employments.—As to my Ballance, I am not paid it to this Day, of which more hereafter.—

Our Captain of the Pacquet had boasted much before we sail'd, of the Swiftness of his Ship. Unfortunately when we came to Sea, she proved the dullest of 96 Sail, to his no small Mortification. After many Conjectures respecting the Cause, when we were near another Ship almost as dull as ours, which however gain'd upon us, the Captain order'd all hands to come aft and stand as near the Ensign Staff as possible. We were, Passengers included, about forty Persons. While we stood there the Ship mended her Pace, and soon left our Neighbour far behind, which prov'd clearly what our Captain suspected, that she was loaded too much by the Head. The Casks of Water it seems had been all plac'd forward. These he therefore order'd to be remov'd farther aft; on which the Ship recover'd her Character, and prov'd the best Sailer in the Fleet. The Captain said she had once gone at the Rate of 13 Knots, which is accounted 13 Miles per hour. We had on board as a Passenger Captain Kennedy of the Navy, who contended that it was impossible, that no Ship ever sailed so fast,

and that there must have been some Error in the Division of
the Log-Line, or some Mistake in heaving the Log. A Wager
ensu'd between the two Captains, to be decided when there
should be sufficient Wind. Kennedy thereupon examin'd rigorously the Log-line, and being satisfy'd with that, he determin'd to throw the Log himself. Accordingly some Days after
when the Wind blew very fair & fresh, and the Captain of the
Packet (Lutwidge) said he believ'd she then went at the Rate
of 13 Knots, Kennedy made the Experiment, and own'd his
Wager lost. The above Fact I give for the sake of the following Observation. It has been remark'd as an Imperfection in
the Art of Ship-building, that it can never be known 'till she
is try'd, whether a new Ship will or will not be a good Sailer;
for that the Model of a good sailing Ship has been exactly
follow'd in a new One, which has prov'd on the contrary
remarkably dull. I apprehend this may be partly occasion'd by
the different Opinions of Seamen respecting the Modes of
lading, rigging & sailing of a Ship. Each has his System. And
the same Vessel laden by the Judgment & Orders of one Captain shall sail better or worse than when by the Orders of
another. Besides, it scarce ever happens that a Ship is form'd,
fitted for the Sea, & sail'd by the same Person. One Man
builds the Hull, another riggs her, a third lades and sails her.
No one of these has the Advantage of knowing all the Ideas
& Experience of the others, & therefore cannot draw just
Conclusions from a Combination of the whole. Even in the
simple Operation of Sailing when at Sea, I have often observ'd different Judgments in the Officers who commanded
the successive Watches, the Wind being the same, One would
have the Sails trimm'd sharper or flatter than another, so that
they seem'd to have no certain Rule to govern by. Yet I think
a Set of Experiments might be instituted, first to determine
the most proper Form of the Hull for swift sailing; next the
best Dimensions & properest Place for the Masts; then the
Form & Quantity of Sail, and their Position as the Winds
may be; and lastly the Disposition of her Lading. This is the
Age of Experiments; and such a Set accurately made & com-
bin'd would be of great Use. I am therefore persuaded that
ere long some ingenious Philosopher will undertake it:—to
whom I wish Success—

We were several times chas'd on our Passage, but outsail'd every thing, and in thirty Days had Soundings. We had a good Observation, and the Captain judg'd himself so near our Port, (Falmouth) that if we made a good Run in the Night we might be off the Mouth of that Harbour in the Morning, and by running in the Night might escape the Notice of the Enemy's Privateers, who often cruis'd near the Entrance of the Channel. Accordingly all the Sail was set that we could possibly make, and the Wind being very fresh & fair, we went right before it, & made great Way. The Captain after his Observation, shap'd his Course as he thought so as to pass wide of the Scilly Isles: but it seems there is sometimes a strong Indraught setting up St. George's Channel which deceives Seamen, and caus'd the Loss of Sir Cloudsley Shovel's Squadron. This Indraught was probably the Cause of what happen'd to us. We had a Watchman plac'd in the Bow to whom they often call'd, *Look well out before, there*; and he as often answer'd *Aye, Aye!* But perhaps had his Eyes shut, and was half asleep at the time: they sometimes answering as is said mechanically: For he did not see a Light just before us, which had been hid by the Studding Sails from the Man at Helm & from the rest of the Watch; but by an accidental Yaw of the Ship was discover'd, & occasion'd a great Alarm, we being very near it, the light appearing to me as big as a Cart Wheel. It was Midnight, & Our Captain fast asleep. But Capt. Kennedy jumping upon Deck, & seeing the Danger, ordered the Ship to wear round, all Sails standing. An Operation dangerous to the Masts, but it carried us clear, and we escap'd Shipwreck, for we were running right upon the Rocks on which the Lighthouse was erected. This Deliverance impress'd me strongly with the Utility of Lighthouses, and made me resolve to encourage the building more of them in America, if I should live to return there.—

In the Morning it was found by the Soundings, &c. that we were near our Port, but a thick fog hid the Land from our Sight. About 9 aClock the Fog began to rise, and seem'd to be lifted up from the Water like the Curtain at a Play-house, discovering underneath the Town of Falmouth, the Vessels in its Harbour, & the Fields that surrounded it. A most pleasing Spectacle to those who had been so long without any other

Prospects, than the uniform View of a vacant Ocean!—And it gave us the more Pleasure, as we were now freed from the Anxieties which the State of War occasion'd.—

I set out immediately w.th my Son for London, and we only stopt a little by the Way to view Stonehenge on Salisbury Plain, and Lord Pembroke's House and Gardens, with his very curious Antiquities at Wilton.

We arriv'd in London the 27.th of July 1757. As soon as I was settled in a Lodging Mr Charles had provided for me, I went to visit Dr Fothergill, to whom I was strongly recommended, and whose Counsel respecting my Proceedings I was advis'd to obtain. He was against an immediate Complaint to Governm.t, and thought the Proprietaries should first be personally apply'd to, who might possibly be induc'd by the Interposition & Persuasion of some private Friends to accommodate Matters amicably. I then waited on my old Friend and Correspondent Mr Peter Collinson, who told me that John Hanbury, the great Virginia Merchant, had requested to be informed when I should arrive, that he might carry me to Lord Granville's, who was then President of the Council, and wish'd to see me as soon as possible. I agreed to go with him the next Morning. Accordingly Mr Hanbury called for me and took me in his Carriage to that Nobleman's, who receiv'd me with great Civility; and after some Questions respecting the present State of Affairs in America, & Discourse thereupon, he said to me, "You Americans have wrong Ideas of the Nature of your Constitution; you contend that the King's Instructions to his Governors are not Laws, and think yourselves at Liberty to regard or disregard them at your own Discretion. But those Instructions are not like the Pocket Instructions given to a Minister going abroad, for regulating his Conduct in some trifling Point of Ceremony. They are first drawn up by Judges learned in the Laws; they are then considered, debated & perhaps amended in Council, after which they are signed by the King. They are then so far as relates to you, the *Law of the Land*; for THE KING IS THE LEGISLATOR OF THE COLONIES." I told his Lordship this was new Doctrine to me. I had always understood from our Charters, that our Laws were to be made by our Assemblies, to be presented indeed to the King

for his Royal Assent, but that being once given the King
could not repeal or alter them. And as the Assemblies could
not make permanent Laws without his Assent, so neither
could he make a Law for them without theirs. He assur'd me
I was totally mistaken. I did not think so however. And his
Lordship's Conversation having a little alarm'd me as to what
might be the Sentiments of the Court concerning us, I wrote
it down as soon as I return'd to my Lodgings.—I recollected
that about 20 Years before, a Clause in a Bill brought into
Parliament by the Ministry, had propos'd to make the King's
Instructions Laws in the Colonies; but the Clause was thrown
out by the Commons, for which we ador'd them as our
Friends & Friends of Liberty, till by their Conduct towards
us in 1765, it seem'd that they had refus'd that Point of
Sovereignty to the King, only that they might reserve it for
themselves.

After some Days, Dr Fothergill having spoken to the Proprietaries, they agreed to a Meeting with me at Mr J. Penn's
House in Spring Garden. The Conversation at first consisted
of mutual Declarations of Disposition to reasonable Accommodation; but I suppose each Party had its own Ideas of what
should be meant by *reasonable*. We then went into Consideration of our several Points of Complaint which I enumerated.
The Proprietaries justify'd their Conduct as well as they
could, and I the Assembly's. We now appeared very wide, and
so far from each other in our Opinions, as to discourage all
Hope of Agreement. However, it was concluded that I
should give them the Heads of our Complaints in Writing,
and they promis'd then to consider them.—I did so soon after; but they put the Paper into the Hands of their Solicitor
Ferdinando John Paris, who manag'd for them all their Law
Business in their great Suit with the neighbouring Proprietary
of Maryland, Lord Baltimore, which had subsisted 70 Years,
and wrote for them all their Papers & Messages in their Dispute with the Assembly. He was a proud angry Man; and as
I had occasionally in the Answers of the Assembly treated his
Papers with some Severity, they being really weak in point of
Argument, and haughty in Expression, he had conceiv'd a
mortal Enmity to me, which discovering itself whenever we
met, I declin'd the Proprietary's Proposal that he and I should

discuss the Heads of Complaint between our two selves, and refus'd treating with any one but them. They then by his Advice put the Paper into the Hands of the Attorney and Solicitor General for their Opinion and Counsel upon it, where it lay unanswered a Year wanting eight Days, during which time I made frequent Demands of an Answer from the Proprietaries but without obtaining any other than that they had not yet receiv'd the Opinion of the Attorney & Solicitor General: What it was when they did receive it I never learnt, for they did not communicate it to me, but sent a long Message to the Assembly drawn & signed by Paris reciting my Paper, complaining of its want of Formality as a Rudeness on my part, and giving a flimsey Justification of their Conduct, adding that they should be willing to accomodate Matters, if the Assembly would send over *some Person of Candour* to treat with them for that purpose, intimating thereby that I was not such. The want of Formality or Rudeness, was probably my not having address'd the Paper to them with their assum'd Titles of true and absolute Proprietaries of the Province of Pensilvania, wch I omitted as not thinking it necessary in a Paper the Intention of which was only to reduce to a Certainty by writing what in Conversation I had delivered *vivâ voce*. But during this Delay, the Assembly having prevail'd with Govr Denny to pass an Act taxing the Proprietary Estate in common with the Estates of the People, which was the grand Point in Dispute, they omitted answering the Message.

When this Act however came over, the Proprietaries counsell'd by Paris determin'd to oppose its receiving the Royal Assent. Accordingly they petition'd the King in Council, and a Hearing was appointed, in which two Lawyers were employ'd by them against the Act, and two by me in Support of it. They alledg'd that the Act was intended to load the Proprietary Estate in order to spare those of the People, and that if it were suffer'd to continue in force, & the Proprietaries who were in Odium with the People, left to their Mercy in proportioning the Taxes, they would inevitably be ruined. We reply'd that the Act had no such Intention and would have no such Effect. That the Assessors were honest & discreet Men, under an Oath to assess fairly & equitably, & that any Advantage each of them might expect in lessening his own

Tax by augmenting that of the Proprietaries was too trifling to induce them to perjure themselves. This is the purport of what I remember as urg'd by both Sides, except that we insisted strongly on the mischievous Consequences that must attend a Repeal; for that the Money, 100,000£, being printed and given to the King's Use, expended in his Service, & now spread among the People, the Repeal would strike it dead in their Hands to the Ruin of many, & the total Discouragement of future Grants, and the Selfishness of the Proprietors in soliciting such a general Catastrophe, merely from a groundless Fear of their Estate being taxed too highly, was insisted on in the strongest Terms. On this Lord Mansfield, one of the Council rose, & beckoning to me, took me into the Clerk's Chamber, while the Lawyers were pleading, and ask'd me if I was really of Opinion that no Injury would be done the Proprietary Estate in the Execution of the Act. I said, Certainly. Then says he, you can have little Objection to enter into an Engagement to assure that Point. I answer'd None, at all. He then call'd in Paris, and after som Discourse his Lordship's Proposition was accepted on both Sides; a Paper to the purpose was drawn up by the Clerk of the Council, which I sign'd with Mr Charles, who was also an Agent of the Province for their ordinary Affairs; when Lord Mansfield return'd to the Council Chamber where finally the Law was allowed to pass. Some Changes were however recommended and we also engag'd they should be made by a subsequent Law; but the Assembly did not think them necessary, For one Year's Tax having been levied by the Act before the Order of Council arrived, they appointed a Committee to examine the Percedings of the Assessors, & On this Committee they put several particular Friends of the Proprietaries. After a full Enquiry they unanimously sign'd a Report that they found the Tax had been assess'd with perfect Equity. The Assembly look'd on my entring into the first Part of the Engagement as an essential Service to the Province, since it secur'd the Credit of the Paper Money then spread over all the Country; and they gave me their Thanks in form when I return'd.—But the Proprietaries were enrag'd at Governor Denny for having pass'd the Act, & turn'd him out, with Threats of suing him for Breach of Instructions which he had given Bond to observe. He however having done it the Instance of the General & for his Majesty's Service, and having some powerful Interest at Court, despis'd the Threats, and they were never put in Execution

Chronology

1706   Born January 17 (Jan. 6, 1705, Old Style) in Milk Street, Boston, opposite Old South Church, where he was baptized Benjamin; youngest son and fifteenth child of Josiah Franklin, tallow chandler and soap boiler who had emigrated from England in 1683 to practice his Puritan faith freely. Eleven brothers and sisters are then living: five of Josiah's seven children by first wife (Elizabeth, b. 1678; Samuel, b. 1681; Hannah, b. 1683; Josiah, b. 1685; Anne, b. 1687) and six of seven so far born to second wife, Abiah Folger Franklin, who came from family of Nantucket Puritans (John, b. 1690; Peter, b. 1692; Mary, b. 1694; James, b. 1697; Sarah, b. 1699; Thomas, b. 1703). Two sisters, Lydia (b. 1708) and Jane (b. 1712) followed.

1714–16   Studies at Boston Grammar School (now Boston Latin) 1714–15, but because of expense, is withdrawn by father at end of school year. Father's widowed brother, Benjamin, comes from England in 1715 and joins household. Attends George Brownell's English school, which follows nonclassical curriculum, for second and final year of formal study (1715–16).

1716–17   Works with father making candles and soap, but dislikes it; tries cutler's trade briefly, but returns to father's shop. Older brother James returns from London, March 1717, and sets up printing business in Boston.

1718–20   Apprenticed to James. Writes broadside ballads "The Lighthouse Tragedy," 1718, and "On the Taking of *Teach* or Blackbeard the Pirate," 1719 (neither extant). December 1719, James hired to print *The Boston Gazette*, second American newspaper; loses contract August 1, 1720. Franklin borrows books to read—among them Bunyan, Defoe, Locke, Xenophon, various histories and religious polemics, as well as such contemporary freethinkers as Shaftesbury and Collins—and improves writing by imitating London *Spectator* essays of Addison and Steele.

1721   Continues working for James when he starts his own newspaper, lively and irreverent *New-England Courant*, August 7, first American newspaper to feature humorous essays and other literary content.

1722   Becomes vegetarian, saving money for books. April to Oc-
        tober, writes fourteen "Silence Dogood" essays for *Cou-
        rant*, submitting them anonymously, believing his brother
        will not print them otherwise. Manages paper while James
        is imprisoned by Massachusetts Assembly (June 12–July 7)
        for suggesting collusion between pirates and local officials.

1723   After *Courant* satirizes ministers and local officials, James
        is forbidden by Massachusetts Assembly to print news-
        paper without prior censorship. James defies order, prints
        Courant, then goes into hiding, leaving Franklin again in
        charge (Jan. 24–Feb. 12). *Courant* hereafter lists Benjamin
        Franklin as editor. Unhappy with James's "harsh & tyran-
        nical" treatment ("Tho' a Brother, he considered himself
        as my Master"), sails secretly September 25 for New York,
        breaking indentures, but fails to find work. Sails for Phil-
        adelphia October 1, encounters squall and spends thirty
        hours on the water; arrives at Perth Amboy, New Jersey,
        next evening with fever. Walks two days across New Jersey
        to Bordentown, then to Burlington; arrives in Philadel-
        phia October 6 with only a Dutch dollar and a few copper
        pence. Finds work the next day with Samuel Keimer as
        journeyman printer. Takes lodging with John Read (father
        of future wife, Deborah) next door to Keimer's shop in
        Market Street.

1724   Encouraged by Pennsylvania Governor William Keith,
        who has sought his acquaintance, to open his own print-
        ing shop; Keith promises to get him public printing. Re-
        turns to Boston near end of April to ask father for money
        to set up business, but Josiah gives him only small pres-
        ents and good wishes. Visits brother James, who takes
        offense at Franklin's display of prosperity. Calls on Cotton
        Mather. Returns to Philadelphia early June, where Keith
        offers to lend money to set up printing shop and suggests
        he go to London to buy materials and arrange for supplies
        from stationers, booksellers, and printers. John Read dies
        July 3. During the fall, Franklin reveals to Deborah Read
        his plan to sail to London; her mother discourages their
        courtship. Sails for London November 5 with friend James
        Ralph and merchant Thomas Denham, relying on letters
        of credit promised by Governor Keith to obtain printing
        equipment. Arrives Christmas Eve and finds that Keith,
        with "no credit to give," had duped him, and sent no

letters; finds employment before January at Samuel Palmer's printing office. Lodges with Ralph in Little Britain section of inner London, next door to bookseller John Wilcox, from whom he borrows books to continue education.

1725   After setting in type William Wollaston's *The Religion of Nature Delineated*, writes and prints rejoinder, *A Dissertation on Liberty and Necessity, Pleasure and Pain*, arguing against free will. William Lyons, surgeon, admires pamphlet and introduces him to Bernard Mandeville and Henry Pemberton, another physician, who promises introduction to Isaac Newton (never fulfilled). Deborah Read marries John Rogers August 5 in Philadelphia; Rogers abandons her in December and is never heard from again. Franklin leaves Palmer's printing shop in fall for larger establishment of John Watts. Moves to Duke Street.

1726   Sails for home July 21 with Thomas Denham, who has hired him as clerk. Keeps journal of voyage July 22–October 11. Following arrival, works for Denham as shopkeeper and bookkeeper.

1727   Denham falls severely ill (dies July 4, 1728); March and April, Franklin critically ill with pleurisy. Returns to printing with Keimer in June. Forms Junto, self-improvement and mutual aid society for ambitious young men of his acquaintance, which meets on Friday evenings; members include three others from Keimer's shop (Hugh Meredith, Stephen Potts, George Webb) along with Joseph Breintnall, Thomas Godfrey, Nicholas Scull, William Parsons, William Maugridge, Robert Grace, Philip Syng, Hugh Roberts, and William Coleman, young men of various occupations and similar interests.

1728   Prints paper currency with Keimer at Burlington, New Jersey, February to May; quits in June and forms printing partnership with friend Hugh Meredith, whose father loans them money to start. Keimer, learning of Franklin's plans for newspaper, hurries into print, October 1, proposal for paper to be called *The Pennsylvania Gazette* (first issue appears Dec. 24). Observing objectionable conduct of freethinkers among his acquaintance, formulates private creed and worship service (*Articles of Belief and Acts of Religion*) November 20, outlining mixture of deistic and polytheistic tenets.

1729   Begins "Busy-Body" essay series February 4 in *The American Weekly Mercury*, Philadelphia newspaper published by Andrew Bradford, hoping to divert readership from Keimer's *Gazette*. Writes *A Modest Enquiry into the Nature and Necessity of a Paper Currency*, published April 10, first of many proposals to stimulate economy by increasing money supply. Buys failing *Pennsylvania Gazette* from Keimer September 25; October 2 issue is first to bear his name. During next decade, it becomes the most widely read newspaper in colonies. About 1729 or 1730, son William is born, out of wedlock, to an unidentified mother.

1730   Named official printer for Pennsylvania January 30. Borrows money from two friends, William Coleman and Robert Grace, to buy out Meredith, who wants to return to farming. Unable to marry Deborah (Read) Rogers in legal ceremony (because Rogers was not known to have died and Franklin, in any case, didn't want to be liable for his debts), forms common-law union with her, September 1; son William is taken into household. Begins to study French and German.

1731   Joins Freemasons in January, beginning lifelong involvement; June, elected junior warden of St. John's Lodge (the first of many Masonic offices he will hold in America and Europe). Drafts "Instrument of Association" for Library Company of Philadelphia, first American subscription library, July 1. Sponsors his journeyman Thomas Whitemarsh as printing partner in South Carolina, advancing necessary equipment and materials in return for one-third of profits, for six-year term (first of several financial sponsorships that will gradually increase his wealth).

1732   Publishes America's first German-language newspaper, *Philadelphische Zeitung*, May 6; it soon fails. Son Francis Folger Franklin born October 20 (baptized in Christ Church, Sept. 16, 1733). Publishes first *Poor Richard's Almanack* December 19 (continued annually by Franklin until he goes to England in 1757). Occasional attendance at Presbyterian services comes to an end.

1733   Conceives "the bold and arduous Project of arriving at
        moral Perfection"; July 1, begins keeping ledger, system-
        atically recording personal faults. In fall, visits family in
        Boston and brother James in Newport, Rhode Island. No-
        vember, sponsors another journeyman, Louis Timothée,
        as South Carolina printing partner succeeding White-
        marsh. Studies Italian, Spanish, and Latin.

1734   Elected grand master of Masons of Pennsylvania June 24.

1735   Brother James dies February 4 in Newport. Franklin pro-
        poses fire protection society in *Pennsylvania Gazette*. Re-
        sumes church attendance during winter and spring to hear
        sermons of Rev. Samuel Hemphill, who emphasizes prac-
        tical morals. After Hemphill is denounced by ministerial
        colleagues as unorthodox in April, Franklin writes pam-
        phlets in his defense; when Hemphill is suspended by
        Presbyterian Synod in September, leaves congregation
        permanently, but continues to contribute money. Suffers
        second pleurisy attack in early summer, with left lung sup-
        purating. Proposes system of paid night watchmen for
        Philadelphia (adopted in 1752).

1736   Prints New Jersey's paper currency in Burlington, July to
        September; to hinder forgeries, devises new nature-print-
        ing technique (reproducing images of tree leaves). Ap-
        pointed clerk of Pennsylvania Assembly October 15. Son
        Francis, age four, dies of smallpox November 21 and is
        buried in Christ Church burial ground. Organizes Union
        Fire Company, Philadelphia's first, December 7.

1737   Begins duties as postmaster of Philadelphia October 5. In-
        creasingly bored with Assembly proceedings, amuses him-
        self by contriving mathematical puzzles.

1738   Accused in *American Weekly Mercury* (Feb. 14) of partici-
        pation in mock Masonic initiation in 1737 which resulted
        in fatal burning of young apprentice. Denies responsibility
        in trial testimony and in *Gazette* account.

1739   Befriends evangelist George Whitefield, English Metho-
        dist preacher, who arrives in Philadelphia November 2 urg-
        ing religious revival in addresses to large outdoor crowds.

Franklin solicits subscriptions to print Whitefield's journals and sermons.

1740 *American Weekly Mercury* (Feb. 12) criticizes Franklin for favoring the popular anti-Proprietary party in his reporting. (Proprietors were descendants of Pennsylvania's founder, William Penn, who lived in England and were privileged by charter to appoint and instruct governor of the colony.) Becomes official printer for New Jersey (appointment continues to 1744). Announces in *Gazette* (Nov. 13) forthcoming *General Magazine*; accuses Andrew Bradford and John Webbe of stealing his plan for first American magazine; Franklin's price (9 *d*. per issue) undercuts Bradford's proposed magazine (announced at 12 *s*. per year).

1741 Designs Pennsylvania fireplace (Franklin stove) during winter of 1740–41; early version advertised for sale to the public February 5. Publishes first issue of *The General Magazine and Historical Chronicle* February 16; it fails after six issues.

1742 Sponsors employee James Parker as printing partner in New York. Organizes and publicizes, March 17, a project to sponsor Philadelphia botanist John Bartram's collecting trips.

1743 Publishes *A Proposal for Promoting Useful Knowledge* May 14, founding document of American Philosophical Society (first scientific society in America). Journeys to New England in late spring, meeting Cadwallader Colden in New York and attending Archibald Spencer's lectures on electricity in Boston. Begins business correspondence with William Strahan that will develop into lifelong friendship; encourages David Hall, young journeyman printer in Strahan's London shop, to emigrate to America, suggesting that he will sponsor Hall in another colony. Daughter Sarah ("Sally") born August 31; baptized in Christ Church October 27.

1744 David Hall arrives in Philadelphia, June 20, and lodges with Franklin. Publishes *An Account of the New Invented Pennsylvanian Fire-Places*.

1745   Drafts presentment of the Grand Jury against public houses and other nuisances, January 3. Father dies January 16, aged eighty-seven. Peter Collinson, member of Royal Society of London, sends pamphlet about recent German experiments in electricity to Library Company in April, together with glass tube, stimulating Franklin to begin electrical experimentation. Publishes woodcut of the "Plan of the Town and Harbour of Louisburgh" June 6, first illustrated news event in *The Pennsylvania Gazette*.

1746   "Immersed in electrical experiments" during the summer. Visits New England in fall and winter.

1747   Sends, May 25, first account of electrical experiments to Peter Collinson, who shows it to members of the Royal Society. November and December, publishes pamphlet *Plain Truth* warning of Pennsylvania's vulnerability to French and Spanish privateer raids on the Delaware River. Organizes voluntary militia for defense.

1748   Refuses position as colonel in militia, January 1, avowing military inexperience, and serves instead as common soldier. Forms printing partnership with David Hall, January 1, placing shop in Hall's hands in return for half the profits, and retires as printer; hereafter devotes himself mainly to scientific research and civic affairs. (Annual income from printing partnerships, real estate investments, and postmastership will amount to almost two thousand pounds in coming years, as much as the salary of Pennsylvania's governor.) Moves to new house away from shop, and acquires first of several black slaves. April, sponsors Thomas Smith, another of his journeymen, as printing partner in Antigua. Elected to Common Council of Philadelphia October 4.

1749   Writes "new Hypothesis for explaining . . . Thundergusts" for Ebenezer Kinnersley, April 29. Kinnersley, lecturing in Annapolis, Maryland, on electricity, first publishes and demonstrates (in miniature) Franklin's lightning rod experiments, May 10. Named Justice of the Peace for Philadelphia, June 30. Appointed provincial grand master of Masons of Pennsylvania, July 10. Writes *Proposals Relating to the Education of Youth in Pensilvania* by October 23, resulting in establishment of Philadelphia

Academy, now University of Pennsylvania (formally opens Jan. 7, 1751). November 7, notes similarities between lightning and electricity in his journal of experiments, and calls for experiment to prove their identity.

1750   Has first attack of gout in February. Proposes use of lightning rods to protect houses in March 2 letter to Collinson. July 29, devises experiment involving sentry-box with pointed rod on its roof, to be erected on hilltop or in church steeple, with rod attached to Leyden jar which would collect the electrical charge, and thus prove lightning to be a form of electricity. Revises lightning rod proposal to include provision for grounding. Severely shocked, December 23, while electrocuting a turkey.

1751   Pennsylvania Assembly passes Franklin's innovative bill, providing public funds to match private contributions, to found Pennsylvania Hospital, February 7. Collection of scientific letters, *Experiments and Observations on Electricity*, edited by Dr. John Fothergill, published in London in April. Elected May 9 and takes seat in Pennsylvania Assembly August 13 (reelected annually until 1764); son William succeeds him as clerk. Initiates proposal to merge city's fire companies into insurance company July 26; representatives of different companies meet on September 7 and organize Philadelphia Contributionship. Elected alderman of Philadelphia, October 1.

1752   Pennsylvania Hospital opens February 6. Mother dies in Boston, May 8, aged eighty-four. June, devises and performs kite experiment proving lightning is electrical. August, sponsors nephew Benjamin Mecom as partner in printing office in West Indies. September, equips his house with lightning rod, connecting it to bells that ring when rod is electrified. *Pennsylvania Gazette* of October 19 explains how to perform kite experiment; writes for *Poor Richard* of 1753 instructions for installing lightning rods. Designs a flexible catheter for brother John, who suffers from bladder stone, December 8.

1753   Abbé Nollet publishes *Lettres sur l'Electricité* in January, disputing Franklin's electrical theories. Second set of electrical experiments (*Supplemental Experiments and Observations*) published in London in March. Sponsors former journeyman Samuel Holland as printing partner in Lancaster, Pennsylvania, June 14. Travels through New England from mid-June to September, receiving honorary Master of Arts degrees from Harvard (July 25) and Yale (Sept. 12). Appointed joint deputy postmaster general of North America August 10, having solicited appointment from England. September 26–October 4, negotiates treaty at Carlisle, Pennsylvania, with Ohio Indians; prints resulting treaty in November. Awarded Copley Medal of Royal Society of London, November 30, for work in electricity.

1754   Disturbed by increasing French pressure along western frontier, devises and prints cartoon of snake cut into sections, over heading "Join or Die," in *Gazette* May 9— America's first political cartoon. Attends Albany Congress as commissioner from Pennsylvania, June–July; meeting brings together representatives from seven colonies to restore alliance with Iroquois and arrange common defense of frontier against French. July 2, conference votes to form colonial union; Franklin proposes plan, which is approved July 10 and sent to colonies for ratification. Pennsylvania Assembly rejects Albany Plan August 17, as do other colonies and British government. Third set of electrical experiments (*New Experiments and Observations on Electricity*) published in September in London, along with second edition of first two parts. Writes series of letters to Massachusetts Governor William Shirley in December protesting taxation without representation and claiming American right to self-government.

1755   Sets up postal communications for Major-General Edward Braddock, commander of British forces in North America; confers with Braddock at Frederick, Maryland, April 22–23, undertaking to supply Braddock's forces with wagons for their march against French at Fort Duquesne. Requisitions wagons at Lancaster and York, Pennsylvania, April 26–May 11. Writes biblical hoaxes "A Parable Against Persecution" and "A Parable on Brotherly Love" by summer. August, joins forces with Quaker party to demand that landholdings of Proprietors be taxed, along with other property, to raise money for defense of frontier. Chosen colonel in October by regiment of foot raised in Philadelphia. Assembly passes Franklin's militia bill, November 25, and approves £60,000 for defense, November 27. Travels to frontier to build forts and organize defenses, December 18 to February 5, with son William as aide.

1756   Unanimously elected to membership in Royal Society of London, April 29, and admitted with waiver of customary fees. Pennsylvania Assembly passes Franklin's bill providing night watchmen and street lighting for Philadelphia on March 9. Meets George Washington, March 21, on way to Virginia on post office business. Receives honorary Master's degree from William and Mary College April 20. Elected corresponding member of Royal Society of Arts, September 1. Undertakes military inspection tour to Carlisle, Harris's Ferry, and New York, October 2–14. Along with other commissioners, confers with Delaware Indians at Easton, Pennsylvania, November 5–18.

1757   Accepts nomination by Pennsylvania Assembly to serve as agent to England, to negotiate long-standing dispute with Proprietors, February 3. Meets with Lord Loudoun, commander-in-chief of British forces in America, March 14– 22, presenting Assembly's position favoring bill to raise taxes for military supplies. Loudoun persuades Pennsylvania Governor Denny to waive instructions of Proprietors (who refused to have their estates taxed) and pass bill. Travels to New York with son William April 4 en route to England; delayed until June 23 waiting for Loudoun to give permission to sail. While at sea, completes preface for *Poor Richard* for 1758, "Father Abraham's Speech" (later known as "The Way to Wealth"), the last of series of almanacs written by Franklin. Arrives in London July 26 and stays with Peter Collinson; sees Lord Granville, president of Privy Council, who alarms Franklin with his claim that King is supreme legislator of colonies. Takes lodgings on July 30 at No. 7 Craven Street with Mrs. Margaret Stevenson, widow with whom he thereafter makes his home in England. Meets with Proprietors Richard and Thomas Penn in August, giving them list of grievances. Late September to early November, ill with severe cold, headaches, and dizziness. Resumes conferences with Thomas Penn November 14.

1758   Establishes routine of club attendance that lasts throughout years in England. On Mondays often dines at George and Vulture with group of scientists, philanthropists, and explorers, including John Ellicot and, occasionally, Captain James Cook. Thursdays, usually dines with favorite group, Club of Honest Whigs, at St. Paul's Coffeehouse; members include John Canton, Richard Price, Joseph Priestley, James Burgh, William Rose, Andrew Kippis, and, occasionally, James Boswell. Sundays, frequently dines with Sir John Pringle, who gradually displaces printer William Strahan as closest friend in England; Alexander Small and David Hume are often guests. January to May, confers with Penns and defends Pennsylvania at Board of Trade; finally, November 27, Penns concede limited taxation, but they write the next day to Pennsylvania Assembly averring that Franklin lacks candor. Spends week at Cambridge in late May performing evaporation experiments with John Hadley, professor of chemistry. Visits ancestral homes at Ecton and Banbury in July with son William, collecting genealogical information. Invents damper for stoves or chimneys, December 2.

1759   Receives honorary degree of Doctor of Laws in absentia from University of St. Andrews in Scotland, February 12; hereafter referred to as "Dr. Franklin." Reports to Joseph Galloway April 7 that Richard Jackson, Englishman who later served as agent of Pennsylvania Assembly in London and then became friend of America in Parliament, proposed to get him elected to Parliament, "but I am too old to think of changing Countries." Takes extensive tour of northern England and Scotland, August 8–November 2, meeting Adam Smith, William Robertson, and Lord Kames.

1760   Third edition of *Experiments and Observations on Electricity* published (reprinted 1762 and 1764). Writes *The Interest of Great Britain Considered* ("The Canada Pamphlet"), published April 17, arguing economic and strategic importance of Canada to colonies and Britain. Meets Dr. Samuel Johnson on May 1 at the Associates of Dr. Bray, a philanthropic organization (of which Franklin had been elected chairman on March 6) that sponsors charity schools for blacks in Philadelphia, New York, Rhode Island, and Williamsburg, Virginia. Board of Trade rejects seven of nineteen acts passed by Pennsylvania Assembly, including taxes on Penn estates, June 24; August, Franklin appeals to Privy Council, which overrules Board of Trade and allows taxation of Penn estates.

1761   Has emerged as active and influential member of Society of Arts (which mainly sponsors farming methods and introduces new crops), of Royal Society of London (premier scientific society of the day), and of Associates of Dr. Bray. Tours Austrian Netherlands and Dutch Republic with son William and Richard Jackson, August–September. Upon return to England, witnesses coronation of George III September 22.

1762   Receives honorary degree of Doctor of Civil Law from Oxford, April 30. Sends Giambatista Beccaria, Italian scientist who disseminated Franklin's electrical theories, a description on July 13 of recently invented musical instrument, glass armonica, which he had been working on since 1761; Mozart and Beethoven later compose for it. Leaves London in August for Portsmouth to embark for Pennsylvania; arrives in Philadelphia November 1. Son William marries Elizabeth Downes September 4 in London, and is commissioned royal governor of New Jersey September 9.

1763   Tours New Jersey, New York, and New England inspecting post offices June 7 to November 5. Visits charity school sponsored by Associates of Dr. Bray in Philadelphia, and reports December 17 that he has "conceived a higher Opinion of the natural Capacities of the black Race, than I had ever before entertained."

1764   Angered by massacre of friendly Christian Indians in Lancaster County by frontier mob ("Paxton Boys"), drafts bill providing for trial of capital offenses between whites and Indians, January 4; bill arouses intense opposition and Assembly quickly kills it. Publishes *A Narrative of the Late Massacres* January 30, denouncing Paxton Boys; they march on Philadelphia, February 5–8. Franklin organizes defense, then meets with leaders of rioters and persuades them to present grievances and disperse. Writes *Cool Thoughts* (April 12), supporting Assembly's recent resolutions in favor of royal charter. Elected speaker of Assembly, May 26; drafts petition to King for change of government, and signs it as speaker after Assembly adopts it. Massachusetts House of Representatives writes Franklin as speaker urging other colonies to oppose Stamp Act, Parliamentary measure to raise revenue by taxing printed matter in colonies; September 12, Franklin lays proposal before Assembly, which instructs its London agent, Richard Jackson, to oppose passage of proposed Stamp Act, to seek modifications of Sugar Act (enacted April 5), and to argue that only the Pennsylvania legislature has the right to impose taxes in Pennsylvania; Franklin signs instructions. August and September, election campaign for Assembly features vicious attacks on Franklin's character (it is alleged that he favored royal government because he coveted governorship; that he had drawn large income from public monies while Assembly agent in England; that he had been careless with public funds given to his supervision; that William's mother was his maidservant Barbara, and that he had buried her in an unmarked grave; in addition, an old ethnic slur—Franklin had called German immigrants "Palatine Boors" in 1751—was brought up), and he is defeated October 1. His party retains a majority and appoints him October 26 to join Jackson as Assembly's agent in London. Minority members impugn Franklin, who defends his integrity November 5 in *Remarks on a Late Protest*. Leaves Philadelphia November 7; wife, Deborah, again refusing to sail overseas, remains in Philadelphia. Arrives at Isle of Wight December 9; reaches London the next day and takes up residence at old lodgings with Mrs. Stevenson.

1765   With other colonial agents, holds interview February 2 with First Minister George Grenville to protest laying of stamp duties in America. Grenville introduces annual budget in Parliament containing proposal for Stamp Act. Franklin and Thomas Pownall, former colonial governor who favored stronger ties between colonies and Great Britain, meet Grenville February 12 and offer an alternative proposal to raise revenue in America by issuing paper money at interest, but are ignored. Stamp Act passes House of Commons February 27, receives royal assent March 22, and is scheduled to take effect November 1. At Grenville's request, Franklin nominates his friend John Hughes as Pennsylvania stamp distributor, leading to rumors that Franklin actually supports the Stamp Act.

Franklin and Pownall succeed in April in getting Quartering Bill amended to eliminate forcible quartering of British troops in private dwellings in America; amended act passes May 3. Burlesques foolish news reports about America in English newspapers by publishing tall tales, May 3, concluding, "The Grand Leap of the Whale in that Chace up the Fall of Niagara is esteemed by all who have seen it, as one of the finest Spectacles in Nature!" Stamp Act protests spread throughout colonies during summer; in Philadelphia, mobs attack stamp distributors, and Franklin's house is threatened, September 16–17; Deborah arms herself, refusing to flee. Mob is dissuaded by readiness of 800 Franklin supporters to combat them. November 1, Stamp Act fails to go into effect as courts refuse to convene and administration of government in colonies breaks down. Franklin presents Privy Council with Pennsylvania petition for change to royal government, but consideration is postponed. Winter, writes newspaper articles defending the colonies and agitating for repeal of Stamp Act.

1766   Designs anti–Stamp Act cartoon and sends messages during early 1766 on cards bearing design. Partnership with David Hall expires January 21, and Hall buys the shop according to terms of 1748 partnership agreement. Examined by Committee of the Whole of House of Commons February 13 concerning the Stamp Act; Franklin's defense of American position contributes to repeal of act February 22, and establishes him as preeminent representative of American colonies. Travels to Germany with Sir John Pringle, June 15–August 16; elected at Göttingen to Royal Academy of Sciences.

1767   Continues to campaign against Parliamentary taxation of colonies in letters to London newspapers. Charles Townshend, Chancellor of the Exchequer, proposes duties in House of Commons, May 13; passed July 2, they intensify the crisis in the colonies. Franklin and Pringle visit Paris, August 28–October 8, where Horace Walpole calls on them (Sept. 13), and they are presented to Louis XV at Versailles. Daughter Sarah marries Richard Bache, Philadelphia merchant, October 29.

1768   Reviews history of relations between Britain and American colonies in *Causes of the American Discontents before 1768*, January 7. Appointed agent of Georgia Assembly April 11 (serves until May 2, 1774). Writes Mary Stevenson July 20 using phonetic alphabet of his own devising. Fall, has maps printed showing the course of the Gulf Stream.

1769   Supervises publication of corrected and enlarged fourth edition of *Experiments and Observations on Electricity*. Elected president of American Philosophical Society in Philadelphia January 2, and reelected annually until his death. Winter, Deborah Franklin suffers stroke, which impairs her memory and understanding; her health deteriorates thereafter. Joins organizers of land company to seek grants in Ohio Valley from King, hoping to sell parcels to settlers. Grandson Benjamin Franklin Bache born August 12. Appointed agent by New Jersey House of Representatives, November 8 (serves until March 1775). November 29, writes Strahan a major statement of American position intended for private circulation to Cabinet and selected members of Parliament.

1770   Elected agent of Massachusetts House of Representatives October 24 (retaining position until leaving England in March 1775), making him agent for four colonies (Pennsylvania, Georgia, New Jersey, and Massachusetts).

1771   Presents credentials as Massachusetts agent on January 16 to Lord Hillsborough, secretary of state for the colonies, who refuses to accept them because Franklin had been appointed by Assembly without governor's concurrence. Elected to Batavian Society of Experimental Science, Rotterdam, June 11. June 17–24, and again July 30–August 13, visits Bishop Jonathan Shipley at Twyford, where, on latter visit, writes first part of *Autobiography*. Tours Ireland and Scotland with Richard Jackson from August 25 to November 30; attends opening of Irish Parliament, October 8; stays with David Hume in Edinburgh, and with Lord Kames at Blair-Drummond. At end of trip, visits mother and sister of son-in-law Richard Bache at Preston in Lancashire, meets Richard for first time, and returns to London with him.

1772   After Board of Trade rejects land company plans, April 29, appeals to Privy Council on June 5, which approves the grant on July 1, but territory is never officially conveyed. Has come to believe that slavery is inherently evil and unjust (1758 will provided for manumission of two slaves he owned, and he evidently freed them sometime during 1760s); first writes against the institution of slavery in "The Sommersett Case and the Slave Trade," June 20. Elected foreign associate of Académie Royale des Sciences, Paris, August 16. October, Mrs. Stevenson moves to No. 10 Craven Street, and Franklin moves with her. Clandestinely obtains correspondence of Massachusetts Governor Thomas Hutchinson and Lieutenant Governor Andrew Oliver with English authorities, finds that it advocates repressive measures, and sends it to Massachusetts Speaker Thomas Cushing.

1773   Hutchinson letters are laid before Massachusetts House June 2; House resolves that they were intended to subvert constitution and appoints committee to petition crown for Hutchinson's and Oliver's removal. Hutchinson surreptitiously obtains copy of July 7 letter from Franklin to Massachusetts Speaker Cushing and sends it to Lord Dartmouth, colonial secretary, who judges it treasonable and asks General Thomas Gage, commander-in-chief in America, to obtain original so Franklin can be prosecuted; Gage fails to obtain it (Cushing may have destroyed the original after copying to protect Franklin). Franklin forwards to Lord Dartmouth petition for removal of Hutchinson and Oliver. Publishes satires "Rules by Which a Great Empire May Be Reduced to a Small One" and "Edict by the King of Prussia" in September. Experiments with use of oil to calm waters of Spithead in October.

1774   January, attends preliminary hearing on petition to remove Hutchinson and Oliver. News of Boston Tea Party reaches London January 20. Accused of stealing the Hutchinson letters, is excoriated and denounced as thief by Solicitor General Alexander Wedderburn before Privy Council during hearing on petition from Massachusetts House; refuses to respond to Wedderburn's accusations. Dismissed as deputy postmaster general for North America January 31. Unsuccessfully petitions House of Commons against Boston Port Bill; March 31 it becomes law, closing port. Attends opening of Theophilus Lindsey's Essex House Chapel, April 17, first enduring Unitarian congregation in England, contributing five guineas for its construction. Effigies of Wedderburn and Hutchinson carted through Philadelphia May 3, hanged, and burned by electricity. First Continental Congress opens in Philadelphia and adopts Continental Association September 5; petitions King through Franklin and other agents. Franklin becomes involved in two series of negotiations to restore calm between Britain and America: one, evidently authorized by Dartmouth, with merchant David Barclay and physician John Fothergill; the other with Lord Howe, secretly meeting at Howe's sister's, under pretense of playing chess. Drafts "Hints for a Durable Union Between England and America" at request of Barclay and Fothergill; forwarded to Dartmouth's office, it is considered and rejected. December 25, asked by Lord Howe to prepare another set of terms for conciliation; these too are not accepted. Deborah Franklin, who had not seen her husband in ten years, suffers a stroke on December 14 and dies in Philadelphia December 19, aged sixty-six; buried at Christ Church.

1775   Confers several times in late January with William Pitt, Earl of Chatham, on Chatham's unsuccessful conciliatory plan. Address to King, adopted by both Houses of Parliament February 9, declares Massachusetts to be in rebellion. Leaves London for Portsmouth March 20 to embark for America. During voyage, begins writing account of peace negotiations; speculates about why sailing from Europe to America takes longer than reverse crossing; measures temperature of air and water, proving that Gulf Stream is warmer than sea on either side of it. Lands in Philadelphia May 5 and next day is unanimously chosen delegate to Second Continental Congress by Pennsylvania Assembly. Active on various committees of Congress, among them one on paper currency, for which he designs devices and mottoes to be used on Continental money. Drafts Articles of Confederation in July, asserting America's political sovereignty, but Congress is unwilling to take such bold action. Submits resolutions proposing free trade, with no duties whatever; resolution is shelved until April 6, 1776, when it is finally adopted with proviso that individual colonies might impose their own import duties.

August 23, King proclaims colonies in rebellion. Congress reconvenes September 13, and Franklin is again active on various committees. Leaves Philadelphia October 4 with committee to confer with George Washington at his Massachusetts headquarters; returns November 9, bringing sister Jane Mecom, who had fled occupied Boston. Reappointed to several committees and offices of Pennsylvania Assembly, and reappointed delegate to Congress November 4. Congress creates standing committee of secret correspondence November 29 to deal with foreign affairs and appoints Franklin to it; committee meets secretly with agent of French court in December. Writes essays, song, and mock epitaph encouraging American war effort; epitaph, published December 14, concludes with words Jefferson adopts as his personal motto: "Rebellion to Tyrants is Obedience to God."

1776   New Jersey militia, acting on resolution of Congress, deprives William Franklin of official functions as royal governor of New Jersey in January; confined to his home in Perth Amboy, he is arrested in June and sent under guard to Connecticut to be imprisoned. Franklin, in Congress, declines to intercede for his son. Argues for "Instrument of Confederation" January 16 in Congress but is defeated. Urges four New England governments to enter into confederation and invite other colonies then to accede to it, February 19. Congress orders new designs for fractional dollars, and Franklin creates device of thirteen linked circles and "Fugio" design (later used on first United States coin, Fugio cent of 1787). Resigns from Pennsylvania Assembly February 26 to devote himself to Congressional duties. Appointed commissioner to Canada by Congress; March 26–May 30, on mission to Montreal, suffering from large boils, swollen legs, and dizziness. Appointed by Congress to committee to draft declaration of independence, June 1; committee chooses Thomas Jefferson to compose draft of declaration. Votes in favor of Richard Henry Lee's motion for independence, July 2. Congress adopts Declaration of Independence, July 4. Elected delegate from Philadelphia to Pennsylvania state convention, July 8; chosen president of Pennsylvania convention July 16; named by convention as Congressional delegate July 20. Asks for and receives Congress's permission to answer personal letter from Lord Howe; writes, July 20: "Long did I endeavour with unfeigned and unwearied Zeal, to preserve from breaking, that fine and noble China Vase the British Empire." Revises draft of Declaration of Rights before August 15, suggesting radical note (rejected by Pennsylvania convention) that claims the state has the right to discourage large concentrations of property as a danger to the happiness of mankind. During Congressional debates on Articles of Confederation, July 30–August 1, unsuccessfully advocates proportional, rather than equal, representation of states in Congress. Appointed by Congress to meet with Lord Howe, September 11, on Staten Island; they are unable to conciliate English and American differences. September, elected by Congress commissioner to France with Silas Deane and Arthur Lee, and is instructed to negotiate treaty. Drafts "Sketch of Propositions for a peace" in fall, suggesting Britain cede Canada to United States. Leaves Philadelphia and sails for France October 27, taking grandsons William Temple Franklin (William's illegitimate son) and Benjamin Franklin Bache (eldest of Sarah's children). Lands at Auray December 3 and proceeds to Paris; meets secretly on December 28 with Comte de Vergennes, French foreign minister.

1777   Commissioners formally request French aid, January 5; Louis XVI approves response to commissioners January 9, and January 13 they receive verbal promise of two million livres. Moves to Paris suburb of Passy about February 27, where he remains during French mission. Elected to Royal Medical Society of Paris, June 17. Combats reports of British victories spread by English Ambassador Lord Stormont by making his name a laughingstock: asked in August if it was true that six battalions in Washington's army had surrendered, Franklin replies, "No, Monsieur, it is not true; it is only a Stormont." Downplays the significance of Sir William Howe's taking of Philadelphia by commenting "it was not he who had taken Philadelphia, but instead Philadelphia had taken him." August 25, orders fifty pounds of type, evidently intending to set up small printing press at home; quantity of type indicates he was planning to print only small notes, forms, and documents. (Purchases additional type in 1778 and 1779, and occasionally employs printers from 1779 to 1783 to work on larger documents, pamphlets, and books. Probably

prints small pieces, including the bagatelles, himself.)
News of British defeat at Saratoga in October arrives December 4, and spurs negotiations leading to French alliance. Establishes several circles of friends in Passy area,
including Louis Le Veillard, Madame Brillon de Jouy (to
whom he writes flirtatious letters and bagatelles), La
Comtesse d'Houdetot (Jean Jacques Rousseau's mistress),
and especially the widow Madame Helvétius, whose salon
includes Anne Robert Jacques Turgot, France's finance
minister, and other notable French intellectuals.

1778   Commissioners report to Congress, January 28, French
grant of six million livres for year. Treaties of "alliance for
mutual defense" and of amity and commerce signed with
France February 6; symbolically, Franklin wears to the
signing ceremony same brown velvet suit he had worn
January 29, 1774, when accused by Wedderburn before
Privy Council. American commissioners formally presented to Louis XVI March 20. Assists at initiation of Voltaire in Masonic Lodge of the Nine Sisters, April 7.
Embraces Voltaire at request of audience at meeting of
French Academy of Sciences, which recognizes them as
leading intellectual exemplars of their nations. In London,
Boswell quotes Franklin's definition of man as "a tool-
making animal" to Dr. Johnson, April 7. Joined by John
Adams, appointed as fellow commissioner to France to
replace Silas Deane. France goes to war with Britain, June
17. Replies scornfully July 1 to offer of official rewards in
return for aid in scheme of reconciliation proposed by secret English agent. Elected sole minister plenipotentiary to
France September 14. Officiates at Masonic funeral services for Voltaire, November 28.

1779   Spain declares war on Britain June 21. Obtains another
three million livres from France. December, Benjamin
Vaughan publishes *Political, Miscellaneous, and Philosophical
Pieces* in London, first general compilation of Franklin's
nonscientific writings.

1780   Reports to Congress August 9 that John Adams, now
commissioner to negotiate peace with Britain, has given
offense to French court by repeated insults in letters to
Vergennes, copies of which Franklin sends to Congress at
Vergennes's request. Adams is thereafter bitterly hostile to

French and to Franklin. Rejects, October 2, surrendering American claims to the Mississippi as price for Spanish aid: "A Neighbour might as well ask me to sell my Street Door."

1781   Writes Vergennes February 13 of America's financial and military necessities, explaining failure of Spanish mission to date, saying "we can rely on France alone." June 4 and 10, again asks Vergennes for money to pay bills of Congress, as well as those of Adams (who is now in Holland) and John Jay in Spain. Congress appoints Franklin, Jay, Henry Laurens, and Thomas Jefferson to join Adams as commissioners to negotiate peace; new instructions require them to act only with knowledge and concurrence of France. General Charles Cornwallis surrenders to Washington at Yorktown, Virginia, October 19.

1782   Continues to request money from France to pay bills presented by Jay and Adams. Edmund Burke writes him as "the friend of mankind," February 28. Holds informal peace negotiations with British emissaries, March–June; suggests on April 18 to negotiator Richard Oswald that Britain should cede Canada to United States. July 10, Franklin suggests to Oswald "necessary" terms for peace without previously communicating them to Vergennes as his instructions from Congress require. July to October, Jay insists on prior recognition of American independence as condition for formal negotiation; Oswald's new commission from Britain, September 21, effectively recognizes United States. Draft articles for treaty prepared and sent to England without consulting Vergennes. August to October, Franklin has severe attack of gout, succeeded by passing gravel in urine. Adams arrives in Paris October 26 and joins negotiations. Oswald and American commissioners sign preliminary articles of peace November 30; when Vergennes complains in December of American failure to consult French, Franklin diplomatically admits impropriety, expresses gratitude to France, and asks for another loan. Vergennes assures Franklin of further six million livres.

1783   Attends signing of Anglo-French and Anglo-Spanish preliminary articles with Adams at Versailles, January 20; commissioners declare armistice. Requests another six

million livres from France January 25, bringing total to
twenty million. Crowned with laurel and myrtle March 6
at Musée de Paris celebration of successful conclusion of
war. Requests permission from Vergennes to print French
translations of American state constitutions together with
Articles of Confederation and treaty with France; presents
copies, translated by Duc de La Rochefoucauld, to all foreign ministers. Signs treaty of amity and commerce with
Sweden April 3. Consulted by papal Nuncio in Paris, July
1783–July 1784, about organizing Roman Catholic Church
in United States; suggests John Carroll (who accompanied
him on 1776 mission to Canada) as its head (Carroll receives appointment as superior of Catholic clergy in
America July 1784, and bishopric shortly thereafter). Fas-
cinated by early experimental balloon ascensions, reports
on them to Sir Joseph Banks, president of Royal Society;
witnesses two of the first manned flights, November 21
and December 1. When asked by scoffing observer, "What
use is it?" replies with defense of pure research: "What use
is a new-born baby?" Definitive treaty of peace between
Great Britain and United States signed September 3 by
David Hartley for the British and by Adams, Franklin,
and Jay for United States. Elected honorary fellow of
Royal Society of Edinburgh.

1784   Mocks aristocratic pretensions of Society of the Cincinnati
            (organization of veteran officers of American Revolution)
            and eagle as symbol of the United States in January 26
            letter to daughter Sarah; facetiously proposes native
            American turkey as better symbol. March, appointed by
            Louis XVI to investigate F. A. Mesmer's theories of ani-
            mal magnetism; *Rapport* of August 11 and *Exposé*, read to
            Academy of Sciences September 4, conclude animal mag-
            netism does not exist. May 12, formal ratification of peace
            treaty with Great Britain exchanged; Franklin requests on
            following day to be relieved from post to return home.
            Writes second part of autobiography, probably during late
            spring. Congress names Adams, Franklin, and Jefferson
            joint commissioners to negotiate treaties with European
            nations and Barbary States; they begin work August 30.
            Elected member of Royal Academy of History of Madrid.

1785   Receives word May 2 that Congress has given long-
            awaited permission to come home and has appointed Jef-

ferson his successor as minister plenipotentiary to France. Describes invention of bifocal glasses May 23. Signs treaty with Prussia July 9, embodying idealistic views on neutrality, privateering, and exemption of private property from capture at sea. Leaves Passy July 12; because bladder stone makes coach travel painful, is furnished with one of Queen Marie Antoinette's litters, borne by Spanish mules. Sails from Havre July 22; arrives at Southampton, England, July 24, and is visited by son William (with whom he reconciled the previous year), Bishop and Mrs. Shipley and daughter Catherine, and by other friends. Sails July 28 for Philadelphia. On voyage, writes "Maritime Observations," containing notes on best form of rigging to improve swiftness of vessels; further observations on course, velocity, and temperature of Gulf Stream; and design of sea anchor for holding ship in wind during rough weather. Lands at Philadelphia September 14, met by cannon salutes, pealing bells, and cheering crowds. Elected to Supreme Executive Council of Pennsylvania for three-year term, October 11; elected its president October 18, and unanimously reelected the next two years. Donates salary to charity.

1786   Designs instrument for taking down books from high shelves, January. Finding Market Street house (now occupied by daughter Sarah Bache, her husband, and six children) too cramped, builds addition, including large dining room and library to house more than 4,000 volumes.

1787   February, helps found Society for Political Enquiries, dedicated to improvement of knowledge of government; elected first president. Named president of reorganized Pennsylvania Society for Promoting the Abolition of Slavery, April 23; devotes much of remaining time and energy to abolition. Serves May 28–September 17 as Pennsylvania delegate to Federal Constitutional Convention. Opposes salaries for highest executive positions. Argues June 11 that representation to Congress should be proportional to population. Moves June 28 that sessions of Convention be opened with prayer; motion, proving controversial, is dropped. July 3, proposes "Great Compromise" on representation, making representation proportional to population in House and equal by state in Senate; approved by

Grand Committee, and enacted by Convention July 16. Argues August 7 and 10 for extending right to vote as widely as possible; condemns property qualification for franchise and for officeholding as unnecessary. James Wilson reads Franklin's closing speech at convention September 17, urging every member to "doubt a little of his own Infallibility," put aside specific reservations, and vote unanimously for approval of Constitution.

1788   Writes last will and testament, July 17, leaving bulk of estate to daughter Sarah and her family; makes smaller bequests to grandsons William Temple Franklin and Benjamin Bache; citing "the part he acted against me in the late war," leaves son William almost nothing (adds codicil, June 23, 1789, making bequests to Boston and Philadelphia). Begins writing third part of *Autobiography* in August. Ends service as president of Supreme Executive Council of Pennsylvania October 14, terminating career in public office.

1789   As president of the Pennsylvania Society for Promoting the Abolition of Slavery, writes and signs first remonstrance against slavery addressed to American Congress, February 12; after debate, committee reports March 5 that Congress has no authority to interfere in internal affairs of states. Congratulates Washington on September 16 on the success of new government under his administration and expresses satisfaction that he has lived to see present situation of United States. Sends copies of first three parts of *Autobiography* to friends in England and France November 2 and 13. Observes to Jean Baptiste Le Roy November 13, "In this world, nothing can be said to be certain except death and taxes." Elected member of Russian Imperial Academy of Sciences, St. Petersburg.

1790   Petitions Congress February 3 as president of Pennsylvania Abolition Society against slavery and slave trade. Restates religious beliefs March 9 in letter to Ezra Stiles, expressing faith in benevolent deity. Last public writing, March 23, satirizes a defense of slavery. In last letter and final public service, April 8, replies to Secretary of State Jefferson's query on northeast boundary as settled at Paris by peace commissioners; sends his copy of Mitchell map used there.

Dies quietly at home, the evening of April 17. Although
painfully afflicted in last years by bladder stone, dies of
pleurisy, accompanied by suppurated lungs. Buried April
21 beside wife, Deborah, and son Francis in Christ Church
burial ground, Philadelphia.

Note on the Text

The text of the *Autobiography* presented here is a newly prepared clear text, derived from the genetic text edited by
J. A. Leo Lemay and P. M. Zall, which was prepared from
the manuscript in the Huntington Library in San Marino,
California (*The Autobiography of Benjamin Franklin: A Genetic
Text*. Ed. J. A. Leo Lemay and P. M. Zall. Knoxville: Univ.
of Tennessee Press, 1981). The genetic text prints Franklin's
cancellations and revisions, using a system of typographical
sigla to indicate interlinear interpolations, marginal interpolations, superscriptions, etc. The cancellations are omitted
here (along with the related editorial sigla), as are punctuation marks associated with cancellations but left uncanceled
themselves. (A few of the more interesting canceled phrases
and passages are reproduced in the notes to the present volume.) Franklin's revisions are printed here without the editorial sigla indicating interlinear interpolations, marginal
insertions, and canceled words or phrases. Conjectural read-
ings of undecipherable words, printed within square brackets
in the genetic text, are accepted here, and printed without
brackets.

Some emendations have been necessary in the preparation
of this clear text, due to the unfinished nature of Franklin's
manuscript. In a number of places, extra punctuation has
been omitted. In some cases, the extraneous punctuation oc-
curs where Franklin evidently finished a sentence, then continued it without canceling his previous mark of punctuation.
In other cases, punctuation associated with a canceled phrase
was left uncanceled itself, or punctuation was rendered super-
fluous or redundant when Franklin revised a passage, but
didn't cancel the superseded punctuation. Where a sentence
plainly ends, but Franklin did not punctuate it, a period has
been added; no period has been added, however, after the last
word of the *Autobiography*. And where Franklin added a word
to an italicized passage (or inserted it in a context where parallel words were italicized) but did not italicize the added
word, the present text italicizes it. Finally, Franklin's notes,
queries, and reminders to himself in the manuscript (e.g.,

indicating the placement of texts to be added) have been omitted.

Certain other emendations have also been made and are recorded below. In a few places the sense of a passage demanded that a mark of punctuation be added, altered, or omitted for the sake of intelligibility. Spelling, if plainly incorrect (or a slip of the pen), is emended. In six places, Franklin inadvertently repeated a word, and in ten places redundancies indicate that he was considering alternative phrasings but neglected to cancel one of them; the present text emends accordingly (choosing in most cases his second alternative as the more likely), and records the emendation. In the following list, the word or words preceding the bracket are those of the present text, and the words after the bracket are those of the genetic text edition: 5.39, beloved."] beloved.; 35.39, if] if if; 36.30, Watson] Watson Watson; 37.18, Task] Task Task; 40.36, ought to] should ought to; 41.23, that] that,; 43.39, advanc'd] advan'd; 46.2, Woman,] Woman; 46.5, revered,] revered; 47.9, Wygate,] Wygate.; 49.26, seeing] see^ging; 49.35, 28,] 28.; 49.37, Stationary,] Stationary; 50.28, Work:] Work; 59.25, Journeyman] Joureyman; 61.16, then] now then; 67.17, Situation,] Situation; 67.25, invalid,] invalid; 75.24, considerable,] considerable.; 80.6–7, Care was employ'd] *Attention was taken up* Care was employ'd; 86.2, But] but; 86.7, exactly] exastly; 86.11, it] *Method* it; 87.17, *Temperance*] *Temperance*.; 87.40, which] whch; 88.28, rare,] rare; 90.3, be] by; 91.31, the] the the; 91.33, wise] wiss; 91.38, BF."—] BF.—; 93.4, Occupations] Occupapations; 97.27, Educating] Eduting; 118.17, *so.*"—] *so.*—; 118.28, for] towards for; 120.26, least] leas; 122.13, obstructed the] obstructed the the; 122.17, flat] flatt flat; 127.28, *pursue.*"] *pursue.*; 131.22, brought] brought,; 131.28, Baggage,] Baggage.; 140.11, you] "you; 140.12, taken?"] taken?; 140.14, Uncertainty."—] Uncertainty.—; 142.16, whimsicall] whimsicll; 143.29, And] Qu and; 144.17, the Sides] th Sides; 144.24, even] evon; 144.31, punctually] puctually; 146.33, Opinion,] Opinion.; 150.19, decry] oppose decry; 154.14, presenting] presenteding; 154.19, conformable; agreable conformable; 155.8, detain'd,] detain'd.; 155.38, the] thr; 157.6–7, others,] others.; 157.24, Business.] Business,;

161.3, occasion'd] accosion'd; 162.15, they] the; 162.39, me,] me.; 163.18, Paper] Pager.

The genetic text edition inadvertently omits four of the black "Spots" from the illustration of a page of the "Book" in which Franklin recorded his daily offenses against virtue (page 83 in the present volume). One of the missing spots is on the line corresponding to the second virtue, "Silence," in the column under "Friday"; two are under "Tuesday," on the lines corresponding to the fourth and sixth virtues, "Resolution" and "Industry"; and the fourth is on the line corresponding to the fifth virtue, "Frugality," in the column under "Thursday." In addition, a question mark was omitted and a period substituted after the word "breakfast" in the diagram of the "Scheme of Employment" (page 85 in the present volume). These have been corrected here.

Franklin never completed his writing and revision of the *Autobiography*, and the text as we have it manifests its unfinished character in various ways. The dashes that appear throughout the manuscript have been retained, even though they may be a manuscript convention that Franklin would not have printed; likewise, manuscript conventions preserved in the genetic text such as ampersands, abbreviations, and superscript characters are printed here as they appeared in the manuscript. Spelling has been neither modernized nor regularized, and original spellings have been retained. Thus the Reverend George Whitefield, for example, appears here variously as *Whitefiel*, *Whitfield*, and *Whitefield*. Ordinary eighteenth-century spellings such as *deny'd*, *publick*, *learnt*, *agreable*, *compleat*, *surpriz'd*, *Cloaths*, *intituled* (or *entituled*), and *chuse*—as well as unusual spellings (some of which are possibly, but not certainly, slips of the pen) such as *werre*, *Sope*, *Wharff*, *Surff*, *beforre*, *Compostors*, *Matras*, *Risque*, *renderd*, *deliverd*, *lenthend*, *Lightnin*, *observ*, *som*, and *Percedings*— have been left unaltered. Some of these spellings have a "phonetic" character and may reflect Franklin's interest in spelling reform. Italics and large and small capitals indicated by Franklin in the manuscript are followed here. The several supplemental texts that Franklin wished to insert in his manuscript (i.e., the note on the name Franklin, his uncle Benjamin's poems, the *Pennsylvania Gazette* editorial of October 9, 1759, the letters from Abel James and Benjamin Vaughan, the Golden Verses of Pythagoras, and the wagon advertisement) have been printed within the text where Franklin indicated; the texts are from the appendices to the genetic text edition. The title, which is customary ("The Autobiography"), has been added by the editor, although it is not in the manuscript and Franklin usually referred to his manuscript as "Memoirs"; the part titles (e.g., "Part One") are also customary and have been added by the editor.

Throughout this volume, conventional features of eighteenth-century writing (spelling and punctuation) and printing, such as italics for proper names and place names and large and small capitals, have been preserved, since Franklin can be presumed to have authorized them. Only obvious typographical and orthographical errors have been corrected, and these corrections are listed below. The long "s" has been printed as the modern short "s" throughout, and ligatures (except æ and œ digraphs) have been printed as separate letters. Footnote symbols have been reordered to correspond, where necessary, to new pagination. In eighteenth-century printing, quotation marks were placed at the beginning of every line of an extended quotation, but in the present volume only the opening quotation mark has been retained (and a closing quotation mark added where needed).

This volume is concerned with presenting the text of the *Autobiography*; it does not attempt to reproduce features of its typographic design, such as the display capitalization of chapter and paragraph openings. It does, however, reproduce capital letters for substantives, italic and boldface type, superscript letters, large and small capitals, and other typographical features, where the original text has preserved them. In a letter to Noah Webster, December 26, 1789, Franklin decried the disuse of these typographical conventions, and explained what he took to be their functions. To the extent that modern typesetting will allow, therefore, this volume preserves those features.

Notes

In the notes below, the reference numbers denote page and line of the present volume. No note is made for material included in a standard desk-reference book. Footnotes in the text are Franklin's own. Translations of classical authors in the notes below are from volumes of the Loeb Classical Library unless otherwise indicated; citations from James Thomson's *The Seasons* are to the line counts in the edition by James Sambrook (Oxford: At the Clarendon Press, 1981). For further biographical information than is provided in the Chronology, see James Parton, *Life and Times of Benjamin Franklin*, 2 vols. (Boston: Ticknor & Fields, 1864), Carl Van Doren, *Benjamin Franklin* (New York: The Viking Press, 1938), Claude-Anne Lopez and Eugenia W. Herbert, *The Private Franklin: The Man and His Family* (New York: W. W. Norton & Company, 1975), and Esmond Wright, *Franklin of Philadelphia* (Cambridge, Massachusetts: The Belknap Press of Harvard Univ. Press, 1986). See also the annotations, background materials, and bibliography in the Norton Critical Edition of Franklin's *Autobiography*, ed. J. A. Leo Lemay and P. M. Zall (New York: W. W. Norton & Company, 1986).

3.2   Twyford]   Bishop Jonathan Shipley's country home, fifty miles north of London, where Franklin stayed while writing Part One of the *Autobiography*, between July 30 and August 13, 1771.

3.5   Son]   William Franklin had been governor of New Jersey since 1762.

3.17   Reputation]   Franklin's autograph manuscript, in the Huntington Library in San Marino, California, shows that he revised his text extensively. For instance, here Franklin first wrote "Fame," then changed it to "Reputation." Other examples of revisions are given in notes at 10.9, 15.8–9, 15.26–27, 15.38, 35.37, 51.7, 56.11–12, 59.23, 60.7, 68.30, 77.11–12, 80.11, and 115.1 below.

6.6   old Stile]   England did not adopt the Gregorian calendar until September 13, 1752. Under the old (Julian) calendar, the new year began on March 25, and the old calendar was, by the eighteenth century, eleven days behind the new. Thus Franklin was born January 6, 1705, "old style," or January 17, 1706, "new style." The Preface to *Poor Richard Improved, 1752*, is an essay on the history of the calendar.

8.31   one . . . printed]   Peter Folger's *A Looking Glass for the Times*, though written in 1676, was not printed until 1725.

9.23   his Character]   His shorthand method.

10.9   against it;]   Franklin first wrote here, "and so it seem'd that I was destin'd for a Tallow Chandler," then canceled the clause.

12.22   By my rambling Digressions]   It may have been at this point, after
writing eight pages of his manuscript, that Franklin felt the need of an outline for his work. Several versions of the outline are extant. The version closest to Franklin's original working outline is a copy in the Pierpont
Morgan Library in New York City, printed in the Lemay–Zall genetic text,
and reproduced here with the genetic text's sigla included. These symbols,
used throughout the genetic text, are omitted in the clear text of the *Autobiography* in the present volume; they are retained in the following outline as
a sample of the genetic text's format.

↑ ↓   single arrows enclose interlinear additions.
< >   angle brackets enclose cancellations.
{ }   braces enclose matter written over by the following matter.
[p. o]   page numbers within brackets indicate the pagination of the original
            manuscript.

Copie d'un {Autographe} Projet très curieux de Bn. Franklin. — 1ere. Esquisse
memorandum de ses mémoires. Les additions à l'encre rouge sont de la main
de Franklin.

My writing. Mrs.. Dogoods Letters — Differences arise between my
Brother and me (his temper and mine) their Cause in general. His News
Paper. The Prosecution he suffered. My Examination. Vote of Assembly. His
Manner of evading it. Whereby I became free. My Attempt to get employ
with other Printers. He prevents me. Our frequent pleadings before our Fa-
ther. The final Breach. My Inducements to quit Boston. Manner of coming
to a Resolution. My leaving him & going to New York. (return to eating
Flesh.) thence to Pennsylvania, The Journey, and its Events on the Bay, at
Amboy, the Road, meet with Dr. Brown. his Character. his great work. At
Burlington. The Good Woman. On the River. My Arrival at Philada... First
Meal and first Sleep. Money left. Employment. Lodging. First Acquaintance
with my Afterwards Wife. with J. Ralph. with Keimer. their Characters. Osborne. Watson. The Governor takes Notice of me. the Occasion and Manner.
his Character. Offers to set me up. My return to Boston. <y> Voyage and
Accidents. Reception. My Father dislikes the proposal. I return to New York
and Philada... Governor Burnet. J. Collins. the Money for Vernon. The Governors Deceit. Collins not finding Employment goes to Barbados much in
my Debt. Ralph and I go to England. Disappointment of Governors Letters.
Col. French his Friend. Cornwallis's Letters. Cabbin. Denham. Hamilton,
Arrival in England. Get Employment. Ralph not. He is an Expence to me.
Adventures in England. Write a Pamphlet and print 100. Schemes. Lyons.
Dr Pemberton. My Diligence and yet poor thro Ralph. My Landlady. her
Character. Wygate. Wilkes. Cibber. Plays. Books I borrowed. Preachers I
heard. Redmayne. At Watts's — Temperance. Ghost,. Conduct and Influence
among the Men, persuaded by Mr Denham to return with him to Philada..
& be his Clerk. Our Voyage. and Arrival. My resolutions in Writing. My
Sickness. His Death. Found D. R married. Go to work again with Keimer.

Terms. His ill Usage of me. My Resentment. Saying of Decow. My Friends
at Burlington. Agreement with H Meredith to set up in Partnership. Do so.
Success with the Assembly. Hamiltons Friendship. Sewells History. Gazette.
Paper Money. Webb. Writing Busy Body. Breintnal. Godfrey. his Character.
Suit against us. Offer of my Friends Coleman and Grace. continue the Business and M. goes to Carolina. Pamphlet on Paper Money. Gazette from Keimer. Junto erected, its plan. Marry. Library erected. Manner of conducting
the Project. Its plan and Utility. Children. Almanack. the Use I made of it.
Great Industry. Constant Study. Fathers Remark and Advice upon Diligence.
Carolina Partnership. Learn French and German. Journey to Boston after 10
years. Affection of my Brother. His Death and leaving me [p. 2] his Son. Art
of Virtue. Occasion. City Watch. amended. Post Office. Spotswood. Brad-
fords Behaviour. Clerk of Assembly. Lose one of my Sons. Project of subordinate Junto's. Write occasionally in the papers. Success in Business. Fire
Companys. Engines. Go again to Boston in 1743. See Dr Spence. Whitefield.
My Connection with him. His Generosity to me. my returns. Church Differences. My part in them. Propose a College. not then prosecuted. Propose
and establish a Philosophical Society. War. Electricity. my first knowledge of
it. Partnership with D Hall &c. Dispute in Assembly upon Defence. Project
for it. Plain Truth. its Success. 10.000 Men raised and Disciplined. Lotteries.
Battery built. New Castle. My Influence in the Council. Colours, Devices
and Motto's.— Ladies. Military Watch. Quakers. chosen of the common
council. Put in the Commission of the Peace. Logan fond of me. his Library.
Appointed post Master General. Chosen Assembly Man. Commissioner to
treat with Indians at Carlisle. ↑ and at Easton. ↓ Project and establish Academy. Pamphlet on it. Journey to Boston. At Albany. Plan of Union of the
Colonies. Copy of it. Remarks upon it. It fails and how. (Journey to Boston
in 1754.) Disputes about it in our Assembly. My part in them. New Governor. Disputes with him. His Character and Sayings to me. Chosen Alderman.
Project of Hospital my Share in it. Its Success. Boxes. Made a Commissioner
of the treasury My Commission to defend the Frontier Counties. Raise Men
& build Forts. Militia Law of my drawing. Made Colonel. Parade of my
Officers. Offence to Proprietor. Assistance to Boston Ambassadors— Journey with Shirley &c.. Meet with Braddock. Assistance to him. To the Officers
of his Army. Furnish him with Forage. His Concessions to me and Character
of me. Success of my Electrical Experiments. Medal sent me per Royal Society and Speech of President. Dennys Arrival & Courtship to me. his Character. My Service to the Army in the Affair of Quarters. Disputes about the
Proprietors Taxes continued. Project for paving the City. I am sent to England.] Negociation there. Canada delenda est. My Pamphlet. Its reception
and Effect. Projects drawn from me concerning the Conquest. Acquaintance
made and their Services to me. Mrs.. S.., Mr Small. Sir John P.
Mr. Wood. Sargent Strahan and others. their Characters. Doctorate from
Edinburg ↑ St. Andrews ↓ <F——d-> [p. 3] Doctorate from Oxford. Journey to Scotland. Lord Leicester. Mr. Prat.— DeGrey. Jackson. State of Affairs in England. Delays. Event. Journey into Holland and Flanders. Agency

from Maryland. Sons Appointment. My Return. Allowance and thanks. Journey to Boston. John Penn Governor. My Conduct towards him. The Paxton
Murders. My Pamphlet Rioters march to Philada... Governor retires to
my House. My Conduct, <towards him. The Paxton Murders.> Sent out to
the Insurgents—Turn them back. Little Thanks. Disputes revived. Resolu-
tions against continuing under Proprietary Government. Another Pamphlet.
Cool Thoughts. Sent again to England with Petition. Negociation there.
Lord H. his Character. Agencies from New Jersey, Georgia, Massachusets.
Journey into Germany 1766. Civilities received there. Gottingen Observa-
tions. Ditto into France in 1767. Ditto in 1769. Entertainment there at the
Academy. Introduced to the King and the Mesdames. Mad. Victoria and
Mrs. Lamagnon. Duc de Chaulnes, M Beaumont. Le Roy. Dali{t}bard. Nol-
let. See Journals. Holland. Reprint my papers and add many. Books pre-
sented to me <by> ↑from↓ many Authors. My Book translated into
French. Lightning Kite. various Discoveries. My Manner of prosecuting that
Study. King of Denmark invites me to Dinner. Recollect my Fathers Proverb. Stamp Act. My Opposition to it. Recommendation of J. Hughes.
Amendment of it. Examination in Parliament. Reputation it gave me. Ca-
ress'd by Ministry. Charles Townsends Act. Opposition to it. Stoves and
Chimney plates. ↑Armonica.↓ Accquaintance with Ambassadors. Russian
Intimation. Writing in Newspapers. Glasses from Germany. Grant of Land
in Nova Scotia. Sicknesses. Letters to America returned hither. the Consequences. Insurance Office. My Character. Costs me nothing to be civil to
inferiors, a good deal to be submissive to superiors &c &c..

    Farce of perpetl. Motion

    Writing for Jersey Assembly.   verte

[p. 4] Hutchinson's Letters. Temple. Suit in Chancery, Abuse before the
Privy Council.—Lord Hillsborough's Character. & Conduct. Lord Dart-
mouth. Negotiation to prevent the War.—Return to America. Bishop of St
Asaph. Congress, Assembly. Committee of Safety. Chevaux de Frize.—Sent
to Boston, to the Camp. To Canada. to <Gu> Lord Howe.— To France,
Treaty, &c

Source: *The Autobiography of Benjamin Franklin: A Genetic Text*, ed. J. A. Leo
Lemay and P. M. Zall (Knoxville: University of Tennessee Press, 1981), pp.
202–05. The headnote in French translates as follows: "Copy of a {Auto-
graph} very curious Project of Bn. Franklin.—1st. Outline memorandum of
his memoirs. The additions in red ink are in the hand of Franklin."

15.8–9   a little . . . sake.]   Franklin first wrote, "because he left me no
Choice," then canceled the phrase and substituted this one.

15.26–27   Spectator.]   A canceled phrase following here indicates that "It
was the Third."

15.38   Stock of Words]   Franklin first wrote "Copia Verborum," then
changed to the English phrase.

18.26–27   *Men . . . forgot*] Alexander Pope, *An Essay on Criticism* (1711), ll. 574–75, substituting "should" for "must."

18.29   *To speak . . . Diffidence*] Pope, *An Essay on Criticism*, l. 567, substituting "To" for "And."

18.30–31   "Immodest . . . Sense."] Wentworth Dillon, Earl of Roscommon, *An Essay on Translated Verse* (1684), ll. 113–14, substituting "Modesty" for "Decency."

19.9–10   The Boston News Letter] *The Boston News-Letter* began publication in 1704; *The Boston Gazette* in 1719; *The American Weekly Mercury* (Philadelphia) later in 1719; and *The New-England Courant* in 1721.

19.25–26   anonymous Paper] The first "Silence Dogood" essay.

20.23   Author] James Franklin twice had serious troubles with the authorities. The first time he was imprisoned for nearly a month, June 12 to July 7, 1722; the second time he hid from the sheriff from January 24 to February 12, 1722/3.

20.35–36   *that . . . Courant*] On January 16, 1722/3, the General Court resolved that James Franklin be forbidden to publish the *Courant* "except it be first supervised by the Secretary of the Province." The *Courant* first appeared under Benjamin Franklin's name on February 12, 1722/3. Franklin gave the "Rulers some Rubs" in his "Rules for *The New-England Courant*" and "To 'your Honour'."

24.34   Sunday morning] October 6, 1723.

27.31   French Prophets] The Camisards, Protestant peasants of the Cévennes region of France, famous for their emotionalism.

30.25   Impropriety of it;] Franklin first continued here, "and said he had advanc'd too much already to my Brother James," then canceled the clause.

35.37   Glutton] Franklin first called Keimer a "Gormandizer," then changed it to "Glutton."

38.15   *Pope* cur'd him] Alexander Pope included unfavorable references to Ralph in *The Dunciad* (1728).

42.4   Woollaston's . . . Nature] Franklin had just set the type for the third edition of William Wollaston, *The Religion of Nature Delineated* (London: Samuel Palmer, 1725), which was advertised for sale at the end of February, 1724/5.

42.39   handsomely] Franklin offered to sell Sir Hans Sloane the purse in a letter of June 2, 1725.

43.24   Young's Satires] Probably Edward Young's *The Universal Passion* (1725–28).

45.1–2   mixing . . . Matter] By mixing his types, putting the manuscript pages in the wrong order, and breaking up the type he had already set.

47.18   Chelsea to Blackfryars] Over three miles.

47.22   Thevenot's . . . Positions] Melchisédec Thévenot, *The Art of Swimming* (1699).

49.18   *Plan*] "Plan of Conduct."

50.13   carried him off] After a long illness, Denham died on July 4, 1728.

50.14   small Legacy] In an oral will, Denham forgave Franklin the £10 Franklin owed him for the return from London.

51.7   Wages] Franklin first wrote "80 Pounds a Year," then canceled the phrase and wrote instead, "Wages so much higher . . . "

55.8   Boyle's Lectures] The English scientist Robert Boyle (1627–91) endowed a lecture series against "notorious Infidels."

55.21–25   *Whatever . . . above.*] John Dryden, *Oedipus* (1679), III, i, 244–48, though the first line is taken from Alexander Pope, *An Essay on Man* (1733–34), Epistle I, l. 294.

56.11–12   Religion.—] Franklin first continued here, "some foolish Intrigues with low Women excepted, which from the Expence were rather more inconvenient to me than to them." After changing "inconvenient" to "prejudicial," he canceled the clause entirely, but returned to the subject later (see p. 67 in the present volume).

57.17–18   Autumn . . . Year] In the fall of 1727.

58.37   Distribution] Putting the letters back into their cases after the printing had been done.

59.23   Friend] Franklin added "She Female" before "Friend," then canceled his revision.

59.38   Busy Body] "The Busy-Body" appeared in Bradford's *American Weekly Mercury* from February 4, 1728, through September 25, 1729.

60.7   singular Number] Franklin had written "my Paper" at 59.36–37, then changed it to "our Paper."

60.15   spirited Remarks*] Franklin's "Remarks" appeared in *The Pennsylvania Gazette*, October 9, 1729, the second issue of the paper after he bought it from Keimer. He did not include the text of this essay in his manuscript. It is reprinted here from the Lemay–Zall *Genetic Text* (pp. 179–81, with the quotation marks added to correspond to Franklin's practice in a similar footnote at 4.36 in the present volume).

63.18   two long Letters] In *The Pennsylvania Gazette*, May 6 and 13, 1731.

63.28–29   the Year 1729.]   The partnership was officially disbanded on July 4, 1730.

68.14   Subscription Library]   The Library Company of Philadelphia was founded on July 1, 1731.

68.30   Beginning]   Franklin first wrote here, "of gratifying the suppos'd Curiosity of my Son; what follows being . . . " After adding "and others of Posterity" after "Son," he canceled the entire clause.

69.1   Part Two]   Franklin wrote the second section of the Autobiography in 1784 at Passy, France (as indicated on pp. 75 and 90 of the present volume).

69.2   Notes]   The "Notes" consisted of a copy of the outline of topics that Franklin had made in 1771 for the Autobiography. See note 12.22.

70.5–75.10   MY . . . VAUGHAN.]   Quotation marks around this letter, presumably added by William Temple Franklin (it is from his edition that the text of this letter derives), have been omitted.

70.36   Art of Virtue]   Franklin never published his "Art of Virtue" as a separate work; when Benjamin Vaughan reminded him of his intention to do so in 1783, Franklin responded by incorporating the elements of his scheme into Part Two of the Autobiography under the guise of his "bold and arduous Project of arriving at moral Perfection" (p. 79).

77.11–12   plucking . . . Owner.]   Franklin first wrote "returning the Reputation thus assumed to its right owner," then rewrote the clause.

77.26–28   "Seest . . . Men."]   Proverbs 22:29.

78.17   Presbyterian]   Franklin was raised as a member of Boston's Congregational Old South Church, but Presbyterianism was more similar to Congregationalism than were most religious denominations.

80.11   our Interest]   Franklin first wrote "my Interest," and, in the next line, "my Slipping."

83.5   Form of the Pages.]   In Franklin's manuscript, the lines of the chart are drawn in red ink; the words, letters, and dots are in black ink.

84.8–11   Here . . . happy.]   Joseph Addison, Cato (1713), V, i, 15–18.

84.13–15   O Vitæ . . . anteponendus.]   Tusculan Disputations 5. 2. 5 (several lines omitted). "O, Philosophy, guide of life! O teacher of virtue and corrector of vice. One day of virtue is better than an eternity of vice."

84.33–38   Father . . . Bliss!]   James Thomson, The Seasons, "Winter," ll. 217–22.

85   Chart]   In Franklin's manuscript, the lines of the chart are drawn in red ink; the words, numbers, and braces are in black ink.

91.1   Part Three]   Franklin began to write this third part of the Autobiog-

raphy in 1788 at home in Philadelphia, and continued it at intervals between then and May, 1789.

93.34–35   connected Discourse]   "The Way to Wealth" (a title supplied by later editors).

94.12–15   Socratic . . . Sense.]   "A Man of Sense."

94.15   Discourse . . . denial]   "Self-Denial Not the Essence of Virtue."

101.16   Paper]   "On Protection of Towns from Fire."

101.25   Articles of Agreement]   Drawn up on December 7, 1736.

105.36   *litera . . . manet*]   The full proverb is *Vox audita perit, littera scripta manet.* "The spoken word passes away, the written word remains."

107.7   Paper]   "A Proposal for Promoting Useful Knowledge Among the British Plantations in America."

112.5   *or other Grain*]   The Assembly so voted on July 25, 1745, although the amount was 4,000 rather than 3,000.

115.1   Providence]   Franklin first wrote "Fortune," then changed it to "Providence."

116.27   Dr Spence's]   Archibald Spencer.

119.3–4   writing . . . Newspapers]   "Appeal for the Hospital."

119.23–36   "And be . . . same."]   Franklin presented the bill to the Assembly on January 23, 1750/1.

125.31   displac'd]   Franklin was fired on January 30, 1774, for his pro-American writings and actions, and especially for surreptitiously obtaining the letters of Massachusetts Governor Thomas Hutchinson and sending them back to America. Since he did not bring the *Autobiography* down to 1774, the topic does not recur.

126.38–40   Degree . . . Compliment.]   The Harvard degree, July 27, 1753, was first; the Yale degree was September 12; these were the highest degrees Harvard and Yale then awarded.

126.18   Plan]   "The Albany Plan of Union."

127.27–28   "Look . . . pursue."]   John Dryden's translation of Juvenal's tenth satire, ll. 1–2, in *The Satires of Decimus Junius Juvenalis. Translated into English Verse. By Mr. Dryden, And several other Eminent Hands . . .* (1693).

129.7–8   Idea of Sancho Panza]   Cervantes, *Don Quixote* (Part 1, chapter 29). Sancho Panza grieves at the idea of governing blacks until he realizes that he can sell them.

135.24   Dº]   "Ditto."

135.29   C.ʷᵗ]   "Hundredweight."

141.14–15   Dialogue]   "Dialogue Between X, Y, and Z, Concerning the Present State of Affairs in Philadelphia."

148.37   Dr Spence]   See note 167.27.

149.17   two Lectures]   "Course of Experiments."

150.3   print . . . Pamphlet]   *Experiments and Observations on Electricity* (1751).

161.8   1757.]   Franklin interrupted his writing at this point and began again sometime after November 13, 1789, with "As soon . . . "

162.9   Clause in a Bill]   The bill containing this clause died when Parliament adjourned in 1744 without passing it.

162.13–16   Conduct . . . themselves.]   The Declaration Act of 1766 asserted Parliament's right to legislate for the colonies.

165.4   Execution]   Franklin stopped writing here, probably shortly before his death on April 17.

Index

The Library of America Paperback Classics Series

**American Speeches: Political Oratory from Patrick Henry to
Barack Obama** (various authors)
Edited and with an introduction by Ted Widmer
ISBN: 978-1-59853-094-0

The Education of Henry Adams by Henry Adams
With an introduction by Leon Wieseltier
ISBN: 978-1-59853-060-5

The Pioneers by James Fenimore Cooper
With an introduction by Alan Taylor
ISBN: 978-1-59853-155-8

The Red Badge of Courage by Stephen Crane
With an introduction by Robert Stone
ISBN: 978-1-59853-061-2

The Souls of Black Folk by W.E.B. Du Bois
With an introduction by John Edgar Wideman
ISBN: 978-1-59853-054-4

Essays: First and Second Series by Ralph Waldo Emerson
With an introduction by Douglas Crase
ISBN: 978-1-59853-084-1

The Autobiography by Benjamin Franklin
With an introduction by Daniel Aaron
ISBN: 978-1-59853-095-7

The Scarlet Letter by Nathaniel Hawthorne
With an introduction by Harold Bloom
ISBN: 978-1-59853-112-1

Indian Summer by William Dean Howells
With an introduction by John Updike
ISBN: 978-1-59853-156-5

The Varieties of Religious Experience by William James
With an introduction by Jaroslav Pelikan
ISBN: 978-1-59853-062-9

Selected Writings by Thomas Jefferson
With an introduction by Tom Wicker
ISBN: 978-1-59853-096-4

The Autobiography of an Ex-Colored Man by James Weldon Johnson
With an introduction by Charles Johnson
ISBN: 978-1-59853-113-8

Selected Speeches and Writings by Abraham Lincoln
With an introduction by Gore Vidal
ISBN: 978-1-59853-053-7

The Call of the Wild by Jack London
With an introduction by E. L. Doctorow
ISBN: 978-1-59853-058-2

Moby-Dick by Herman Melville
With an introduction by Edward Said
ISBN: 978-1-59853-085-8

My First Summer in the Sierra and Selected Essays by John Muir
With an introduction by Bill McKibben
ISBN: 978-1-59853-111-4

Selected Tales, with The Narrative of Arthur Gordon Pym
by Edgar Allan Poe
With an introduction by Diane Johnson
ISBN: 978-1-59853-056-8

Uncle Tom's Cabin by Harriet Beecher Stowe
With an introduction by James M. McPherson
ISBN: 978-1-59853-086-5

Walden by Henry David Thoreau
With an introduction by Edward Hoagland
ISBN: 978-1-59853-063-6

Democracy in America by Alexis de Tocqueville
The Arthur Goldhammer Translation, in two volumes
Edited and with introductions by Olivier Zunz
Volume 1 — ISBN: 978-1-59853-151-0
Volume 2 — ISBN: 978-1-59853-152-7

The Adventures of Tom Sawyer by Mark Twain
With an introduction by Russell Baker
ISBN: 978-1-59853-087-2

Life on the Mississippi by Mark Twain
With an introduction by Jonathan Raban
ISBN: 978-1-59853-057-5

Selected Writings by George Washington
With an introduction by Ron Chernow
ISBN: 978-1-59853-110-7

The House of Mirth by Edith Wharton
With an introduction by Mary Gordon
ISBN: 978-1-59853-055-1

Leaves of Grass, The Complete 1855 and 1891–92 Editions by Walt Whitman
With an introduction by John Hollander
ISBN: 978-1-59853-097-1

For more information, please visit **www.loa.org/paperbackclassics/**

▵ The Library of America

The contents of this Paperback Classic are drawn from *Benjamin Franklin: Autobiography, Poor Richard, & Later Writings*, volume #37B in the Library of America series. It is joined in the series by a companion volume, #37A, *Benjamin Franklin: Silence Dogood, The Busy-Body, & Early Writings*.

Created with seed funding from the National Endowment for the Humanities and the Ford Foundation, The Library of America is a non-profit cultural institution that preserves our nation's literary heritage by publishing, and keeping permanently in print, authoritative editions of America's best and most significant writing. Hailed as "the most important book-publishing project in the nation's history" (*Newsweek*), this award-winning series maintains America's most treasured writers in "the finest-looking, longest-lasting edition ever made" (*The New Republic*).

Since 1982, over 215 hardcover volumes have been published in the Library of America series, each containing up to 1600 pages and including a number of works. In many cases, the complete works of a writer are collected in as few as three compact volumes. New volumes are added each year to make all the essential writings of America's foremost novelists, historians, poets, essayists, philosophers, playwrights, journalists, and statesmen part of The Library of America.

Each volume features: authoritative, unabridged texts • a chronology of the author's life, helpful notes, and a brief textual essay • a handsomely designed, easy-to-read page • high-quality, acid-free paper, bound in a cloth cover and sewn to lie flat when opened • a ribbon marker and printed end papers.

For more information, a complete list of titles, tables of contents, and to request a catalogue, please visit **www.loa.org**